Manufacturing Threats
Case Studies of State Manipulation and
Entrapment in Canada

Manufacturing Threats
Case Studies of State Manipulation and Entrapment in Canada

Alexandre Popovic

KERSPLEBEDEB
2023

Manufacturing Threats:
Case Studies of State Manipulation and Entrapment in Canada
By Alexandre Popovic

ISBN 978-1-989701-24-9

Produire le menace, copyright Alexandre Popovic, 2017

Translated as Manufacturing Threats, copyright Kersplebedeb 2023

First appeared as "Produire la menace: Agents provocateurs au service de l'État canadien" (Sabotart, 2017)

Cover art by Leplesh

To order copies of the book:
    Kersplebedeb
    CP 63560, CCCP Van Horne
    Montreal, Quebec
    Canada
    H3W 3H8

    info@kersplebedeb.com
    www.kersplebedeb.com
    www.leftwingbooks.net

To my dear mother

We shall provoke you to acts of terror and then crush you.
—Sergei Vasilyevich Zubatov
head of the Moscow Bureau of the Okhrana,
the secret police in Tsarist Russia

Keeping provocation an absolute secret is of course one of the main concerns of the police.
—Victor Serge

Contents

Introduction: In the Name of the Law   1

1. Confederation and Provocation   19

2. Seeing Red   34

3. On the Trail of the FLQ   51

4. An Agent Provocateur "Made in the USA"   71

5. Moles Come Out of Their Holes   81

6. The Birth of a Monster   92

7. Paid by the CSN … and CSIS   99

8. A Big Thank You from the Neo-Nazis   119

9. Terror Threats, Courtesy of CSIS   156

Conclusion   173

Endnotes   198

Bibliography   282

Introduction:
In the Name of the Law

Yo wassup.

I saw that u were going to be in my hood on sunday for da march & I appreciate fo'sho. We gotta stick together no matter what. My boyz are ready to do war. You dunno da area, so together we can make some noize. Government will understand that we ain't happy with da shit thats happening in montreal north.

Write me back so we can organize sumthin fucktup.

holla back

—Will J

August 5, 2009. I am answering emails for the Coalition Against Police Repression and Abuse (Coalition contre la répression et les abus policiers—CRAP), a group that came together following the death of Fredy Villanueva, an 18 year-old young man shot by a Montreal police (SPVM) officer in Montreal North on August 9, 2008. So I get to this email, from a guy calling himself "Will J." We are a few days from the first anniversary of the death of young Villanueva and there is tension in the air. The young man's death, the previous summer, had set off a riot the likes of which has not often been seen in Quebec. First, because the riot broke out in the middle of a residential neighbourhood—the northeast of Montreal North. Second, because several shots were fired in the direction of the SPVM personnel deployed on the scene, with one policewoman taking a bullet in the leg. Tensions were still running high in the area, and Montreal North had been the scene of fresh incidents between youth and the SPVM in the early summer of 2009.

It was in this somewhat stormy context that CRAP, in conjunction with Montréal-Nord Républik,[1] was organizing a march through the streets of the borough to mark the first anniversary of Fredy Villanueva's death. Not a riot. A march. A demonstration. All in collaboration with the Villanueva family. And then this "Will J" comes along like a bull in a china shop. His tone with CRAP is rather feisty, as if he sees us as a bunch of hooligans who just use political causes to stir up trouble. Wasn't "Will J" aware that just the day before, Wendy Villanueva, one of Fredy's sisters, had called for calm at a press conference organized jointly by CRAP and Montréal-Nord Républik?

Reading this, I already knew that this same "Will J" had also contacted Montréal-Nord Républik just three weeks earlier, emailing to offer to "distribute flyers." On that occasion, he introduced himself as "Will M. Joseph Jr.," but he also sometimes called himself "Jimmy James." It turns out that his real name is James Noël. And that he is a police officer with the SPVM—badge number 5787.

Yep, that guy trumpeting that his "boyz are ready to do war" and generously offering to organize "sumthin fucktup" was a cop. But what this undercover cop didn't know is that Montréal-Nord Républik was well aware of that fact. Constable Noël was certainly unlucky: one of the members of the collective had been with him in the Royal Canadian Air Force cadets back in the 1990s and knew that he had subsequently joined the ranks of the SPVM. Furthermore, this undercover agent made a mistake that proved fatal to his cover as a "hood" guy: he was careless enough to send two emails to Montréal-Nord Républik from a computer that, as his IP address revealed, was located at 2580 St. Joseph Boulevard East, where the offices of the SPVM's Operational Communications Centre are to be found.

I had been an activist working against police abuse for almost fifteen years, and now I was confronted for the first time with a cop playing agent provocateur. I now knew first-hand that the phenomenon of police provocation was not just an urban legend.

Agent Noël never showed up at the August 9, 2009, event. He must have learned, somehow, that he had been found out. It was a great demonstration; there were maybe 600 of us, and the lively crowd seemed to only grow larger as we moved toward the northeast end of the borough, where Fredy Villanueva had died before his time. However, there was one point when things could have gotten out of hand: it was when I was giving a speech, on Pascal Street, near Jubinville. Some cops had the gall to arrest a young man in front of the packed crowd. I feared a confrontation as I saw more and more people massing around the patrol car. "This is what they want, don't get in there," I shouted into the megaphone to try to defuse the situation. The police vehicle sped off, but not without smashing into a protester's bike.

ALEXANDRE POPOVIC

The isolated incident was later blown up by columnist Richard Martineau of the *Journal de Montréal*, who was not even present at the scene. "You would have liked it if it had blown up, if it had exploded," he wrote, in the hallucinatory style that is his bread and butter.[2] "Will J," aka "Will Joseph Junior," aka "Jimmy James," aka James Noël, might have wanted that. But CRAP didn't. Nor did Montréal-Nord Républik. And the Villanueva family certainly didn't.

Unexpectedly, Agent Noël did make an appearance at the very end of the march, when Will Prosper of Montréal-Nord Républik—the *real* Will—was giving a speech. "The police have infiltrated us, as if we were terrorists," he said, exposing the double game of "Will Joseph Junior." Furious, the man of many aliases phoned one of the organizers to threaten that Will Prosper had "better watch his back."

This was going too far. On March 19, 2010, I filed a complaint with the Police Ethics Commissioner to denounce all the acts and actions that the undercover agent had taken against members of CRAP and Montréal-Nord Républik. An exercise in futility: "The Commissioner cannot conclude that a derogatory act was committed," wrote Assistant Commissioner Hélène Tremblay in a decision dated July 18, 2013.[3] "It is not the Commissioner's place to call into question police investigative techniques," Tremblay also wrote, without deigning to mention the thinly veiled threats to the Montréal-Nord Républik spokesperson. Normally, the person who files a complaint can appeal a rejection to the Police Ethics Committee after its investigation is complete. But not this time, since the Commissioner simply shelved the investigation.[4] Police ethics at its finest: a machine for rejecting complaints. The Police Ethics Commissioner showed a complete lack of interest in reining in undercover cops who push the envelope a little too far when playing pretend protester.

The "police watchdog" had already demonstrated its toothlessness in its handling of a complaint against three Sûreté du Québec police officers dressed as members of the "Black Bloc" in 2007.[5] In Montebello on August 20 of that year, hoping to blend in with a demonstration against a summit between the Prime Minister of Canada and the presidents of the United States and Mexico, Sergeants Jean-François Boucher, Joey Laflamme, and Patrick Tremblay dressed in black and hid their faces behind black scarves while Boucher carried a large rock in his hand. The trio was soon spotted by protesters, including David Coles, president of the Communications, Energy and Paperworkers Union of Canada (CEP), who asked them to leave. After

3

INTRODUCTION: IN THE NAME OF THE LAW

insulting and shoving Coles, the officers eventually took refuge behind a line of riot cops, who then pretended to arrest them. Later, a photo showing that the boots of one of the three undercover officers were the same as those worn by the SQ would force the provincial police to admit what everyone already suspected: the three men were indeed cops.[6]

On April 14, 2008, Mr. Coles filed a complaint with the Police Ethics Commissioner against the three plainclothes officers, as well as against Inspector Marcel Savard, the most senior officer of the "flagrante delicto"[7] squad. Despite overwhelming video evidence, the Commissioner dismissed the complaint out of hand. When the file went to review on October 19, 2009, the Police Ethics Committee had to admit that "while the infiltration of police officers is acceptable to arrest the perpetrators of criminal acts, not every action committed by them for this purpose is legitimate just because the original goal is commendable."[8]

The Commissioner had to reluctantly cite the three plainclothes officers before the Police Ethics Committee, for having violated three sections of the Code of Ethics of Québec Police Officers.[9] But in its decision, rendered on March 14, 2011, only the insults uttered by Sergeant Boucher to Coles were deemed derogatory. As for the rock he was holding, the Committee did not even see this as an incitement to violence.[10] And the matter did not end there, as Sergeant Boucher appealed the decision to the Court of Quebec.

On February 9, 2012, Judge Daniel Dortélus would overturn the one and only conviction handed down by the Police Ethics Committee in this case, interpreting the officer's insults as a ploy "to continue to cover his tracks, until he could get safely out of reach of potential assailants."[11] The court also expressed the view that Sergeant Boucher's conduct would only have been derogatory had it occurred "after he had successfully crossed to the side of the police squad."[12]

Does this mean that cops are only subject to ethical standards when they are in uniform? The reasoning put forth by the court seems to suggest that the duties and standards of conduct set out in the Code of Ethics of Québec Police Officers no longer apply when police pose as protesters at demonstrations or take part in undercover operations. That is just a small step from saying that the law no longer applies to covert operations carried out by police and other intelligence services.

And it is a step that has been taken throughout Canadian history. Indeed, the Canadian secret services have always acted as if their operations were above the law. When the first secret service was created in Canada in the nineteenth century, there was no law or official policy governing its surveillance activities.[13] This did not stop the Canadian secret police from illegally opening people's mail during the First World War.[14] The Commission of Inquiry into Certain Activities of the Royal Canadian Mounted Police (RCMP)—commonly known as the McDonald Commission—revealed that the federal police was still doing the same thing six decades later.[15] The McDonald Commission reported numerous instances where the RCMP, specifically its Security Service (SS), had acted outside the law.[16] It noted, for example, that in June 1970, RCMP members were concerned about a memo that stated that

> Certain tasks performed by S.I.B. [Security and Intelligence] or C.I.B. personnel [required] that the law be transgressed, whether it be Federal, Provincial or Municipal law, in order that the purpose of the undertaking may be fulfilled.[17]

Agents were worried that the "tasks" in question might result in criminal or civil proceedings against them. The Legal Services Branch reassured them that if such an unfortunate event were to occur, the Attorney General would be asked to waive criminal charges so long as the acts were committed during an operation approved by a superior. If ever they were convicted, the RCMP would pay their fine and there would be no dismissal. Senior RCMP officers wanted this opinion to be circulated throughout the force, so a memo was prepared for the approval of the RCMP's top man, Commissioner William Leonard Higgitt, explaining that "a member has the right to refuse to perform an illegal act." Higgit, however, refused to sign the memo, warning that

> Under no circumstances should anything of this nature be circulated in written or memo form. The reasons ought to be obvious. I do not believe this is the problem it is being made out to be. Members know or ought to that whatever misadventure happens to them the Force will stand by them so long as there is some justification for doing so.[18]

RCMP agents were thus reassured that they did not have to worry about breaking the law. In his testimony before the McDonald Commission, Commissioner Higgitt stated that this unwritten policy had been in place for over thirty years.[19]

This revelation came on the heels of comments made by SS Director General John Starnes during a meeting of the Cabinet Committee on Priorities and Planning, on December 1, 1970. There, Starnes had boasted that the RCMP "has been doing S & I [Security & Intelligence] illegal things for 20 years but [was] never caught."[20] It should be noted that amongst those present when Starnes made these remarks were Pierre Elliott Trudeau, Prime Minister of Canada at the time, and his Minister of Justice, John Turner. Like so many others, these two men subsequently suffered from memory lapses when called to testify before the commission. But Starnes remained adamant: "Ministers were aware or had been made aware, that we had been breaking the law."[21] "The problem was placed on Ministers' desks," added Commissioner Higgitt.[22] And the McDonald Commission concluded that "on December 1, 1970, Mr. Trudeau, Mr. Turner and other persons present were told that the Security Service had been doing illegal things for twenty years."[23]

While Ottawa chose to feign ignorance, certain judges showed no compunction about openly condoning illegal acts by police. To cite the 1993 findings of the Alberta Court of Appeal in *Bond v. The Queen*:

> Police involve themselves in high speed chases, travelling beyond posted speed limits. Police pose as prostitutes and communicate for that purpose in order to gather evidence. Police buy, possess, and transport illegal drugs on a daily basis during undercover operations. In a perfect world this would not be necessary but, patently, illegal drug commerce is neither successfully investigated, nor resisted, by uniformed police peering through hotel-room transoms and keyholes or waiting patiently at police headquarters to receive the confessions of penitent drug-traffickers.[24]

Still, there are limits to what Canadian courts will tolerate in terms of police crimes. One example is the unanimous decision of the Supreme Court of Canada in December 1988, in *The Queen v. Mack*, which continues to serve as a key reference in regard to police entrapment, which it defines as follows:

> Entrapment occurs when (a) the authorities provide a person with an opportunity to commit an offence without acting on a reasonable suspicion that this person is already engaged in criminal activity or pursuant to a bona fide inquiry, and, (b) although having such a reasonable suspicion or acting in the course of a bona fide inquiry, they

go beyond providing an opportunity and induce the commission of an offence. It is essential that the factors relied on by a court relate to the underlying reasons for the recognition of the doctrine in the first place.[25]

It is the case of *The Queen v. Campbell*, however, that is probably the most significant. Arrested in Ontario in 1991 during an undercover RCMP operation, John Campbell and Salvator Shirose had been caught in a trap set by plainclothes cops who claimed they were trying to sell them 50 kilos of hashish resin worth $1 million on the open market. The two men appealed their conviction, setting off a judicial saga that led to a series of interactions between the three branches of government (executive, legislative, judicial), the ultimate consequences of which are still being felt today.

In January 1997, the Ontario Court of Appeal upheld the convictions of the two accused, but at the same time noted that while under the Narcotic Control Regulations police are allowed to be in possession of illegal drugs when conducting undercover operations, they cannot offer to sell prohibited substances.[26] In other words, the RCMP had broken the law. On May 15, Jean Chrétien's Liberal cabinet responded to the ruling by passing the Controlled Drugs and Substances Act (Police Enforcement) Regulations, which authorized police to engage in drug trafficking, as well as the production, import, and export of any prohibited substance, "for the purposes" of an investigation. The regulation, which has far-reaching implications, was quietly adopted by Order-in-Council without any public debate in Parliament—not even a press release.[27]

In 1999, however, the Campbell case made its way to the Supreme Court of Canada. In a unanimous ruling on April 22, the country's highest court concluded that "the police stepped outside the lawful ambit of their agency," adding that "it should be left to Parliament to delineate the nature and scope of the immunity" granted to police officers to commit criminal offences.[28] In other words, an executive order is not sufficient to allow the police to commit crimes: such a thing would have to be sanctioned by a vote in parliament. The courts had spoken: the police had to obey the law during their investigations. The ruling apparently threw a spanner in the works of how things were normally done: one government document admitted that as a result of the Campbell decision, "some law enforcement investigations have been suspended, substantially modified, or stopped altogether."[29] According to

RCMP Inspector Raf Souccar, it was "absolutely necessary" for police to have immunity to commit criminal offences in order to carry out their duties.[30]

Ottawa got the message: On June 22, 2000, after the House of Commons had adjourned for the summer, Justice Minister Ann McLellan introduced draft legislation in the Senate that would allow police to commit crimes legally.[31] The RCMP had worked closely with the government to craft the proposed legislation.[32] Michel Belhumeur, the Bloc Québécois justice critic, objected that the draft legislation "goes far beyond the war on drugs and organized crime. It leads straight to a police state."[33]

On April 5, 2001, Minister McLellan introduced Bill C-24—*An Act to amend the Criminal Code (organized crime and law enforcement) and to make consequential amendments to other Acts*—also known as the "Second Anti-Gang Law." C-24 proposed to amend the Criminal Code to extend immunity to the police for a wide range of criminal offences.[34] The Bloc Québécois proposed amending C-24 to limit the crimes that could be committed by police to those that occurred during investigations targeting organized crime. This proposed amendment was supported by the New Democratic Party (NDP) but was rejected by the governing Liberal Party and the Canadian Alliance, the official opposition at the time.[35] The Ligue des droits et libertés issued a statement that C-24 ran "contrary to the principle of equality before the law and the rule of law" in that it created "two classes of citizens, some of whom can commit offences with impunity."[36]

The bill even raised some eyebrows within the ranks of the police—Toronto Detective John Irwin expressed concern police might try to take advantage of the immunity afforded by C-24.[37] Such reservations were, however, drowned out by the excitement at the new powers that had been granted by the government. Vincent Westwick, counsel for the Canadian Association of Chiefs of Police, responded to Detective Irwin's comments by asserting that the bill enjoyed broad support among Canadian police forces.[38] Yves Prud'homme, president of the Fédération des policiers et policières municipaux du Québec, even complained that the immunity proposed by C-24 did not go far enough:

> We strongly suggest that the government not create a list excluding certain offences from this immunity. We are concerned that criminal organizations will require undercover officers to commit one of the excluded offences in order to expose them.[39]

The measures granting immunity to police to carry out criminal acts came into effect on February 1, 2002. In the name of combating organized crime, Ottawa made it legal for police to do things that are illegal for the rest of us. Except, it is true, for those select members of the civilian world with a special status—those known as "sources" or "undercover civilian agents" (UCOs) in the legal world—who act under police orders during undercover operations...

Yet, as has been noted by Université de Montréal law professor Anne-Marie Boisvert, "there is no legal definition of an undercover civilian agent,"[40] despite the often crucial role played by UCOs in major police investigations into organized crime. UCOs should not be confused with informants, who are simply referred to as "human sources" in police jargon.[41] (Popular culture has the merit of being more direct, referring to these people as "snitches".) UCOs collect evidence that leads to charges, while informants "only" provide confidential information. However, as Jacques Shore of the Law Union of Ontario has observed, "too often, it seems, the information obtained is self-serving, with the informant generally being rewarded for his or her work. Too often the testimony of such informants cannot be corroborated."[42] Unlike UCOs, informants are not called upon to testify in court, and their identities are closely guarded secrets. Only under exceptional circumstances—for example, to prove the innocence of a person facing charges following police entrapment—can a court lift the cover of secrecy on their identity.[43]

With Bill C-24, the purview of police provocateurs grew significantly more broad. Cops and informants, who already had a penchant for entrapment, certainly took this as a sign of state approval for their actions. The ends justify the means—this is the message that the Canadian state seemed to be sending. So who was left to hold the police accountable when they took advantage of this dangerous immunity?

The accountability mechanism provided by Parliament is unfortunately very weak. Government authorities are only required to publish an annual report containing information on the number of times police or their UCOs have been authorized to commit criminal offences under C-24. Unfortunately, the media does not seem to be at all interested in these statistics. My own research using newspaper databases shows that the criminal offences contained in these annual reports have only been reported in the print media on two occasions since C-24 was passed.[44] Despite assurances that we live in a democratic society and all the hype about the "fourth estate," the fact is that the media have failed to even pretend to be interested in this subject.

INTRODUCTION: IN THE NAME OF THE LAW

And without the media paying any attention, the police can do whatever they please with nothing to prevent them from committing the worst abuses.

The annual reports are not very difficult to obtain. Many of them are actually available online. This is the case for all those concerning the RCMP. As for the annual reports concerning Quebec police forces, a simple access to information request is enough to obtain them. I did so myself. The documents obtained were very illuminating. First, they revealed that Quebec police forces did not avail themselves of the criminal immunity provided by C-24 during the first two years following the bill's coming into force, which would seem to indicate that this immunity was not really necessary for the police to carry out their investigations. Second, the annual reports show that this immunity was not just used to fight drug trafficking and organized crime. For example, in 2004, Quebec police forces reported that they had granted ten authorizations "for the purpose of committing mischief on a vehicle, but in six of these cases, no mischief was committed." Not exactly the kind of crime traditionally associated with the mafia …

In 2005, thirteen more authorizations were granted by police in Quebec, this time "for the purpose of committing mischief, vehicle theft, postering, painting and graffiti. In all cases, no acts were committed." The authorized criminal offences therefore remained at the discussion stage. Does this mean that an UCO had infiltrated a group that had proven itself inclined to *not* engage in illegal activities? The report does not go into enough detail to allow us to answer this question. However, the document does state that "the investigations involved activities related to receiving stolen property, attempted murder, homicide, narcotics, demonstrations, and theft over $5,000." So we know that on at least one occasion the police planned to use a law supposedly targeting organized crime against protesters.

As for the other annual reports obtained, up to 2020 they reveal that Quebec police forces have given the green light to a wide range of criminal offences: fraud and forgery, sale of tobacco and alcohol without a permit, sale and trafficking in weapons, theft, drug trafficking, breaking and entering with criminal intent, offences committed for the benefit of a criminal organization, breach of trust, corruption in municipal affairs, intimidation, laundering the proceeds of crime, etc. All in all, 406 authorizations to commit a criminal offence were granted in Quebec between 2004 and 2021. It should be noted that the 2012 report discloses that four offences were committed "without the written authorization of senior officials."[45] The said offences were: theft;

breaking and entering with criminal intent; commission of offence for a criminal organization; obstructing justice; mischief; and mischief in relation to data.[46] It happened again in 2021: a theft was committed without authorization during a police investigation into the illegal production of cannabis. As for the RCMP, reports indicate that a total of 159 authorizations were granted between 2002 and 2021. However, the reports do not indicate how many offences have been committed. On the one hand, certain authorizations are not subsequently acted upon. On the other hand, a single authorization can sometimes include several offences. For example, in 2018, seven authorizations resulted in the commission of fifty-five offences.[47] However, the peak was reached the previous year, with seventy-three offences committed. Note that no offences were authorized in 2019 and 2020, and that none of the twenty authorizations granted in 2021 were acted upon.

The Canadian Security Intelligence Service (CSIS)—Canada's version of the CIA—has a similarly murky relationship with the law. This history was revealed (in large part) by a comprehensive judgment by Justice Patrick K. Gleeson of the Federal Court in May 2020.[48] For example, when Parliament enacted the *Anti-terrorism Act* of 2001[49] with the consequence, among other things, of criminalizing "the provision of property or financial services or other related services" for the purpose of benefiting any person facilitating or carrying out any terrorist activity or knowing that doing so would benefit a terrorist group (*Criminal Code*, section 83.03), this "posed a difficulty for [CSIS]," reports the judge. "Gaining access to the subjects of national security terrorism investigation at times requires the provision of money or property to these individuals," he writes. Consequently, "this raised the possibility of criminal liability attaching to certain of [CSIS's] activities."[50]

Lawyers from the National Security Litigation and Advisory Group (NSLAG), however, did not see things the same way. The NSLAG is made up of Department of Justice lawyers whose role it is to provide legal advice to CSIS and represent the agency in court. These lawyers use a "legal risk assessment framework" to advise CSIS in its covert operations. However, as the judge wrote, "the legal risk assessment framework does not capture the concept of illegality." In the bureaucratic language of NSLAG lawyers, it is simply a question of determining whether "the overall legal risk level is low, medium, or high."[51] For Judge Gleeson, this framework "is poorly suited to assessing and addressing potentially illegal activity" since it "suggests that the risk can either be accepted or mitigated."[52]

INTRODUCTION: IN THE NAME OF THE LAW

In April 2002, the Department of Justice produced a legal opinion stating that "the *Criminal Code* provisions passed under the *Anti-terrorism Act* do not bind the Crown." This position was based on the "Crown immunity doctrine," which "creates a presumption that the Crown is not bound by statute unless the statute expressly states that it binds the Crown; the statute clearly intends to bind the Crown; or the statute would be frustrated, or an absurdity would result, if it did not bind the Crown."[53] However, the reasoning was based on an old judgment from 1959[54] which, by the very admission of the authors of the legal opinion, was now obsolete. "It is not entirely clear that the Supreme Court would arrive at the same decision today if a case were to raise squarely the issue," the government's lawyers warned. Despite this, "in [CSIS's] view, it was in a position to conduct activities in carrying out its mandate that on their face contravened the *Criminal Code* on the basis that Crown immunity shielded the [CSIS] employees and human sources from criminal liability and therefore allowed it to operate within the law," wrote Justice Gleeson.[55]

There seemed to be some doubt, however, since in 2004 CSIS sought advice from Department of Justice lawyers "on the potential liability of human sources and their handlers who may engage in activities which on their face contravene the *Criminal Code*'s anti-terrorism provision." The new legal opinion was, however, based on that of 2002. Although Crown immunity was again invoked, the jurists nevertheless affirmed that this principle "should not be seen as a panacea for potentially illegal actions."[56] They also argued that "legislative reform" would be necessary to "resolve the uncertainty."[57] Just like the *Campbell* decision led Parliament to pass C-24.

In April 2005, the NSLAG was even clearer towards CSIS, not only saying that "the 2002 opinion is weak," but that there was "a lack of academic and recent judicial support for the Crown immunity doctrine." Then, in April 2013, the Justice Department "concluded that the likelihood of the Service successfully relying on Crown immunity was low and recommended a legislative solution."[58]

This "legislative solution" took the form of Anti-terrorism Bill C-51, introduced by Stephen Harper's Conservative government on January 30, 2015. C-51 provided a form of immunity for criminal offences when CSIS decides to take "measures to reduce threats to the security of Canada." CSIS was thus granted disruptive powers, which it could even use outside the country. CSIS agents were now allowed to commit any offences to the *Criminal Code*, except those that result in bodily harm or death to a person, that violate the sexual integrity of an individual, or that pervert or obstruct the course of justice. Those three exceptions to immunity are the same that were provided in C-24. "If those measures will contravene a right or freedom guaranteed by the Canadian Charter of Rights and Freedoms or will be contrary to other Canadian law," CSIS must then seek judicial authorization from the Federal Court.[59]

However, the relationship between CSIS and the Federal Court has not been particularly reassuring to date. Thomas D'Arcy "Ted" Finn, the first Director of CSIS, was forced to resign on September 11, 1987, after the Canadian secret service admitted to the Court that it had submitted "inaccurate and unsubstantiated" information in order to obtain a wiretap warrant.[60] There is no indication that CSIS has learned from its past mistakes. On the contrary, in a decision on November 22, 2013, Justice Richard Mosley criticized CSIS for violating its "duty of candour" by deliberately concealing from the court the scope and scale of an operation to intercept foreign communications.[61] Then, in November 2016, Justice Simon Noël ruled that CSIS had breached its duty to inform the Federal Court by concealing the fact that it had illegally retained personal data collected under court orders for ten years.[62]

CSIS has repeatedly proven itself resistant to judicial review. A document leaked by the Wikileaks website revealed that then–CSIS Director Jim Judd complained to a US State Department official in 2008 that Canadian courts were undermining his agency's work.[63] CSIS officials have even referred to a "judicial jihad."[64] But it is not as if judges have ever been particularly zealous in monitoring the activities of Canada's intelligence agencies. From 1993 to 2003, the Federal Court granted 99.3% of the 2,544 warrant applications submitted by CSIS to spy on people it had in its sights.[65] In short, it is doubtful that the courts are up to the difficult task of ensuring that CSIS does not abuse the immunity granted by C-51.

CSIS's new powers naturally sparked controversy. However, the public debate on C-51 was off to a bad start. Indeed, journalists, columnists, and national security experts have all questioned the immunity CSIS enjoys, expressing concern that such powers could result in a repeat of the misdeeds perpetrated by the RCMP in the 1970s. Unfortunately, these critics have only referred back to those earlier abuses, as if CSIS had no history of entrapment itself. But one needn't go back forty years, to a time before CSIS even existed, to find spectacular cases of abuse by Canadian intelligence agencies.

INTRODUCTION: IN THE NAME OF THE LAW

In the 1980s, a union organizer acting as a CSIS informant did jail time for participating in plans to plant bombs in the Quebec City area. In the 1990s, another CSIS informant was revealed to be a leader of a white supremacist group in Toronto, and in Montreal, a Canadian intelligence mole posing as a Muslim community leader made numerous death threats and calls for terrorist attacks. These agents provocateurs and the scandals surrounding them—all of which will be discussed in greater detail later in this book—were never mentioned when the expansion of CSIS's already broad powers was being publicly debated in the wake of C-51. This unfortunate amnesia suggests that journalists are not paying enough attention to what CSIS is up to. And when the media turn a blind eye, the secret services' agents provocateurs will simply take advantage of the situation to do whatever they please.

Bill C-51 was passed by the House of Commons on May 6, 2015. The NDP, Bloc Québécois, and Green Party all voted against it, but the Liberals sided with the Conservative government in supporting it, while promising to amend it if they came to power. Such an eventuality did indeed come to pass when Justin Trudeau won the general election on October 19 of that year (more on this below).

That said, CSIS remained unsatisfied. The immunity conferred by C-51 only related to "measures to reduce threats," and not to all of CSIS's activities. As Justice Gleeson reports, CSIS attempted, in June 2015, to take advantage of an update to the written directives issued by the Public Security minister to the Canadian secret services to include "language that would recognize a Crown immunity exception to the requirement that [CSIS] and its human sources comply with the law." The request then led to the production of a new legal opinion. "It marks the first time that the Department of Justice unequivocally told [CSIS] that it likely did not benefit from Crown immunity," writes the judge.[66]

However, in October 2015, the NSLAG issued another written advisory to CSIS on the issue of Crown immunity that "contradicted" the legal opinion of the previous June, concluding that CSIS "may rely" on Crown immunity, with caveats relating to the uncertainty surrounding the applicability of the doctrine and the "medium to low chance" of success should the matter be reviewed by a court."[67] In the fall of 2016, the NSLAG warned CSIS that "reliance on illegally collected information" might have legal repercussions, noting in particular that the intelligence agency "could engage a whole host of liabilities, including impacting the outcome of criminal prosecutions."[68]

Then, in January 2017, a new legal opinion "concluded that [CSIS] did not benefit from Crown immunity," wrote Justice Gleeson. Fearing that this lack of immunity could "have a significant impact on Service operations," CSIS's director, Michel Coulombe, "sought a meeting with the Deputy Minister of Public Safety and Emergency Preparedness, the Deputy Minister of Justice, and the National Security and Intelligence Advisor to discuss the opinion and potential legislative solutions."[69] In the meantime,

> [CSIS] continued to conduct previously approved high legal risk operations. Having ceased the approval of new operations following the receipt of the January 2017 opinion, approvals recommenced in late March 2017. These were operations that the opinion had concluded were illegal.[70]

Justice Gleeson was also highly critical of the NSLAG, noting "the Department of Justice's equally troubling reluctance to clearly and unequivocally communicate that certain proposed operational activity was illegal, and that the Service lacked the authority to undertake the activity."[71] Gleeson went on to say that "The Department of Justice also appeared content with the status quo,"[72] before concluding that "The Department of Justice's apparent inaction in the face of this information where it had reached the conclusions set out in the January 2017 opinion fall well short of its obligations to ensure that public affairs are administered according to law."[73]

While CSIS lobbied behind the scenes to change the law, the newly elected Liberal government launched a public consultation on "national security." In a green paper published in 2016, the Liberals announced that they wanted to repeal the "problematic elements" of C-51.[74] During the fall of 2016, tens of thousands of Canadians expressed their opinion on the government proposals. "Most participants in these Consultations have opted to err on the side of protecting individual rights and freedoms rather than granting additional powers to national security agencies and law enforcement, even with enhanced transparency and independent oversight," says the consultation report.[75] In May 2017, the House of Commons Standing Committee on Public Safety and National Security tabled its own report in which it recommended limitations to CSIS's new powers, namely to "remove the ability to violate the Charter" and to impose on CSIS the dual obligation to "exhaust all other non-disruptive means of reducing threats" and to obtain the "Minister's approval," in addition to a warrant from the Federal Court, before engaging in "disruption activities that violate Canadian law."[76]

Those who had high expectations for this consultation process must have been sorely disappointed when they learned of Bill C-59, *An Act respecting national security matters*, which was intended to be the Liberal response to C-51. Filed in June 2017, C-59 maintains criminal immunity for CSIS when it applies "measures to reduce a threat," but adds three new classes of offences that Canadian secret services are not authorized to commit: torture and other cruel, inhuman or degrading treatment or punishment; the detention of a person; and "caus[ing] the loss of, or any serious damage to, any property if doing so would endanger the safety of an individual."[77] CSIS also retained the power to take measures "that would limit a right or freedom guaranteed by the *Canadian Charter of Rights and Freedoms*," as long as they are authorized by a warrant issued by a judge.[78] It should be noted that the hearing to apply for a mandate, or for its renewal, is "held in private" by the Federal court.[79]

The "measures" requiring obtaining judicial authorization have been divided into seven classes of activities, namely "altering, removing, replacing, destroying, disrupting or degrading a communication or means of communication," "altering, removing, replacing, destroying, degrading or providing—or interfering with the use or delivery of—any thing or part of a thing, including records, documents, goods, components and equipment," "fabricating or disseminating any information, record or document," engaging in "financial transaction" or sabotage thereof, or "personating a person, other than a police officer."[80] Clearly, most of these "measures" are actually deeds forbidden under the *Criminal code*. Thus the need for CSIS to obtain immunity.

Worse, C-59 even extends CSIS's criminal immunity to the agency's "information and intelligence collection activities" so that its "employees effectively carry out [...] information and intelligence collection duties and functions." It is up to the Public Security Minister to "determine the classes of acts or omissions that would otherwise constitute offences and that designated employees may be justified in committing," or even justified in "directing another person to commit" if they want to have someone else do the dirty work, excluding the six classes of forbidden offence mentioned above.[81] It is also this same minister who appoints the employees or senior officials who can break the law with impunity, although the Director of CSIS or one of his senior employees can also make such designations "for a period of not more than 48 hours" when "exigent circumstances" make it "not feasible for the Minister to designate the employee." The CSIS Director or a designated senior employee may also "authorize designated employees, for a period of not more than one year, to direct the commission" of an offence.[82]

However, the "designated employee" may give the order to break the law without having received authorization if "it is not feasible in the circumstances to obtain" it and if the commission of the offence is "necessary," either to "preserve the life or safety of any individual," or the anonymity of a CSIS employee or a "human source," or to "prevent the imminent loss or destruction of information or intelligence." Thus the door is open to several exceptions to the authorization process. Furthermore, criminal immunity also extends to "a person, other than an employee," who has been ordered to commit an offence by a "designated employee" of CSIS.[83]

Curiously, C-59 generated considerably less public controversy than C-51, even though it broadened the possibility for CSIS to commit criminal offences. "When the Trudeau government announced this week that, in effect, it was keeping the most contentious elements of C-51, there was little outcry. Neither the *Star* nor the *Globe and Mail* thought the story worthy of page 1. Even the British Columbia Civil Liberties Association was muted in its criticism," wrote Thomas Walkom in the *Toronto Star*.[84]

Meanwhile, David Vigneault, who was appointed Director of CSIS in June 2017, had no intention of having his agency take a break from illegality while waiting the entry into force of C-59. "Pending passage of the Bill, CSIS will continue to rely on its historic interpretation of Crown Immunity to conduct such operational activities," he wrote in a letter to the Minister of Public Safety, in September 2017, adding: "I will immediately notify you of high risk operations I approve, should any be identified."[85]

The bill was approved by the House of Commons on June 19, 2018, with 176 votes in favour and 126 votes against. The Liberals, of course, came out in favour of its adoption, with the support of the Bloc Québécois, the Green Party, and the independent MP Darshan Singh Kang. The opposition came from the Conservatives and the New Democrats, as well as from members of Québec Debout and the sole MP representing the Cooperative Commonwealth Federation. The "legislative solution" much desired by CSIS came into force a year later. No more contradictory legal opinions from the Ministry of Justice! By a simple wave of a magic wand, Parliament legalized what had until then been unlawful conduct for CSIS.

As we saw, CSIS was not waiting for the passage of Bill C-51 to give itself permission to commit criminal acts, just as the RCMP had not waited

INTRODUCTION: IN THE NAME OF THE LAW

for C-24 to get involved in drug trafficking. If CSIS was already having a field day before C-51, it must undoubtedly be a carnival for the provocateurs now, what with the carte blanche they currently enjoy to commit almost any offence under the Criminal Code. Cops and CSIS are now on an equal footing: the police are officially authorized to fight crime with crime, while the secret service has a parliamentary green light to fight subversion with subversion and terrorism with terrorism—like pyromaniac firefighters who enthusiastically fan the flames instead of bringing out the hoses.

This book is a call to stop giving CSIS a free pass. In other words, it is a call to document the illegal activities of the Canadian secret service, to fight against amnesia, in short: a call to raise awareness with the goal of offering some protection against, and if possible even rolling back, the powers of those who seek to surveil and manipulate us, our movements, and our communities. It is also an invitation to take a trip back in time, to learn how provocation and entrapment, far from being the unique prerogative of CSIS or the RCMP, are at the very heart of the police as an institution—and go back as far as the state that they act to protect. This book does not purport to provide an exhaustive list of all the cases of police provocation or entrapment in this country's history, but rather to demonstrate that these practices have existed for as long as Canada has existed, regardless of the name under which the secret services were operating.

Welcome to the bizarro world of intelligence, where the masters of manipulation and professional provocateurs make—and *break*—the law ...

Alexandre Popovic
Montreal, February 2023

1. Confederation and Provocation

The origins of the secret police in Canada can be traced back to the nineteenth century, when Quebec was a British colony called Lower Canada. In 1837, the British colonial power's hostility to demands for reform (for universal suffrage, an end to corruption, abolition of the death penalty, etc.), as well as a hardening of political repression, led to the Patriotes rebellion, which took its name from the Patriot Party, led by Louis-Joseph Papineau. Although the movement was mostly composed of francophones, there were also several anglophones, including the physician Robert Nelson, who proclaimed the independence of Lower Canada in February 1838. After brutally suppressing the rebellion, the colonial authorities set up the Lower Canada Rural Police in 1839, modelled after the Royal Irish Constabulary. Its main objective was to combat any further attempts at subversion. The civil secretary of the colony at the time stated the mandate of the country's first political police force as follows:

> To prevent the recurrence of those combinations of the people which in the two preceding years had led to such disastrous results, and to supply the government with a means of intelligence in those locations where discontent and disaffection appeared to have taken deepest roots.[1]

In its counter-insurgency efforts between 1839 and 1842, the Lower Canada Rural Police—originally 80% anglophone—intercepted mail, carried out surveillance to identify potential plots, dispersed public gatherings deemed suspicious, closely monitored taverns—considered to be "hotbeds of idleness, immorality, and disaffection"—identified newspapers read by "ill-intentioned" people, and shut down speeches made by "apostles of sedition" in church squares after Sunday mass.[2] This "pacification" quickly bore fruit, and colonial officials were pleased with the results of their new police force:

> I attribute the present tranquility of the district entirely to the presence of the Rural Police; to the fact that no illegal meeting can be

1. CONFEDERATION AND PROVOCATION

held without their knowledge ... and to the immediate assistance of a military force if required ...³

Conservative leader John A. Macdonald, then Attorney General of the Province of Canada (also known as the United Province of Canada) was similarly inspired by the Royal Irish Constabulary when he established the Western Frontier Constabulary in September 1864.⁴ Generally considered to be Canada's first secret service, the organization was set up without fanfare or public debate. Its mandate was to protect the Canadian frontier and to ensure the neutrality of the British colony in regards to the civil war that was then raging in the United States to the south. Macdonald put Gilbert McMicken, an ambitious Conservative MP with no police or military experience but with a reputation for discretion, in charge of the constabulary.⁵ In the fall of 1865, McMicken ordered his agents to seek employment in the towns where they were operating, so as not to raise any suspicions about their true source of income.⁶

The end of the American Civil War gave way to a new threat: Irish nationalists (known as Fenians) in the US had come up with a plan to invade Canada and use it as a bargaining chip to wrest their mother country from the hands of the British Empire. Most of the Fenians' daring schemes ended in failure. In April 1866, when some of them attempted a landing on the small island of Campobello, New Brunswick, they were forced to retreat in the face of a massive mobilization of British troops. On June 1, about 700 Fenians invaded Ridgeway on the Niagara Peninsula; they initially were met with poorly trained Canadian volunteers, but nonetheless retreated to the city of Buffalo, New York, two days later in the face of the imminent arrival of battalions of Canadian militiamen and British soldiers.

When Irish-born Conservative MP Thomas D'Arcy McGee, one of the "thirty-six fathers of Canadian Confederation," was found murdered in Ottawa on April 7, 1868, the Fenians immediately came under suspicion. It was in the wake of this incident that the Western Frontier Constabulary gave way to the Dominion Police—Canada having acquired British "Dominion" status following Confederation in 1867.⁷

The Canadian secret service had been keeping a close eye on the Fenians, spying on them in both Canada and the United States. To this end, McMicken retained the services of the Pinkerton private detective agency, founded in 1850 by Allan Pinkerton—who had distinguished himself by organizing the secret service of Abraham Lincoln's Unionist army during the Civil War.[8] Their surveillance was so successful that John A. Macdonald was reputed to have known more about the Fenians' plans than the Fenians themselves.[9] "I will spare no expense in watching them," said Macdonald, who served as Prime Minister for a grand total of nineteen years.[10]

No less than four Canadian spies worked to collect evidence against Michael Murphy, a Fenian leader in Toronto, where the movement had seventeen cells. Following Murphy's arrest, the Canadian secret service even went so far as to place an undercover agent in prison to continue spying on him. By the end of 1868, the Canadian government had three undercover agents amongst the Fenians in the United States. John W. McDonald had penetrated the organization in Philadelphia and William McMichael worked inside the Fenian headquarters in New York City, but it was Thomas Billis Beach, better known as Henri Le Caron, who went the furthest in infiltrating the Fenian movement.[11]

Born in England in 1841, Beach was not himself Irish. As a teenager, he went to live in Paris, where he befriended several Americans, joining them as they returned home when the Civil War broke out, despite his being largely ignorant as to the nature of the conflict. Once in New York City, the young adventurer enlisted in the Northern army under the pseudonym Henri Le Caron.[12] In 1865, shortly after the end of the conflict, Le Caron met up with one of his former comrades-in-arms, General John O'Neill, who had also led the Fenians at Ridgeway. O'Neill told him about the plan to invade Canada.[13] When Le Caron returned to his family in England in the fall of 1867, it was suggested that he infiltrate the Fenians in the United States as a secret agent of the United Kingdom. As he would later put it, given his "adventurous nature" he seized the opportunity. Back in the United States, he offered his services to O'Neil as a military man; delighted, the latter promised him a position.

In March 1868, under the pseudonym Donald Mackay, Le Caron wrote directly to the Canadian Prime Minister informing him that the Fenians were plotting to assassinate the Prince of Wales. Thus began Le Caron's relationship with the young Canadian state. Three months later, Commissioner McMicken suggested to Macdonald that Le Caron be retained, noting that he had expressed willingness to become an "organizer" within the Fenians. The Prime Minister agreed to pay the recruit a monthly salary of $150, but not without reservations: "A man who undertakes to do what he offers to do, which is to betray the people he is dealing with, cannot be trusted."[14] This mistrust no doubt explains why Canadian spies were soon being assigned to keep an eye on Le Caron in the United States, unaware that he was himself a secret agent.[15]

By August 1868, Le Caron had risen to the rank of commander, giving him access to all the documents produced by John O'Neill, who had become president of the Fenian Brotherhood.[16] O'Neill had Le Caron relocate to the organization's headquarters in New York. Le Caron explains that his role was then enlarged:

> Commissioned at the very outset as Major and Military Organiser of the Irish Republican Army (at a salary of sixty dollars per month, with seven dollars per day expenses), I was instructed to proceed to the Eastern States in company with a civil organiser, in order to visit and reorganise the different military bodies attached to the rebel society.[17]

Le Caron liked the idea of being paid by the Fenians as well as by the governments of Canada and Great Britain, as each plotted against the other. When he was promoted to second-in-command of the IRA, the salary he received from the Fenians even exceeded what he got from Ottawa.[18] He was less happy about having to make speeches to Fenian assemblies—part of his duties in the organization. Not only was the secret agent by his own admission "absolutely ignorant of Irish affairs,"[19] but he also felt nothing but contempt for his audience, bordering on hatred. "Night after night have to speak & associate with a pack of low dirty foul mouthed beings—worse than n----rs,"[20] Le Caron wrote, flaunting his racism.

According to McMicken, Le Caron was by far the "best card" held by the Canadian secret service.[21] Indeed, the agent had been entrusted with a crucial responsibility for the impending invasion of Canada: supervising the establishment of arms and ammunition caches along the Canada-US border. As such, the Canadian state was now in a position to nip any new Fenian incursion in the bud. By November 1868, the Fenian Brotherhood was beginning to falter; according to Le Caron, a quarter of its members had resigned, disappointed that no invasion of Canada had been attempted for over two years.[22] The Commissioner of the Dominion Police, however, was of the opinion that "it is better to let the raid take place so as to give the raiders a lesson which will not be easily forgotten"—a view shared by the British authorities.[23]

When the Fenians finally planned their next raid for the morning of

April 26, 1870, Le Caron would later recall that he was "laughing to myself at [their] coming discomfiture."²⁴ On the day in question, between 400 and 500 Fenians gathered at St. Albans, Vermont, as part of an expedition that was set to land in Franklin, New Brunswick. They were walking into an ambush: once within a few feet of the border, the Fenians came under heavy fire from Canadian forces. Caught by surprise and unable to return fire, the insurgents had no choice but to retreat.²⁵

Despite this humiliating setback, O'Neill refused to give up. In June 1871, he informed Le Caron of his intention to attempt a new incursion onto Canadian soil. The secret agent immediately notified McMicken—"If it pays, I'm in."²⁶ That's all it took to convince Ottawa. Penniless and isolated, O'Neill could only get forty-one diehards to agree to carry out what looked like a desperate attempt at invasion. There was "one great difficulty, however, and that was the want of arms," reported Le Caron.²⁷ But the secret agent had a solution in mind: "I cheerfully agreed to let him have 400 breech-loaders and ammunition, and accompanied him to the points where they were, for the purpose of their delivery."²⁸

This time, O'Neill wanted to attack Canada via Manitoba; this province had been established less than a year previous, and at the time was only one eighth of the size it is today. Most of its inhabitants were Métis, a people who emerged in the eighteenth century when French and Scottish fur traders married Indigenous women, particularly Cree and Anishinaabe (Ojibwe). The descendants of these marriages developed a distinct culture and collective identity, and together they came to form a nation. O'Neill hoped to ally himself with the man who was known as the "Father of Manitoba," Louis Riel,²⁹ leader of the Métis nation. At only twenty-five years of age, Riel had led the Red River Rebellion, the first crisis to confront the Macdonald government following Confederation. The uprising came on the heels of Ottawa's 1869 acquisition of Rupert's Land, a territory of 3.9 million square kilometers that was defined by the drainage basin of Hudson's Bay, including lands that today are part of Quebec in the east and Alberta in the west, the US states of Minnesota, North Dakota, and Montana in the south to Nunavut in the north. Rupert's Land had been controlled by the Hudson's Bay Company since 1670; it was renamed the North-Western Territory³⁰ by Ottawa, which appointed the lawyer William McDougall as its representative there. The Macdonald government had not bothered to consult with the people already living on the land—45% of whom were Indigenous, followed

1. CONFEDERATION AND PROVOCATION

by people of French descent and Métis francophones (40%), and only 5% of whom were anglophones—nor did it inform them of the implications of this transfer of sovereignty. It was against this backdrop that members of the Red River Métis Nation, most of whom were francophone, took up arms to form a provisional government, headed by the young Louis Riel. Given Lieutenant-Governor McDougall's inability to establish his authority, Ottawa decided to negotiate with the rebels, which led to the creation of Manitoba on July 5, 1870.

By the time O'Neill attempted to join forces with Riel, the latter had already gone into exile in the US and the Métis leader showed no interest in the Fenian venture. "The Fenians, as a body, were met with refusal or silence when they offered their assistance," wrote the Archbishop of St. Boniface.[31] With only twenty men at his disposal, O'Neill's desperate foray ended in failure.[32] O'Neill died at the age of forty-four in 1878, never suspecting the duplicity of his "friend" Le Caron over the years.[33] In his autobiography, Le Caron denied having ever acted as an agent provocateur:

> Although I always voted for politic reasons on the side of the majority, even to the joining in the vote which meant dynamite, on no single occasion was I instrumental in bringing an individual to the commission of crime.[34]

He failed to mention, however, that the last Fenian expedition had been financed by the robbery of a Hudson's Bay Company trading post in Pembina, North Dakota. Without the weapons provided by the secret agent, O'Neill and his men would never have been able to commit this armed robbery. Despite his protestations to the contrary, at that point Le Caron had clearly crossed the line separating defensive espionage from provocation.

Le Caron continued to infiltrate the Irish nationalist movement for many years, now exclusively on behalf of the British government. His career as a secret agent came to light when he was summoned to testify before a commission of inquiry in London in 1889. The retired spy passed away on April 1, 1894, having spent his last years in constant fear of being murdered.[35]

A few years later, relations between the Métis Nation and the Canadian authorities once again become dangerously fraught, this time with the help of a certain Lawrence Clarke, a complicated character who could in many ways be described as an agent provocateur. Ambitious and well-educated, Clarke had settled in the North-Western Territory, where he worked for the Hudson's Bay Company. When he was transferred to the supply post at Fort Carlton, in the centre of what is today the province of Saskatchewan, he was promoted to senior company manager. His generosity and oratory skills had earned him the respect of the Métis population, as evidenced by his December 1871 election as president of the village council of St. Laurent, where the Métis of Red River had settled.[36] Events in the summer of 1875, however, indicate that Clarke's true loyalties lay with the Hudson's Bay Company, not with the Métis nation.

Gabriel Dumont, Chief of the Métis Council, had been forced to intervene with employees of the Hudson's Bay Company to enforce the rules of the St. Lawrence Council intended to protect the buffalo. This now-endangered species had been the primary means of subsistence for the First Nations of the region for millennia. After a written warning was ignored, the Métis fined the offenders and seized their hunting equipment. One of the Hudson's Bay employees complained in writing to Lawrence Clarke, the newly appointed Justice of the Peace. Outraged, Clarke denounced the rules in an inflammatory letter to Lieutenant-Governor Alexander Morris: "[They] have assumed for themselves the right to enact Laws and regulations for the Government of the Colony and adjoining Country of a most tyrannical nature," he wrote, lamenting that he was "without protective force to compel Lawbreakers to respect the Laws of Canada." Accusing Dumont's group of having "levied by violence and Robbery large sums of money of inoffensive persons,"[37] Clarke warned that "life and property will be endangered" unless a "protective force" was deployed to the Fort Carlton area the following winter.[38] The letter ended up with the Department of the Interior,[39] which authorized the dispatch of a "party of observation" of about fifty officers from the newly formed North West Mounted Police (NWMP) to the area to put an end to the "spread of mischievous complications with the half-breeds."[40]

The Macdonald government had created the NWMP in May 1873 in response to a report by Colonel Robertson-Ross recommending the establishment of an armed force to ensure the safety of those building the Canadian Pacific Railway, particularly in the presence of

> a half-breed population of about 2,000 souls in the Saskatchewan unaccustomed to the restraint of any Government, mainly depending as yet upon the chase for subsistence, and requiring to be controlled nearly as much as the Indians.[41]

1. CONFEDERATION AND PROVOCATION

As with the Lower Canada Rural Police, this new police force was modeled on the Royal Irish Constabulary.[42]

The NWMP investigation soon found that the whole story had been fabricated by Lawrence Clarke. In a letter to the Lieutenant Governor, NWMP Commissioner George Arthur French was blunt: "His Honour, and I fear the Dominion Government have been unnecessarily agitated by the alarming reports received."[43]

The case against Gabriel Dumont was dropped with an order to keep the peace and obey the law—Canada's law, of course. As for the regulations passed by the St. Lawrence Council to protect the buffalo, Commissioner French approvingly noted that they were "absolutely necessary ... in a country where no law virtually exists, and where the few Justices of the Peace are Hudson's Bay Company officials inimical to them (as they suppose), settlements should band themselves together for mutual protection."[44]

Although Clarke had most of his allegations dismissed out of hand, he won his main point: the St. Lawrence Council was to cease all activities as of the summer of 1875.[45] According to a priest in the community,

> The humble legislation of the Colony of St. Laurent, having no longer the right to punish the delinquents naturally lost all sanction .... Every one took their freedom and ran on the buffalo without any other guide than their insatiable keenness, passion for killing, greed and avarice.[46]

So much so that six years later, the buffalo herds in the Prairies had been wiped off the map.[47]

In 1875, the NWMP established a headquarters at Battleford, north of the Saskatchewan River.[48] The arrival of a police presence, which the region had previously lacked, was, as we have seen, in keeping with Clarke's wishes. But it also suited Lieutenant-Governor Morris, who had previously called for the mobilization of a substantial police force to pressure the First Nations to relinquish their territories. As the lieutenant-governor argued in a letter to the federal Minister of the Interior, the absence of such a force would reinforce "the Indians' belief in the weakness of Canada from a military point of view."[49] Indeed, several treaties would be signed with the Prairie First Nations in the months and years to come, with the gradual extinction of the buffalo convincing many that the Indigenous ways of life were no longer viable.[50] The path was now clear for a mass influx of European settlers and ambitious economic development projects in the North-Western Territory, including the construction of the Canadian Pacific Railway. Land speculators close to Macdonald's Conservative Party—not the least of whom, of course, was Lawrence Clarke himself—made a killing, while the region's First Nations were gradually decimated by the genocidal food rationing policies of the federal authorities.[51]

The disappearance of the buffalo also affected the Métis, who were forced to switch to subsistence farming, and whose repeated requests for financial assistance were ignored by Ottawa.[52] In 1884, when the Métis decided to appeal to Louis Riel, who had sought exile in Montana, Lawrence Clarke made sure to inform Macdonald. Clarke even invited himself, unannounced, to the dinner held to welcome Riel back amongst the Métis. After donating twenty dollars, the justice of the peace went so far as to advise the Métis to "Bring on your rebellion as soon as you can."[53] But Riel would soon disappoint those who were counting on him to take an insurrectionary stand; in his first public addresses, he adopted a conciliatory tone and a diplomatic approach, focusing his energies on organizing a coalition with various First Nations leaders to try to get Ottawa to listen to their concerns.[54]

On September 26, Sergeant Keenan, who was monitoring Riel on behalf of the Macdonald government, wrote that "Riel holds frequent meetings in which he employs measured and cautious words, unlike those in the private sessions of his Council"[55] (suggesting that these were likely infiltrated). In a letter to Macdonald, Ansdell Macrae, the most senior of the government's "Indian agents," noted that many settlers were considering abandoning the area if repressive measures were not put in place to control Riel and his supporters. His letter also mentioned the existence of several spies keeping tabs on the Métis nation, including one "L. Clarke." It was in this context that the NWMP opted to reinforce its northern section with 200 additional men. "Many of the new arrivals were quartered in Fort Carlton, the Hudson's Bay Company post supervised by Lawrence Clark," wrote Captain Chambers.[56] Billeting these police reinforcements would of course have been good for business.

That fall, rumours circulated that the NWMP was preparing to arrest Riel. The tense situation pushed the movement in a more combative direction, which in turn led more moderate elements to pull back—everyone was on edge. When news spread that the police might try to arrest Riel and suppress a Métis assembly at St. Laurent on December 23, more than one hundred armed men rallied within a half hour to protect the Métis leader.[57]

In late 1884, Riel wrote to Ottawa, sending a "Bill of Rights" containing a list of demands: provincial status for the region, the construction of schools and hospitals, and the resolution of Métis and First Nations land claims. Macdonald would have the gall to deny that his government had even received the document.[58] So the Métis decided to send an emissary to Ottawa to directly argue the merits of the "Bill of Rights," the person chosen being ... Lawrence Clarke. There was a certain logic behind this: Clarke was the first elected member of the Northwest Territories Legislative Assembly, he had represented the Saskatchewan riding of Lorne from 1881 to 1883, was considered a local Conservative Party leader, and was well known in the federal capital. Riel, on the other hand, was routinely being slandered in various local newspapers.[59] Furthermore, seeing how the government was no more receptive than it had been prior to his return, Riel had concluded that his presence had become useless, counter-productive even. At a meeting in Batoche on February 24, 1885, he announced his intention to return to the United States; this was taken as disastrous news, and Riel, moved by the support he was receiving, abandoned the idea.[60]

March came, and the Métis had yet to hear anything from Clarke, despite his having been in Ottawa for several weeks.[61] No one had informed the Métis of the federal government's decision to set up a commission to investigate their claims. On March 3, Riel travelled to Halcro, an English-speaking Métis community south of Prince Albert, accompanied by an armed escort; explaining that the NWMP wanted to arrest him, Riel pointed to his companions, saying, "These are the real police." Three days later, in a secret meeting, he asked eleven members of the Métis nation to swear an oath to "save our country from a wicked government by taking up arms if necessary." At a public meeting in St. Laurent on March 8, Riel announced the creation of a provisional government, in a scenario not unlike the first Red River Rebellion. "No hostile movement would be made unless word was received from Ottawa refusing to grant the demands in the bill of rights," he promised.[62]

On March 10, the Regina Regional Police sent a telegram to Ottawa: "Métis excited, more turbulent than usual; weapons are being prepared. The cause or purpose of these preparations is not known."[63] On March 13, Superintendent Leif Crozier of the NWMP wrote to Lieutenant-Governor Dewdney requesting reinforcements. "Halfbreed rebellion likely to break out any moment," he warned. "If Halfbreeds rise Indians will join them." Dewdney replied that the government had prohibited the sale of arms and ammunition to Treaty 6 First Nations.[64] Meanwhile, Prime Minister Macdonald appealed to the Hudson's Bay Company to make Fort Carlton available to lodge the police reinforcements requested by Crozier.[65] On March 15, Commissioner Acheson Irvine of the NWMP left Regina for Fort Carlton with one hundred men.[66]

On March 17, Lawrence Clarke finally made his return. When some Métis went to meet him to ask about Ottawa's response, Clarke warned them that "Within 24 hours, 500 men from the Mounted Police will bring redress to their grievances in the form of chains for their chief and bullets for their councillors."[67] As we have seen, this was untrue: while the government's decision to create a commission to examine the Métis nation's grievances was a far cry from what had been hoped for, it was nonetheless a political response not a repressive one. Clarke's statement set off a dangerous spiral of violence. When Gabriel Dumont told him the news, Riel is said to have shouted "To arms! To arms!" A council of Métis leaders was immediately convened, and all available weapons in the area were requisitioned from the local merchants. In addition, people suspected of spying for the authorities were taken hostage.[68] As Duck Lake storekeeper Hillyard Mitchell explained:

> Mr. L. Clarke of the HBC is the cause of the whole excitement, viz. on Wednesday he, on driving from Grey, stopped at the Settlement at the South Branch, and told the people that the Government was sending 500 Police from Troy to fight the half-breeds. The people, of course, got excited and said they were going to fight the said 500 men. And they are now waiting at Batoche expecting them to arrive.[69]

While Clarke would deny making the comments attributed to him, contemporary Métis accounts, including the testimony of Riel himself, place responsibility for triggering the armed uprising at the feet of the controversial Hudson's Bay representative.[70] Moreover, Clarke could not have been unaware of the arrival of police reinforcements since, as we have seen, Macdonald had asked the Hudson's Bay Company to house them at Fort Carlton. According to Murray Dobbin, project coordinator for the Batoche Centenary Corporation, "Many historians […] have come to the conclusion that Clarke if not both a government spy and an agent provocateur was certainly the key figure in fomenting the violence."[71]

1. CONFEDERATION AND PROVOCATION

Clarke's statement was all the more significant given the tension that prevailed in the region in March 1885. After all, a flame is a lot more dangerous beside a powder keg. Riel had made no secret of his plans to launch an uprising in the event of a negative reply from Ottawa. By telling the Métis that the government was not only unwilling to hear their demands, but had actually opted for repression, Clarke had provided the missing ingredient for the explosion. Clarke had not directly supplied the Métis with weapons, as Henri Le Caron had done with the Fenians in 1871, but he deliberately provided the impetus for their immediate use. Moreover, given that Clarke made a point of not passing on information about the government's decision to set up a commission to examine the concerns of the Métis, while also more than doubling the number of police reinforcements, he was engaging in more than just misinformation: he was inventing facts outright, just as he had done in 1875 to invalidate the St. Laurent Council. In each case, Clarke was clearly worried that things might be resolved peacefully, and so he worked hard to exacerbate matters and to provoke armed confrontation between the Métis nation and the Canadian state.

Within days, the Métis rebels controlled a forty-kilometer stretch of territory east of the Saskatchewan River. Still, shots had yet to be fired. Superintendent Crozier, stationed at Fort Carlton, opted for caution and decided to await the arrival of the reinforcements led by Commissioner Irvine. Once these reinforcements joined his own, he would then be able to make a show of force, which he hoped would deter the insurgents.[72]

Clarke had his own ideas, however. Before witnesses, he challenged Crozier to "teach the rebels a lesson if he were not afraid of them."[73] Crozier had no desire to be known as a coward or to lose face. Especially since Clarke was supported by forty civilian volunteers from Prince Albert, who were eager to fight the rebels. This final act of manipulation seems to have worked, as Crozier soon set off with a troop of fifty-six police officers and forty-three volunteers.[74]

Alerted by his scouts of Crozier's approach, Dumont had positioned his men strategically on a road located two and a half kilometers from Duck Lake. After a brief verbal exchange between representatives of the two groups, a firefight broke out. Pinned down in a trap, Crozier's forces suffered heavy casualties, despite their superior firepower. Clarke, who had been charged with looking after the horses, deemed discretion to be the better part of valour: he fled the battlefield so quickly that he left his coat behind in the snow. After thirty minutes, Crozier ordered a retreat. The tally: twelve dead on Crozier's side alongside five Métis freedom fighters.[75] It was now open war between the two groups—each of which, ironically, had been manipulated by the same man.

In western Saskatchewan, the rebel victory had a ripple effect on many Plains First Nations. Starving Plains Cree from Mistahimaskwa's band took up arms under the leadership of war chief Kah-paypamhchukwao (Wandering Spirit); they were soon joined by members of the Assiniboine nation. On March 30, two settlers were killed south of Battleford, and businesses and homes that had been abandoned by the white population were looted. On April 2, nine residents of the village of Frog Lake were killed. On April 24, Métis freedom fighters, supported by Cree and Dakota, succeeded in repelling government forces at Fish Creek. On May 2, Cree led by Chief Kah-Me-Yo-Ki-Sick-Way (Fine Day) defeated a ragtag militia under the command of Colonel Otter.

The Métis uprising ended on May 12, 1885, when, after three days of fighting, the Canadian army successfully recaptured Batoche. On May 15, Riel surrendered himself to the government, while Dumont fled to the United States. The Cree insurgents alone confronted vastly superior military and police forces at the Battle of Butte aux Français on May 28. The final battle was fought at Loon Lake on June 3 and resulted in a Cree defeat. As Gabriel Dumont's biographer Adolphe Ouimet has pointed out, the balance of power clearly favoured the Canadian state:

> In order to suppress the Saskatchewan insurrection and subdue 250 poorly armed, ill-disciplined Métis and 500–600 Savages [sic!], who lacked food and ammunition, the Canadian government had to raise a force of 5,456 non-commissioned officers and soldiers, 351 officers, 586 horses, 8 cannons, including two Gatling guns, 6,000 Snider rifles, quantities of Winchester rifles and Colt revolvers, 1,500,000 rounds of ammunition, not counting the 20 rounds distributed to each man before his departure, and, in addition, 2,000 rounds of cannon and projectiles.[76]

The clashes were costly in terms of human life: at least twenty-two Métis and First Nations warriors died in combat. On the Canadian side, sixty-two people, including fourteen civilians, were killed.[77] And then there were the executions. Louis Riel was sentenced to death following a trial for high treason.

1. CONFEDERATION AND PROVOCATION

Macdonald ignored pleas for clemency from the French-speaking population of Quebec, declaring, "He must be hanged, even if all the dogs in Quebec barked that he should not be."[78] The execution took place on November 15, 1885. Eleven days later, Kah-paypamhchukwao, alongside five of his fellow Cree and two Assiniboine warriors, met the same fate and were buried in an unmarked grave near Fort Battleford.[79]

The Macdonald government came under heavy criticism, both in Canada and abroad. The Official Opposition expressed outrage when it was revealed that the Conservatives had kept from Parliament the many written requests made to them by the Métis nation. According to Don McLean, a researcher at the Gabriel Dumont Institute, the Macdonald Conservatives had a lot to gain from an armed uprising by the Métis Nation and First Nations on the Prairies: "The rebellion was created by the federal government as a means of making it possible politically to get further funding for the bankrupt CPR."[80]

The Canadian Pacific Railway was of vital importance to Macdonald; its completion was essential to the government's National Policy, which had been the Conservatives' main plank in the 1878 general election that had returned them to power.[81] Moreover, the railroad was the foundation on which Macdonald hoped to build Canada as a nation.[82] Although Ottawa had provided a total of $47.5 million in credits and loans, by March 1885 the ambitious project found itself so desperately short of capital that its very existence was in doubt. What's more, important Conservative supporters faced bankruptcy if the railroad was not completed.[83] But Macdonald was worried about his chances of convincing not only Parliament but even his own caucus to dip into the public purse yet again to avert such a calamity.[84]

David Cruise and Alison Griffiths, who co-authored *Lords of The Line: The Men Who Built the CPR*, explain how everything suddenly changed with the rebellion:

> The CPR was saved, not by any financial legerdemain, but by Louis Riel. On March 26, 1885, a second Métis uprising led by Riel, the Northwest Rebellion, gave Van Horne, at long last, the chance to demonstrate the CPR's value to Canada. Until then the public and politicians alike had seen the enterprise as little more than a massive and unending drain on the Treasury. Fifteen years earlier, General Wolseley's army had slogged through bush, rock and muskeg for three months to reach Winnipeg from Montreal in order to crush

the first Riel Rebellion. In April, 1885, Van Horne dedicated every resource of the CPR to the astonishing transportation feat of hauling nearly 3,000 troops over the still-uncompleted line. The first contingent reached Winnipeg in only seven days. The soldiers were chilled to the marrow, but they'd arrived months earlier than Riel had expected, and the revolt was crushed by May 14th.[85]

To support this argument, McLean cites various documents suggesting that the Macdonald government would have been in serious trouble if its role in the rebellion had come to light. For example, Joseph Royal, Conservative MP for the federal riding of Provencher (Manitoba), wrote a letter to the Archbishop of St. Boniface, suggesting that the Canadian Prime Minister had committed illegal acts in connection with the rebellion. "My Quebec friends are anxious and ask me questions," he wrote. "What should I do? Should I say everything, and have Sir John [A. Macdonald] put on trial, a very real possibility?" The Archbishop "advised him to keep quiet."[86] Apparently, Royal's career did not suffer as a result of his silence, as he was appointed Lieutenant-General of the North-West Territories in 1888.

And then there is this letter, from the Governor General of Canada, Sir Henry Charles Keith Petty-Fitzmaurice, addressed to Macdonald in August 1885:

> You see the recent unrest in the Northwest simply as "domestic unrest" that should not be elevated to rebellion. The disturbance has undoubtedly been confined to our own territory and can therefore be described as an internal disturbance, but I am afraid we have all done all we can to elevate it to a rebellion so successfully that we cannot now reduce it to an ordinary riot.[87]

Lawrence Clarke died on October 8, 1890, at the age of 58; he was never held accountable for his actions.

It is time to face the role played by agents provocateurs in the building of Canadian Confederation. Provocateurs like Lawrence Clarke and Henri Le Caron did all they could to fan the flames of discord in order to crush resistance movements, such as those of the Fenians, the Métis, and the First Nations of the Prairies. Given that provocation and manipulation have been such useful tools, it is no wonder the Canadian authorities remained enthusiastic about their use in the next century.

2. Seeing Red

"In labour circles, when any man stands up at a meeting and begins to talk violence he is immediately suspected by the labour people of being a spy," explained James S. Woodsworth, a Member of Parliament for the Independent Labour Party, in an address to the House of Commons on April 4, 1922.[1] A measure of the apprehension that existed in the labour movement at that time in regard to agents provocateurs.

At the time, the Royal North West Mounted Police (RNWMP)[2] did not hesitate to employ undercover agents to infiltrate the ranks of labour organizations. The police force had taken advantage of the First World War to develop an intelligence network to investigate, harass, and arrest not only labour activists, but also socialists, pacifists, those refusing to submit to military service, or simply those from "enemy countries." By the end of the war, intelligence, which until then had been largely the responsibility of the Dominion Police, was now entirely under the purview of the RNWMP.[3]

By 1918, the RNWMP employed eight secret agents and six detectives. In addition, there were an unknown number of civilians secretly providing information to the Canadian government. Language skills were one of the most sought-after assets in an undercover agent;[4] after all, in order to know what was being said in the "enemy country" communities, one had to understand what people were saying. Yet as of 1914, 79% of RNWMP personnel had been born in the United Kingdom.[5]

Guidelines for intelligence work emerged from trial and error.[6] The officers in charge often felt it better to use two informants: in a court of law, the word of two people carried more weight than just one, plus this allowed for the verification of each informant's account.[7] RNWMP Commissioner Aylesworth B. Perry advised that officers should "be constantly on their guard against being purposely misled by the informants."[8] Clearly, trust was in somewhat short supply ...

In Alberta and Saskatchewan, the only two provinces where the force performed the provincial policing function, RNWMP reports focused on the content of public speeches—specifically, any references to communism or sedition—and the impact of the speech on its audience, which the police tried to gauge by the amount of applause and the amount of money in the hat that would be passed around the audience.[9] Once an agent was able to infiltrate a target organization, his success was measured not only by the information he was able to obtain, but also by his ability to move up the group's hierarchy.[10]

In addition to the political surveillance conducted by various Canadian state bodies, private detective agencies were also used, on behalf of both government authorities and private employers. In 1921, 70–80% of the information in the individual files on members of the Toronto branch of the Communist Party of Canada was obtained by private agencies, and the Employers Detective Agency was able to obtain a detailed account of the Party's founding meeting, held secretly in a barn in Guelph, Ontario, in May of that year.[11]

On August 14, 1913, British Columbia's Acting Premier William J. Bowser (of the Conservative Party) called on the Pinkerton Agency, requesting they send him a "roughneck who could get in among the mob of men and yell and throw a stone occasionally in order to be one of them."[12] The Pinkertons sent one of their detectives—fitting Bowser's requested profile—to the small town of Ladysmith, on Vancouver Island, where a coal miners' strike had resulted in some violence. The investigator, known as 29-S, was tasked with identifying the perpetrators of a dynamite attack on the home of a strikebreaker, as well as monitoring the activities of both the striking workers and the strikebreakers.[13]

For five and a half months, 29-S lived under an assumed name among the striking workers. Because the local hotel administration opposed the strike, "the strikers themselves cannot obtain a drop of anything and this fact alone helped me out greatly," 29-S reported, using whisky to try to loosen tongues.[14] The investigator also tried to alienate the strikers from the United Mine Workers of America (UMWA); this went beyond his original mandate, or perhaps reveals it to have been more extensive than was otherwise indicated. 29-S believed that the local population belonged to an "inferior class of people ... displaying the traits employed by the ignorant and savage."[15] His attitude may explain why he was never able to get close enough to the people living there to obtain any information of use to his mission.

History does not record whether, in addition to buying drinks, 29-S had to throw a few rocks to win acceptance among the striking miners. Still, the point is that a government leader gave the green light to a private investiga-

2. SEEING RED

tor to play rioter in order to gather intelligence. It is also worth noting that Bowser had been the Attorney General of British Columbia for several years as well as being the province's Acting Premier at the time.

Another case in point is Robert Raglan Gosden, a British immigrant who earned a reputation as an agent provocateur in the labour movement at the same time, also in British Columbia. Dubbed "Secret Agent No. 10" by the RNWMP, Gosden was active in several revolutionary unions, including the Industrial Workers of the World (IWW) from 1910 to 1914.[16] However, the exact date that Gosden began spying for the RNWMP remains unknown.

While Gosden himself did not have a job, he was nonetheless involved in IWW-affiliated unions such as the Prince Rupert Industrial Association (PRIA).[17] And the secret agent certainly was able to rouse a crowd; it was thanks to his skilful oratory that he became president of the Miners' Liberation League (MLL), formed in the fall of 1913 by trade unionists and socialists seeking the release of some 200 miners arrested for demonstrations and riots during a long and bitter strike at the Canadian Collieries coal mining company. In December 1913, Gosden delivered a fiery speech to a crowd of roughly a thousand people at a Vancouver carnival, in which he made thinly veiled threats on the lives of the province's political leaders:

> By the end of this month every last peaceful appeal which is necessary or possible for us to make as citizens of this Dominion for the release of our brothers in prison will have been made. By the end of this year all peaceful measures will have been exhausted. If they are not released by the time the New Year is ushered in, if [Conservative provincial premier] Sir Richard McBride, Attorney-General Bowser, or any of the minions and politicians go hunting, they will be very foolish, for they will be shot dead. These men will also be well advised to employ some sucker to taste their coffee in the morning before drinking it if they value their lives. In addition, it will cost them one million dollars a week for every week that our brothers remain in jail after the New Year.[18]

Although the McBride government was certainly not known to be averse to repression, not only was Gosden never troubled by the authorities for this incendiary speech, but he was even able to get a job in 1915 as a janitor in the British Columbia legislature, where the same politicians were apparently destined to die if the MLL did not have its demands met. In his autobiography,

British Communist organizer George Hardy would recount that Gosden had also offered to get him a job for the provincial government, an offer that Hardy rejected out of hand.[19] Not exactly subtle.

It was with a similar lack of tact that Gosden boasted of having "helped kill the IWW" when he testified before a parliamentary committee of inquiry in May 1916.[20] The committee was not investigating the labour movement, however, but rather allegations of electoral fraud in connection with two by-elections won by members of the Liberal opposition. The scandal was a windfall for McBride's Conservatives, who were in dire straits after thirteen years in office and knew they would have to face the provincial electorate the following September. In his testimony, Gosden said he was hired by a Liberal campaign manager with a salary of $20 a week to compile lists of people who were dead or ineligible to vote, so that their identities could then be fraudulently used to cast ballots for the Liberals. The scandal did not prevent the Liberal Party from defeating the Conservatives in the election, but Gosden would later face perjury charges, for which he was acquitted in not one but two trials.[21]

Constable Frank Zaneth (the "Canadian" version of his birth name, Franco Zanetti) was another RNWMP spy who earned infamy as an agent provocateur. Known as the "Man of a Thousand Faces" and referred to as a "master of disguise" by his colleagues, Zaneth seemed to have had a natural gift for infiltration. Over the course of his long career as a secret agent, he posed as a Chicago gangster, a Quebec drug dealer, and even a bumbling Italian bureaucrat.[22] But it was while infiltrating union and socialist circles, under the alias Harry Blask, that he first cut his teeth in the world of intelligence work.

Born in Italy in 1890, Zaneth immigrated to Canada in 1911 after living in the United States for a few years. He was hired by the RNWMP in December 1917, becoming the first recruit to the force's new Secret Service, which had been created as a direct response to the "communist threat." As the Secret Service officers saw it, Zaneth's short stature and being an Italian immigrant made him the ideal secret agent, as he looked nothing like the typical gendarmes of the RNWMP, who were generally tall, imposing, and of British origin. The spy reported directly to Commissioner Perry, a measure of his importance.[23]

Zaneth's first undercover assignment was during the Quebec Conscription Crisis in the spring of 1918, during which he arrested several young men

2. SEEING RED

who were refusing military service.[24] For his second assignment, in September of that year, the secret agent was sent to the mining town of Drumheller, Alberta, where he was to infiltrate the Wobblies (as IWW members were known).[25] To this end, Zaneth was given an IWW membership card that had been confiscated from a prisoner. Posing as an Austrian, the secret agent was to work in the coal mines, a demanding and dangerous job, but one with higher pay than the RNWMP—Zaneth soon learned how stingy his employer could be when he was ordered to reimburse the wage difference. Undeterred by this blatant injustice, Zaneth persevered in his mission and managed to win the trust of a local union leader who taught him the Wobblies' secret handshake.[26]

When the war ended, the Conservative government, under Robert Borden, was determined to bring the full weight of the Canadian state to bear to crush the radical left. On September 28, 1918, Ottawa invoked Order-in-Council PC 2384 under the War Measures Act—which was still in effect, despite the fact that the war was over—to ban sixteen organizations, including the IWW and the Socialist Party of Canada, while also imposing drastic restrictions on the right to strike.[27] This hardline state offensive came at a time of increasing unemployment, as a result of many arms factories closing at the same time as thousands of Canadian soldiers returning home from the front were struggling to find work.[28] This was also the time when the "red scare" was sweeping across North America in the wake of the Russian Revolution of 1917—the world's largest country was now called the Soviet Federated Socialist Republic of Russia. And when monarchists and a host of other movements opposing the new regime took up arms, plunging Russia into civil war, Canada was among the many countries that joined the anti-Soviet forces in the conflict, dispatching an expeditionary force to Siberia that included 174 cavalry units of the RNWMP.[29]

John Leopold joined the RNWMP in September 1918, one of many young men who volunteered to fight against Bolshevism in Russia.[30] Born in 1890 in Bohemia (a region corresponding today to the western half of the Czech Republic), Leopold had immigrated to Canada in 1912; he could speak German and Czech and could get by in Polish and Croatian. Like Zaneth, Leopold was small in stature: at five feet four inches, he didn't even meet the RNWMP's height requirements.[31] In fact, his application would have been rejected had it not been for his desire to join the Siberian campaign: as Leopold was about to set sail, a detective informed him that he had been selected to become an undercover agent.³² In the eyes of the RNWMP, Leopold's language skills and "cool temperament" made him an ideal candidate for infiltrating foreign-born activists; such promising potential should not be wasted as mere cannon fodder.³³ As of February 1919, Leopold, now Secret Agent No. 30, began to frequent Regina's militant labour milieu under the alias "Jack Esselwein," pretending to be a simple house painter with radical political ideas.³⁴ Thus began an undercover mission that would last nine long years.

Both Leopold and Zaneth would target the "One Big Union" (OBU) in their information gathering. The OBU, which had grown out of a split in the Trades and Labour Congress of Canada, embraced the IWW's call to unite all members of the working class in a single labour organization. "To find out if the One Big Union plotted violence they planted undercover men in almost every local," wrote Alan Philips in a tribute to the RCMP.³⁵

Robert Gosden was also contracted by the RNWMP to monitor OBU members in various cities in British Columbia and Alberta. He was paid up to $5 a day by the RNWMP for this work, as much as double what he would have earned doing manual labour. Ironically, Gosden's penchant for verbal radicalism caused other spies to report on his activities, oblivious to the fact that he was also an undercover agent.³⁶

After growing a moustache in the hope of going incognito, Gosden was chosen as a delegate to a union convention in Calgary in March 1919, which aimed to lay the groundwork for the OBU. His plans went awry, however, when a delegate from the United Mine Workers of America unmasked him, informing convention members that Gosden had recently visited Fernie under the alias "Smith" and Hillcrest under the alias "Brown." A former Vancouver Island coal miner then accused Gosden of attempting to "stir up trouble" during a strike and of having given "certain persons the formula of a chemical composition intended to be spread on the floor of buildings to start a fire." A motion calling for his expulsion was defeated, however, after some interventions to the effect that the members of the convention had nothing to hide since they were not engaged in illegal activities.³⁷

Gosden saw things differently, however, reporting to the RNWMP that the OBU was "stamped[ing] organised labor in the direction of mass action, with the idea that it shall terminate in social revolution of the Bolsheviki type."³⁸ The secret agent recommended the government make use of the traditional old guard of the trade union movement to marginalize the OBU. But Gosden went further than just that: claiming that the "Reds" lacked the

2. SEEING RED

"physical courage of their convictions and they possess the fear of the consequences of their acts," he suggested kidnapping some of their leaders in order to terrorize their supporters.[39] There is no indication that the RNWMP ever pursued such a plan, and Gosden's value as an undercover agent was considerably diminished after he was exposed.[40]

Gosden was not the only RNWMP spy at the Calgary convention, however. Zaneth, who had been transferred to that city as of January 1, 1919, was also present, and, unlike Gosden, his cover remained intact. Gradually climbing the ranks of the union world, Zaneth had become secretary to George Sangster, leader of the International Association of Machinists, a position that gave him access to Sangster's correspondence, as well as to all the radical and subversive literature circulating on the Prairies. He even became vice-president of the Calgary Trades and Labor Council. As a member of the recently outlawed Socialist Party of Canada, the secret agent distributed banned literature, such as Lenin's *Political Parties in Russia*.[41]

On April 13, 1919, after a Socialist Party meeting, Zaneth met with Joe Knight, a British-born Marxist activist, and his new friend, a man named Jim Davis, who had bragged to the secret agent that he had broken into a safe in Chicago and turned over the jewels it contained, worth half a million dollars, to the IWW. Knight suggested that the two men go check out the arrival of a shipment of rifles destined for the Canadian military. That evening, Zaneth and Davis went to the site and made plans to abscond with the weapons stored there. The undercover agent wrote in his report that the two men did not enter the building; perhaps that is why the RNWMP never followed up on the report, despite the fact that one of its constables had been on the verge of stealing army weapons.[42]

In May, Commissioner Percy learned of rumours circulating in Calgary that a spy had managed to get close to the union leadership. The head of the RNWMP was getting worried about Zaneth, so a plan was devised to enhance his credibility amongst his targets: the undercover agent was arrested in Regina and charged with violating immigration laws. Newspapers at the time reported on Zaneth's hearing, describing him as a "well-known agitator." Receiving a fine, as he left the court the spy was greeted warmly by socialist and trade union comrades.[43] P.F. Lawson, publisher of the socialist miners' newspaper *Searchlight*, remained suspicious nonetheless, noting that Zaneth was always willing to carry out political work but never expected to be paid in return.[44]

While Zaneth languished behind bars, the Winnipeg Trades and Labour Council called for a referendum on a general strike to demand an eight-hour workday, the right to a living wage, and collective bargaining. Eleven thousand people, including members of the municipal police force, voted in favour of the general strike, while five hundred voted against it. On May 15, 30,000 people went on strike, bringing Winnipeg to a standstill. Business and government authorities responded with a propaganda campaign portraying the strike as the beginning of a violent revolution instigated by Bolsheviks.

Shortly after being appointed Deputy Minister of Justice by the Borden government, Alfred J. Andrews, then head of a citizen's committee opposed to the strike, ordered a series of arrests for "seditious conspiracy."[45] On the night of June 16–17, police apprehended several strike leaders, and a few days later the RNWMP, supported by police auxiliaries, attacked a silent march, killing two and injuring dozens. Demonstrations and public meetings were banned and the army was deployed in the streets.[46] The Winnipeg General Strike had been crushed.

In December 1919, when the trial of those "Reds" arrested in June commenced, Special Prosecutor Andrews felt that Zaneth would make the perfect witness. The RNWMP was cool to the idea, which would mean blowing the cover of their secret agent, who after long years had managed to attain a sensitive position in the labour movement. The prosecutor had the last word, however, and called on Zaneth (who had meanwhile been promoted to the rank of corporal-detective) to testify. The entrance of Frank Zaneth—alias Harry Blask—in his red RNWMP uniform caused an uproar in the courtroom, most especially among the accused.

Zaneth's testimony made headlines across Canada.[47] His reputation as an agent provocateur would now stick with him on the Canadian left. "Corporal Zaneth himself engaged in typical tricks of the agent provocateur. He would sell banned literature for instance and then charge the people who bought it for having it in their possession," wrote Lorne and Caroline Brown in a book chronicling the "unauthorized history" of the Royal Canadian Mounted Police.[48] The case was also reported on at length in the pages of *Searchlight*. "One of Blask's favorite tricks," Lawson wrote, was to show his pistol to socialists. "He advised the boys that it was always safer to go with a gun for one could never tell what might happen."[49] The RNWMP obtained issues of *Searchlight* before they were even released, as the publication's staff had been infiltrated. However, Inspector Spalding of the RNWMP was not pleased to read that "Blask" had been one of those who had advocated throwing sulphuric acid on businessmen during a strike in Calgary. Zaneth was asked to explain himself, as he had never informed his superiors of this plan. He insisted that the idea was Jim Davis's, and that it was to pour acid on the tires of vehicles to prevent the authorities from transporting police or military personnel during the strike:

> While Davis was making statements of this nature in the presence of others, I never concurred with him in his statements. As a matter of fact at this particular time I pretended to be reading a book, but I must admit that when I met Jim Davis alone, during our conversations, I used to drift back to his statements of this nature, in order to find out what materials he was made of, and how far he dared to go to carry out his threat.[50]

What is telling about Zaneth's rebuttal is what he does not deny that he incited vandalism and that he privately acquiesced to Davis's criminal plans. Moreover, wasn't it with Davis that Zaneth had planned to steal guns from the army in April 1919? It should be noted that, in that case, the spy did not conceal this aborted project from his superiors. By failing to inform them of the scenarios involving acid, was the secret agent trying to cover his tracks? The assumption that Zaneth's conduct was not aboveboard is further supported by the fact that the RNWMP never attempted to prosecute Davis, a possibility that might have been quite embarrassing for both the agent and the police force.

On February 1, 1920, the government amalgamated the RNWMP with the Dominion Police, creating the Royal Canadian Mounted Police (RCMP). The Winnipeg General Strike was certainly an important factor in the Borden government's decision to create a federal police force with Canada-wide jurisdiction.[51] The survival of the RNWMP had been in jeopardy in 1916 and 1917, as a number of voices suggested that it should be disbanded and its functions divided among the provinces.[52] The rise of labour unrest after the end of the war, culminating in the Winnipeg events, was thus used to justify the consolidation of a national police force.

Against all expectations, the new police force did not relieve Zaneth of his duties as a secret agent after the trial, and even went so far as to give him another mission to infiltrate the socialist milieu, this time in Montreal, in April 1920.[53] Using the pseudonym James Laplante, the secret agent even attended a talk given by Heaps, one of the accused against whom he had testified in Winnipeg, on May 29. Despite the insistence of military intelligence that Zaneth's cover was definitely blown, the RCMP was not about to give up its famous spy. It wasn't until the weekly B.C. *Federationist* published an article on October 19, complete with photo, revealing the true identity of "James Laplante" that the RCMP resigned itself to removing its favourite secret agent from the field—after five months of infiltration into the Montreal labour movement. For the next three years, Zaneth would continue his intelligence work on the left, but as a case officer with informants and agents provocateurs in Montreal.[54]

A spider spinning its web is engaged in a lengthy process, one that requires patience and much attention to detail. In September 1921, the web that secret agent John Leopold had woven in Regina was beginning to snare its victims. At the third annual OBU convention, Leopold had met Matthew Popovic (no relation to the author), a Bolshevik activist from the Ukraine.[55] Soon after, Popovic sent a letter to Leopold, inviting him to join the newly formed Worker's Party of Canada:

Dear Comrade,

The urgent need in Canada for a militant Worker's party which would unite the working masses ... so as to lead towards the overthrow of the capitalist system, and the establishment of the workers republic has long been apparent ....

You, Comrade, as an active worker in the class struggle, have, we are certain, felt this need. You have wished that such a party established ... so that you could throw all your energies into the work. Now, such a party is actually here in Canada ....[56]

The letter from Popovic, a member of the party's Provisional Organizing Committee, went on to mention the upcoming visit to Regina of "Comrade Jack Macdonald, one of the best speakers in the east."[57] Leopold was offered the task of organizing and promoting this visit. The RCMP was aware that the Worker's Party of Canada was the name being used by the Communist Party of Canada, following directives issued by the Comintern in Moscow.[58] The fact that Secret Agent No. 30 now had an opportunity to infiltrate the Communist Party posed a legal dilemma; participation in such a political organization was clearly against the law. Sergeant Salt expressed his concerns to the spy in an interview he forwarded to an official with the RCMP's Southern Saskatchewan Detachment:

> It would be impossible for him to carry on without doing criminal actions occasionally. On being questioned, he assured me that he would never in any away promote the Communist Party unless forced to do so by circumstances and that he would use every discretion in the matter.[59]

Perhaps to reassure his superiors, Salt portrayed Leopold as a real nuisance to the left, pointing out that the secret agent had already destroyed leaflets, wasted funds, and sabotaged meetings.[60] Impressed by such brilliant prowess, Commissioner Perry, the RCMP's number one officer, was quick to grant his blessing: "The opportunity offered of gaining access to Communist plans must not be allowed to escape us." Leopold "should throw himself into the movement and his aim should be to obtain an appointment as organizer."[61]

For his part, Leopold pledged to "do so with the least amount of effect as possible."[62] However, being a slacker is not a very effective approach to inserting yourself in the group you're infiltrating, or getting your hands on valuable information. In reality, the facts show that Leopold actually did everything he could for the Party, just like Popovic had asked him to. This is what Philips argues in his book extolling the accomplishments of the RCMP:

> The Mountie became the party's first secretary in Regina. He chaired meetings, recruited members, sold pamphlets. He was campaign manager for a Regina alderman who became the first Communist elected to office in North America. For a time—the worst time—Leopold acted as bodyguard for the Moscow agent, Charles Scott. They shared the same bed, the policeman constantly fearful of talking in his sleep. Soon he reported to his RCMP superiors that the party was really two groups, A and Z. A group was the Workers' Party. It was the legal front; it did the recruiting, Z group contained the leaders. It did the plotting, mainly plans to infiltrate unions and widen their membership. Leopold was a Z. The inner circle held no secrets from him. He corresponded with national secretary Jack Macdonald and drank with him or Tim Buck, another Communist bigwig, whenever they came to town. Twice a week, through an undercover contact, he would send the RCMP his notes, party pamphlets and

copies of personal correspondence. Jack Esselwein became a well-known radical, a marked man with the western police. Only four or five RCMP officers—the direct chain of command from Leopold's Regina inspector to the commissioner in Ottawa—knew Esselwein's real identity. His non-Communist friends forsook him. His bewildered fiancee, a Saskatchewan school-teacher, tried to persuade him to quit Communism. Leopold could not tell her who he was and eventually she married another man. (Leopold never married.) With party members and leaders he was popular. He gave his money generously. Once a month a messenger brought him his Mounted Police pay in cash. If party funds were tight he would pay his own way to eastern conventions.[63]

Leopold took part in all the national party conventions up until 1928.[64] "For years, we had no suspicion. We liked him and trusted him," said Jack Macdonald, the party's national secretary from 1923 to 1929.[65] The key to the secret agent's success was the connections he was able to make with the party's leading figures. Of course, access to leadership meant access to high-level intelligence. The RCMP had its weight in gold: it now had privileged access to all the party convention reports.

All that remained was to identify the membership. This was the task assigned to Constable Harry Catt, number 9322, when he infiltrated the Toronto branch of the party in December 1921, six months after its founding. By getting close to William Moriarty, the party's general secretary, Catt was able to ascertain the true identities of the party's key members (who were using pseudonyms at the time), the number of members, information about its finances, and the countermeasures used to combat infiltration.[66]

Catt ended his intelligence activities in the winter of 1922–23. But like a weed that comes back no matter how many times you pull it out, police infiltration never really goes away.

In the spring of 1924, having infiltrated the party only two months earlier, Constable James T. Goudie sat on the central committee of its Toronto branch. He had also befriended members of the party core, which gave him access to valuable information.[67] In the summer of 1924 and 1925, Goudie helped organize anti-war demonstrations on behalf of the party. He even acted as a spokesman in an interview with *The Globe* (the predecessor to *The Globe and Mail*), during which the reporter noted that the demonstrations

2. SEEING RED

would go ahead despite opposition from the mayor of Toronto. Hundreds of people took part in the protests, which resulted in several arrests. Toronto police came close to arresting Goudie after he had the gall to ask two detectives to clear the sidewalk. In an August 1925 report, a Toronto police inspector wrote:

> Goudie made an appeal for membership, stating that it was hoped enough members would come forward as they are desirous of forming a branch there. He also appealed for anyone who witnessed the arrests, if they were willing to give evidence on behalf of the accused, to come forward and give their names.[68]

The constable's "militant" zeal propelled him to new heights within the party. Goudie presided over assemblies of up to 1,500 people and proved to be an outstanding orator. He was even briefly brought into the party's highest body, the Central Executive Committee, where decisions were made that affected not only the political formation from coast to coast, but also its relations with the international communist movement. Nonetheless, his rise would be short-lived: in the fall of 1925 his position began to decline within the party, and in early 1927, the RCMP would remove him from counter-subversive operations.[69]

As for Leopold, by 1926 some RCMP officers were beginning to fear that he was slipping out of their control. "This man is somewhat willing to work alone and without sufficient consultation with his superiors," Commissioner Starnes lamented after Leopold took a trip to Winnipeg without informing the RCMP.[70] Another sign of lack of discipline was his lackadaisical approach to filing reports. However, RCMP National headquarters preferred to be lenient with him. So when the Leopold would fail to show up for meetings with his supervisor, the secret agent's superiors were instructed to sit tight and judge him solely by the merit of his reports.[71]

In May 1927, the RCMP decided to transfer Leopold to Toronto. On August 9, in front of the US consulate, the secret agent and four others were arrested by Toronto police at a demonstration in support of Sacco and Vanzetti.[72] The five were convicted of "vagrancy" the next day and fined $50 each. When called to account by his superiors, the secret agent produced a report full of half-truths in which he claimed that the demonstration was "spontaneous" and that the party had appointed him to carry the lead banner without him being able to do anything about it. On September 8, Leopold's conviction was overturned on appeal.[73]

In November, the Party received a tip from a former RCMP officer living in California that Leopold was a government agent.[74] Leopold denied the accusation, and the matter was left at that. But the Party would now be keeping an eye on him.[75] The truth was finally discovered six months later by a man named Otto, a fellow countryman of Leopold's, who had agreed to take him in. While Leopold was out, Otto went through his belongings, finding several RCMP documents. Believing that Moscow would pay him a fortune for this find, Otto contacted the Party.[76] On May 15, 1928, Leopold received a letter from the Party:

> This is to inform you that the C.E.C. [Central Executive Committee] at a recent meeting decided to expel you from the Party. You are aware that there have been suspicions against you for some time, but we were not in possession of any evidence to substantiate same. We now have incontrovertible evidence that you are and have been for some considerable time in the employ of a certain department of the Government. We are notifying your group secretary and the general membership and also through the columns of the *Worker* the labor movement at large.[77]

In August 1931, Tim Buck and eight other members of the party's political bureau were arrested and charged with "seditious conspiracy" and membership in an illegal organization, an offence punishable by up to twenty years in prison.[78] The evidence presented by the prosecution at trial focused not so much on the individual actions of the defendants, but rather on the fact that they acted under the authority of the Comintern, which advocated violent revolution.[79] Sergeant Leopold, the prosecution's star witness, testified for three days, offering his own interpretation of the writings of Marx, Engels, and Lenin.[80] The Canadian state thus used the court system to put communist ideology on trial, arrogating to itself the right to decide which political doctrines were so dangerous that regular people should not be exposed to them, other than to subject them to general opprobrium.

In his testimony, Leopold tried to downplay his involvement in the Communist Party, but the defence was able to establish that the former spy had set up its Regina branch, had recruited several members (including one of the accused, Malcolm Bruce), and had financially contributed to the organization on numerous occasions.[81] If the Canadian state deemed it a

2. SEEING RED

crime to join and assume positions of authority in the Communist Party of Canada, then both Leopold and the RCMP should have been in the dock. On November 13, Tim Buck, Malcolm Bruce, John Boychuck, Sam Carr, Tom Ewen, A.T. Hill, and Matthew Popovic were sentenced to five years in prison each, Tom Cacic received a two-year sentence, while the eighth accused, Michael Golinski, was acquitted. The Communist Party was essentially decapitated, deprived of its leadership.

The RCMP was not particularly keen on such overtly political trials, which risked creating martyrs for the left and exposing its intelligence activities. But while Commissioner Starnes was concerned that sedition charges would give the Communists too much publicity, he was in favour of the deportation proceedings.[82] Deporting members of the Communist Party had become easier since it had been designated an illegal organization by the courts, and beginning in the fall of 1931, the pace of deportations of radical left-wing activists intensified. The RCMP played a major role in this, both by providing lists of names to immigration officials and by having its undercover officers testify at removal hearings.[83]

Leopold's career came to a sorry end. Transferred to the Yukon, he contracted a venereal disease and went through periods of alcohol abuse, all of which led to his being demoted. In early 1936, Leopold was reprimanded for insubordination and being intoxicated at work. In fact, the only reason the RCMP did not get rid of him was out of the fear that the Communists would use his dismissal for propaganda purposes. Leopold remained employed by the RCMP until his death in 1958.[84]

In Toronto, the RCMP proved unable to infiltrate the Communist Party for many years after the Leopold debacle.[85] Meanwhile, in western Canada, undercover operations were initiated when "relief camps" for unemployed single men proved fertile ground for unrest. Established by the Conservative government of R.B. Bennett, these austere barracks, isolated from major urban centres, were bound to stir up discontent, as the tens of thousands of outcasts confined to them were required to perform hard physical labour for low pay.[86]

For example, RCMP Constable H.M. Wilson infiltrated the "relief camp" set up on the outskirts of Saskatoon, prior to the May 8, 1933, riot in which an RCMP officer was killed. "I have firmly established myself as a radical," boasted Constable Wilson,[87] whose role would come to light in his testimony at the rioters' trial. This approach was not without controversy: "Canadian public opinion is strongly against what might be referred to as secret police," wrote the Regina *Leader-Post*.[88] A "relief camp" in Dundurn, also in Saskatchewan, was similarly infiltrated by an undercover RCMP agent. The constable, seeking to pass himself off as a communist, apparently never missed an opportunity to speak out against the government, but only succeeded in alienating the residents, who told him he would have to either keep his mouth shut or leave the camp.[89]

Former RNWMP agent provocateur Robert Gosden—the same man who once delivered fiery speeches for the IWW—snuck into the "relief camp" at Deroche, located between Mission and Hope, British Columbia, in 1932. He subsequently provided the provincial police with a list of activists, described as "secret, dangerous and irreconcilable."[90] Gosden clearly hoped to use the "relief camp" as a springboard for a comeback onto the espionage market, conducting his work independently, hoping to sell his information to the highest bidder. Any further investigations "necessitate me being given carte blanche action," Gosden said, adding that "your camps will burn and your commiserate [sic] will be looted" if the authorities did not heed his warnings.[91] The available historical record does not indicate whether this freelance informant ever found a buyer.

During the interwar period, the radical left was the most important target of RCMP political intelligence operations, accounting for tens of thousands of pages of intelligence documents.[92] The RCMP's anti-communist crusade was fuelled by conspiracy theories; for instance, Superintendent A.J. Mead explained in an article published in the *RCMP Quarterly* in July 1935 that Communists were behind 90% of all strikes in Canada.[93] Such was the RCMP's obsession with the Communists that when constables failed to find evidence of their being behind a particular act of wrongdoing, their superiors assumed this could only be due to the incompetence of their subordinates or to some sophisticated ruse on the part of the Communists.[94]

It should be noted that this same period was also marked by the rise of fascist movements in Canada, notably those inspired by Adolf Hitler's Nazi Party. The RCMP tended to ignore, underestimate, or even condone the far right.[95] For example, according to former Vancouver Police Chief Colonel C.E. Edgett, whose views the RCMP saw fit to publish in the January 1937 edition of the *RCMP Quarterly*:

2. SEEING RED

> The typical Fascist is not perfect by any means nor very admirable from the standpoint of the normal Democrat. But at least he has applied his violence and ferocity to the enemies of traditional family life—to the enemies of religion—and the Fascist states, as now established, are ruled neither by mere businessmen nor yet by fanatical revolutionaries.[96]

Clearly, not all "extremists" were equal in the eyes of the RCMP, hence the difference in the attitude of law enforcement, to the disadvantage of the far left, particularly the Communist Party, which remained the main target of political surveillance. And so it would remain until the rise of the Quebec independence movement in the 1960s.[97]

3. On the Trail of the FLQ

Following the end of the Second World War, there was a wave of anti-colonial national liberation movements, particularly in Africa and Asia. It was only a matter of time before this reached Quebec. During the 1960s, groups advocating Quebec independence multiplied, some of which operated outside the law. Of these, the Front de Libération du Québec (FLQ) was undoubtedly the most radical.

On the night of March 7–8, 1963, the FLQ carried out its first major attack by simultaneously firebombing three Canadian Army barracks in different parts of the island of Montreal. "Only a total revolution can bring about the necessary changes in an independent Quebec," the organization proclaimed in its April 16 manifesto.[1] The Patriotes' Rebellion of 1837–1838 was often invoked as a "model" by the FLQ, as evidenced by its adoption of the green, white, and red flag that had been the symbol of Louis-Joseph Papineau's party.

No sooner had the FLQ begun to organize itself into cells than it found itself being infiltrated by the Montreal police. When the leadership held a clandestine strategy meeting on June 1, 1963, nobody suspected that one of those present, Jean-Jacques Lanciault, would soon receive a $60,000 reward for his betrayal. Twenty-three arrests followed soon after.[2] The repression marked the end of the first *felquiste* wave.[3] But the next would not be long in coming; indeed, from 1963 to 1970, the FLQ would experience six successive waves, during which eighty bombings, causing a total of four deaths and thirty-six injuries, were attributed to it, as well as twenty-three robberies, two fires, and two train derailments.[4]

In 1964, the RCMP, the Sûreté du Québec (SQ), and the Montreal police combined forces to fight the FLQ by establishing the Combined Anti-Terrorist Squad (CATS). The RCMP had already set up its own special squad, made up of constables from the Criminal Investigation Bureau and the Security and Intelligence Service,[5] to fight the *felquistes*. But the RCMP cast a wide net, as evidenced by their having a file on René Lévesque, the future premier of Quebec.[6] The RCMP was not about to employ half-measures against separatism, which in its view had now replaced communism as the greatest threat to the Canadian state.[7]

In collaboration with the Montreal police, the RCMP launched a massive eighteen-month undercover operation in October 1966, targeting Jacques Désormeaux. An assistant accountant, Désormeaux had participated in the founding of the Rassemblement pour l'indépendance nationale (RIN)[8] and was active in the network around the FLQ's newspaper, *La Cognée*. Désormeaux, who was associated with the nationalist tendency of the FLQ,[9] had already served five months in prison in 1964 when police arrested him for complicity in the robbery of the International Firearms gun shop in Montreal, during which two people had been killed.

The RCMP assigned Lieutenant Bernard Sicotte, a railway security officer from the Canadian Army, to entrap Désormeaux. Sicotte proposed blowing up the "Confederation Train," which was passing through Montreal in 1967 as part of Canada's hundredth-anniversary celebrations. He then provided Désormeaux with twenty sticks of dynamite from which the federal police had removed the nitroglycerine, thereby rendering them inert. As it turned out, the fake explosives were used in a bombing of a Royal Bank of Canada branch on February 12, 1968, which obviously did not cause any damage—except to Désormeaux, who was arrested for possession of explosives on March 14, 1968, while riding in the car of the spy Sicotte.[10] He was acquitted after a long trial during which his lawyer, Serge Ménard, stressed the important role played by the RCMP agent provocateur.[11]

By the end of the decade, the police had no shortage of informants around the FLQ. Towards the end of 1968, the RCMP recruited a thirty-year-old "cab driver" who was able to draw up organizational charts of networks active in left-wing circles and to compile up-to-date files on activists, their associates, and their psychological and character profiles. In his book on the history of the FLQ, Louis Fournier writes that this informant "asserts that he only provided certain information and that he never acted as an agent provocateur, although the RCMP occasionally asked him to do so. Other testimony casts doubt on this assertion."[12]

As for the Montreal police, it was able to get itself an informant after arresting three student activists on March 18, 1970. One of these, Jean-Marc Lafrenière, a student at the Université du Québec à Montréal (UQAM), buckled under the threat of beatings and agreed to become coded source 945-168. Lafrenière's tips proved to be particularly valuable as he was friends with certain activists on the edge of the networks of Jacques Lanctôt and Paul Rose, two FLQ militants who would find themselves at the centre of the October Crisis of 1970.¹³

Indeed, it was the October Crisis that revealed the full extent to which the FLQ had been infiltrated. The Crisis began on October 5, 1970, at 8:20 a.m., when members of the FLQ's Libération Cell kidnapped British diplomat James Richard Cross from his home in Montreal's affluent Golden Square Mile. The FLQ issued seven demands to the authorities, the final one being that they be given the name of the informant who had "sold out" the six FLQ associates who had been arrested the previous June 21 in Prévost.¹⁴ A raid that CATS had described as a "major breakthrough against terrorism"—a testament to the importance the organization accorded its undercover operations.¹⁵

On October 7, the Quebec government authorized the reading of the FLQ manifesto, which was then broadcast in its entirety on CKAC radio. According to the Centre d'analyse et de documentation (CAD), a controversial intelligence and data collection agency set up by Robert Bourassa's Liberal provincial government in 1971 which tracked public sentiment during the October Crisis, "the first kidnapping provoked a reaction of curiosity rather than disapproval," which "was compounded by a certain sympathy after the manifesto was read."¹⁶

The Montreal Police's Anti-Terrorist Section (SAT) was assigned to the investigation and worked in liaison with the SQ and the RCMP within the CATS. It should be noted that the RCMP Security Service (SS) alone had 300 agents in Montreal, compared to about twenty agents for the SAT and about thirty for the SQ. The three police forces were also supported by the Canadian Army's intelligence services, as well as those of the United States and Great Britain, namely the CIA and MI6. CATS soon identified almost all the members of the Libération Cell—Marc Carbonneau, Jacques Cossette-Trudel, Nigel Hamer, Jacques and Louise Lanctôt—thanks to information provided by the "cab driver" and the 945-168 source.¹⁷ Locating them, however, would prove to be a different matter altogether.

On October 10, at six p.m., the Quebec Minister of Justice, Jérôme Choquette, while flatly refusing to accede to the entirety of the FLQ's demands, promised that members of the Libération Cell would receive safe conduct to Cuba. Eighteen minutes later, the Chénier Cell kidnapped one of his colleagues, Minister of Labour Pierre Laporte, at his home in

3. ON THE TRAIL OF THE FLQ

Saint-Lambert. Both this kidnapping and that of Cross "were carried out in quasi-artisanal conditions and by numerically small groups," the CAD later wrote.[18] By October 13, the SQ had identified the four members of the Chénier Cell: Francis Simard, Bernard Lortie, and the brothers Paul and Jacques Rose.[19]

Using the pretext of an "apprehended insurrection,"[20] the federal Liberal government of Pierre Trudeau (father of the current Canadian Prime Minister) proclaimed the War Measures Act on the night of October 15–16. This allowed Trudeau to suspend the Canadian Bill of Rights (which preceded the Canadian Charter of Rights and Freedoms), grant special powers to the police, and send 8,000 soldiers into Quebec, many of whom would patrol the streets of Montreal. From October 16 to November 27, no less than 465 people were arrested, of whom a little over 400 were released after periods of detention ranging from a few days to several weeks, without ever being charged with any offence.[21] In addition, some 4,600 searches were conducted throughout the province.[22] Marc Lalonde, Prime Minister Trudeau's chief of staff at the time and a key player in the decision to introduce the emergency legislation, would say three decades later:

> The insurrection was not the FLQ as such, it was the shift in public opinion in Montreal: the demonstration at the Paul-Sauvé Centre with three thousand people,[23] then the student strikes at UQAM and the University of Montreal. One could not help but think of what had happened in France in 1968, two years before, where everything had started with student demonstrations.[24]

On October 17, Laporte's lifeless body was found in the trunk of an abandoned car in a vacant lot on the south shore of Montreal, near a Canadian Army base. "This murder aroused general disapproval and shifted public opinion to the law and order camp. The sympathy that the kidnappers had enjoyed disappeared," Fournier wrote.[25] On October 24, the police authorized the release of a "dubious communiqué" signed by the "Papineau and Chénier" Cells, calling for "selective assassinations," while news of Communiqué #10 from the Libération Cell, issued on October 16 and announcing the suspension of the decision to execute Cross, was suppressed.[26]

In the meantime, the police show of force—which had resulted in a series of raids, mainly against people who were not involved in the events in question—had largely avoided targeting individuals who were seriously suspected of belonging to the FLQ. This is made particularly clear in the report of lawyer Jean-François Duchaîne, who was commissioned by the Quebec government in 1977 to shed light on the October Crisis. Based on statements of Montreal police and SQ officers, Duchaîne reported that,

> The RCMP had known for some time where the Roses were hiding. However, the RCMP never informed the Sûreté du Québec, which was in charge of this investigation, of the location of the Rose's hideout. This omission seems completely inexplicable to us. Since we did not obtain the cooperation of the federal authorities in our investigation, it was impossible for us to obtain answers from the RCMP to our questions.[27]

Duchaîne also criticized the "amateurism" of the Sûreté du Québec, as well as the "disorganized improvisation" of the Montreal police. "The only real success of the Montreal Police in the investigations they conducted was the recruitment of Carole Deveault [sic] as an informant," wrote Duchaîne.[28]

Carole de Vault was a twenty-four-year-old history student at UQAM; a Parti Québécois activist, she had campaigned for Jacques Parizeau, a PQ candidate in the April 1970 general election, with whom she had also had an affair that same year.[29]

In her autobiography, de Vault claims that she sympathized with the FLQ manifesto but not with the kidnappings.[30] Yet she ended up in an *felquiste* cell through a most unlikely combination of circumstances. According to de Vault, Robert Comeau, a history professor at UQAM, had requested that she act as a go-between to put him in touch with Michel Frankland, a PQ activist whom she knew from the Ahuntsic riding association. Soon after, she attended the creation of a new cell, named André Ouimet, with Comeau and Frankland. Comeau "seemed to take my collaboration in the terrorist struggle for granted," wrote de Vault, who, if her account is to be believed, never verbalized any intention to either join or reject the FLQ.

But there are serious reasons to doubt her account: It is difficult to believe that Comeau would have proposed to a young woman, with whom he had never spoken in his life, that she join an underground movement during a period of police repression unequalled in modern Quebec history. Nor does it make sense that Comeau, a member of the Viger Information Cell,[31] would have given this same young woman shocking details about the death of Minister Laporte after spending only a few hours with her. Yet this is the version put forth by de Vault in her autobiography. Indeed, the Duchaîne report offers a different view, stating that previously "Carole Deveault [sic] had told a university professor of her desire to participate in the FLQ action."[32]

Whatever the facts may be, after she told Comeau that her part-time job with the Caloil oil company involved accompanying a guard who made cash deposits at various banking institutions, de Vault found herself drawn into a robbery scheme to fund the Libération Cell. This is a turning point in de Vault's story. "Now I knew it was more than fantasy," she wrote. "It was from that moment that I began to consider going to the police."[33] She did so on November 6, when she went to Station 17 to meet with Sergeant Fernand Tanguay. De Vault provided valuable information about Cross's captivity and about a planned kidnapping of Jean Pellerin, an editor at *La Presse* and an old friend of Prime Minister Trudeau. Skeptical, Lieutenant Julien Giguère filed the source report in the "crackpot" pile.[34] However, he soon changed his mind after seeing that some of the information provided by de Vault was included in the Libération Cell's Communiqué #11.[35]

On November 7, 1970, de Vault would be identified as coded source 945-171, in an undercover operation named "Poupette," after a restaurant on Mont Royal Street where SAT members used to meet.[36] "Soon they started calling me Poupette, and it was under this name that I was known henceforth at the SAT," wrote de Vault.[37] The robbery finally took place on November 12. The robber grabbed the wrong bag, however, and it was with de Vault's purse, containing only $12, that he would flee before being quickly intercepted by police. "I felt relieved of a great weight. It was over! Now I could return to a normal life. I could forget about the FLQ and the police," wrote de Vault.[38] However, the opposite was about to happen.

While the purse-snatcher's arrest might have raised suspicions, Comeau did not cut ties with de Vault. On the night of November 13–14, he even asked her to help draft the Viger Information Cell's Communiqué #2, in which the FLQ intended to reveal a monumental blunder the police had made: while they had struck a blow by arresting Bernard Lortie, one of Laporte's kidnappers, in an apartment on Queen Mary Street in Montreal on November 6, the three other members of the Chénier Cell had remained hidden in the back of a closet and had managed to flee after the police left to go eat. Once the draft was complete, de Vault rushed to phone Detective Lieutenant Giguère to give him the scoop. "I couldn't conceal a trace of irony and of triumph. I am very pleased with myself," she wrote.[39] Giguère reluctantly admitted the

FLQ's story was true, except for the part about the *felquiste* fugitives taking the weapons left by the police in the apartment. "He did not want the communiqué to mention the guns that the police were supposed to have left in the apartment. He told me that the FLQ would make itself look foolish if it wrote something like that," she said.⁴⁰ So now an official from the Anti-Terrorist Section was worried about the FLQ's credibility!

"Done! I have transcribed my first statement. I look at it, I must confess, with a touch of pride," de Vault wrote. When he delivered the communiqué, Comeau was followed by no less than ten police officers in five different undercover cars. Back at de Vault's place, Comeau hinted to the informant that he knew where Cross was being held. He also told her about the financial difficulties the Libération Cell was experiencing. "They have to pay the rent on Monday and they have no money. They hadn't expected to keep Cross for such a long time," he explained. De Vault then undertook to play the generous soul, offering to pay the rent. "Still hoping to find out where James Cross was detained, I offered to lend Robert the money," she wrote.⁴¹

At a November 18 meeting, Montreal police informed members of the RCMP and SQ that they had a source inside an *felquiste* cell. Those present at the meeting were also given an apparently complete account of two interviews between Montreal police investigators and de Vault. The Montreal police would subsequently share the information they received from "Poupette" with the other two police forces.⁴²

On November 25, the RCMP thought they had identified both the location where Cross was being held—on Des Récollets Street in Montreal North—and the hideout of the three members of the Chénier Cell on the run, in a country house on the South Shore. By December 2, the hideout of Cross's captors was surrounded. The British diplomat was released after fifty-nine days' captivity while most members of the Libération Cell flew to Cuba.⁴³ One however remained in Montreal: Nigel Hamer, a McGill University engineering student who was not present on Des Récollets Street when the police moved in.

The day after Cross was kidnapped, source 945-168 told the Montreal police that Hamer was one of the five people she suspected of having taken part in Cross's kidnapping. But apart from intermittent surveillance in November 1970, Hamer was left alone. On December 4, de Vault confirmed to Detective Lieutenant Giguère that Hamer was one of Cross's kidnappers and even provided the address where he was hiding, but nothing came of it.

3. ON THE TRAIL OF THE FLQ

"One wonders why it took until 1977 for an investigation to be opened on him," Duchaîne would note. "Hamer was not charged until July 1980 with the kidnapping of James Cross."[44] There is no evidence of any collusion between Hamer and the police or foreign intelligence services, which obviously leaves one wondering why he was able to benefit from this strange immunity for a decade.[45] Duchaîne speculated that "an investigation of Hamer would have risked revealing the identity of a former FLQ member recruited in May 1972 as a police informant within left-wing groups."[46] Hamer was eventually sentenced in May 1981 to one year in prison after admitting to his involvement in the kidnapping.[47]

In the weeks following the October Crisis, RCMP officials held discussions with members of the federal government about future strategies for dealing with groups like the FLQ. "The question of the commission of crime in the national interest was clearly discussed by Ministers. There is no doubt about that," according to John Starnes, Director General of the RCMP Security Service (RCMP-SS).[48] On December 17, 1970, an RCMP memorandum, entitled "RCMP Strategy for Dealing with the FLQ and Similar Movements," was sent to the Cabinet for Security and Intelligence, a body chaired by the Prime Minister. One passage is of particular interest:

> An increased effort to penetrate movements like the FLQ by human and technical sources will have to be undertaken. We have had only limited success in being able to penetrate the FLQ and similar movements with human sources. Changes in existing legislation will be required if effective penetration by technical means is to be achieved. The greatest bar to effective penetration by human sources is the problem raised by having members of the RCMP, or paid agents, commit serious crimes in order to establish their bona fides with the members of the organization they are seeking to infiltrate. Among other things, this involves the difficult question of providing some kind of immunity from arrest and punishment for human sources (usually paid agents) who have ... to break the law in order successfully to infiltrate movements like the FLQ.[49]

Another RCMP document, entitled "Law and Order—Enhancing the RCMP's Capacity to Act," which was distributed to the Interdepartmental Committee on Law and Order and elsewhere, was blunt:

> It is to be recognized that penetration of terrorist cells by police agents will inevitably involve commission of crimes on their part to establish their *bona fides*. [...] The question that must be asked is whether we as a police force can go outside the rule of law to detect criminal activities.[50]

As 1970 drew to a close, the SQ finally located the South Shore hideout of the three Chénier Cell fugitives in Saint-Luc. Francis Simard and Paul and Jacques Rose surrendered after a nighttime siege, their only request being that those still detained under the War Measures Act be released. Paul Rose and Francis Simard were both sentenced to life imprisonment, Bernard Lortie received a twenty-year sentence, and Jacques Rose was sentenced to eight years in prison after his fourth trial.[51] In addition, fourteen people who had assisted the Chénier Cell in various ways received sentences ranging from six months to eight years in prison.

The decision to strike at the Chénier Cell's support network was made at a strategy meeting of senior security and intelligence officials from the Montreal police, the SQ, and the RCMP. Perhaps most importantly, representatives of the three police forces agreed to not crack down on the Libération Cell's support network, which included the Viger Information Cell, which included Comeau, Nigel Hamer, and François Séguin. As Detective Lieutenant Giguère explained, "I don't think the ones we control are dangerous. I think we might as well sit back and watch them move ... When the time comes that we lose control, OK then we will strike."[52]

The people whom the SAT investigator did not consider to be dangerous had stolen a large quantity of dynamite from the Demix Agregats quarry in Saint-Hilaire a few months earlier. This big haul had been stored in a garage rented by Hamer in Montreal. In December 1970, de Vault informed Giguère that Comeau and Hamer knew where the dynamite was hidden. They were never questioned, although the War Measures Act gave the police the power to do so.[53] In addition, from mid-November to the end of December, police and military forces jointly conducted Operation Sweep to locate caches of weapons and explosives. No less than 22,539 searches were conducted, yet the garage rented by Hamer was never touched.[54] The Montreal police were equally unconcerned about another dynamite theft committed, again, by members of the Viger Information Cell.[55]

But Detective Lieutenant Giguère was not content to just sit back and

3. ON THE TRAIL OF THE FLQ

watch what the *felquistes* were getting up to. On December 2, 1970, the SAT investigator gave $225 to de Vault so that she in turn could give it to the André Ouimet Cell, which had been set up by Frankland and "Poupette," in order for it to have "a good reputation in the FLQ."[56] At the time, the cell, duly subsidized by the Montreal police, was planning a kidnapping. "Let Frankland make his kidnapping plans! When he and his gang come knocking in the morning to kidnap their guy, it's [me and my] men who will open the door for them," boasted the detective.[57]

Since December 1970, de Vault had been paid by the Montreal police for the information she delivered, $30 each time she met with her controller, which was usually twice a week. She also received a lump sum of $15,000 in November 1971, a "nice surprise" according to the informant.[58] The federal government agreed to partially reimburse the Montreal police for the remuneration it provided to three sources active during the October Crisis, including "Poupette."[59] In her memoirs, de Vault discussed her double life as follows:

> I became an informant by accident, against my will. Now, I was enjoying the game.[60] [...] It had become a challenge to get to know all the people in the FLQ and to become privy to their secret plans. There was a lot of romanticism involved: the romanticism of the Felquistes who played at revolution, at grandiose clandestine acts. But my role was even more complicated: I lived a double secret life, as part of the FLQ, and as a spy. [...] Insofar as FLQ actions had serious consequences, I seriously wanted to counter the FLQ. And insofar as they were only playing a game suited to naïve adolescents, I, too, was playing the game.[61]

With funds sent to it by the SAT through Carole de Vault, the André Ouimet Cell would soon be in a position to undertake its first direct action: firebombing Brink's, the cash courier company.[62] De Vault took part in the preparations, scoping out the scene and providing the use of her bathroom to make the firebombs. On January 6, 1971, no less than thirty-eight SQ officers, divided into three teams, were dispatched to tail Frankland. All these dozens of police nonetheless managed to lose his trail between 10:31 and 10:54 p.m., and it was during this period that Frankland threw a Molotov cocktail at the door of the Brink's garage on Ottawa Street in downtown Montreal. The damage was superficial, but that did not stop twenty-seven SQ officers from tailing Frankland and de Vault when they delivered the communiqué claiming responsibility for the attack. While the attack went unpunished, Brink's did not fail to seize the opportunity to increase its security measures.[63]

The next month, de Vault took part in another operation, this time targeting a post office on Papineau Street in Montreal. Working with Detective Lieutenant Giguère, she replaced the FLQ's dynamite with fake explosives. During the preparations, Giguère urged de Vault to persuade the *felquistes* not to place the bomb on the roof of the post office; as a result, it was placed in the alleyway. "Poupette" even assisted in activating the detonator. "I returned to the lane to ignite the fuse," she recounted, while a strikeforce of about twenty police officers waited nearby without intervening.[64] The action, which took place on the night of February 19–20, would nonetheless lead to the conviction of *felquiste* Jacques Primeau later that month, charged with making and planting an explosive device. At the time that it sentenced Primeau to six months in prison, the court was unaware that the bomb had been made with fake explosives.[65]

In November 1971, de Vault also participated in an extortion attempt to finance the FLQ. The plan was to warn the authorities that a time bomb had been placed on a plane in flight and to demand $200,000 from Ottawa in exchange for information as to how to defuse the device. In reality, it was a simple detonator, provided by the informant, and a communiqué, co-authored by the informant, that were placed in a baggage locker at Dorval airport. The operation was scheduled for November 9, but Frankland backed out of going to the airport that day after being stopped by a patrol car for a broken headlight. Looking back some years later, the Commission of Inquiry on Police Operations in Quebec Territory, commonly known as the Keable Commission, would note that, "This incident shows how easy it would have been to get Mr. Frankland to abandon his plans. However, it does not appear that Mr. Giguère was willing to take preventive measures against Mr. Frankland."[66]

The scheme was finally carried out on November 19. Inexplicably, three hours passed between the time KLM and Air Canada received the phone calls from the *felquistes* and the arrival at Dorval Airport of Sergeants Aldo Ghirotto and Louis Arsenault of the Criminal Research Section (Subversive Activities), or CRS(SA), the new name of the Montreal Police's Anti-Terrorist Section.[67] The two investigators tried to be reassuring, but failed to assuage the concerns of airport officials, as recounted by de Vault:

3. ON THE TRAIL OF THE FLQ

The police, filled in by Julien Giguère, told the officials that they had every reason to believe that there was no bomb on a plane. The Dorval authorities, however, were reluctant to expose passengers to even the slightest risk, so Staff Sergeant Donald McCleery of the RCMP phoned the force's superintendent in Ottawa. He, in turn, spoke to senior management at the airport to tell them that the communiqué was not to be taken seriously.[68]

"Inquiries in this case did not lead us to any suspects," concluded Constable Robert Lemieux of the SQ's Security Squad, who was never informed that a police source was involved. This is curious, to say the least, in light of the fact that "in November and December 1971, the reports written on the basis of information from 'Poupette' were regularly forwarded to the RCMP and the SQ."[69]

In December, de Vault organized another fundraiser, the robbery of a bingo game held in the basement of St. Catherine's Parish Church on Robin Street in Montreal. The robbery was carried out by a new group, the Michèle Gauthier Cell,[70] all of whose members were aged 21 or under, two of whom had been recruited by de Vault.[71] "Poupette" also provided a toy gun, a pair of handcuffs, and chloroform to Michel Guay, the "leader" of the cell.[72] Detective Lieutenant Giguère would later admit that his informant had gone "too far" on this occasion.[73] Forewarned by the police, the parish priest made sure that the bingo box contained only a small amount of cash. As a matter of fact, on December 7, 1971, when Guay carried out the robbery (without violence), it contained only $31.90. Guay and his three accomplices were quickly apprehended by CRS(SA) detectives. They were convicted of theft and fined $25 each ...[74]

During his testimony to the Keable Commission, Detective Lieutenant Giguère attempted to justify the police's non-interference in various FLQ actions by citing the need to protect his valuable source. But despite Giguère's willingness to protect "Poupette" from suspicion, Comeau eventually began to distrust de Vault.[75] "[François 'Fritz' Séguin] told me that Robert Comeau had spread it around that I was a woman cop, but that he, Fritz, did not believe it," she wrote.[76] This conversation was the prelude to a romantic affair between the informant and Séguin. This intimate relationship did not prevent de Vault from later providing Giguère with information about Séguin after she learned that he was in Cornwall, Ontario, "on FLQ business."[77]

Betraying a comrade and intimate partner like this says a lot about where "Poupette" was coming from.

In fact, de Vault went so far as to talk about "Fritz" as someone "whose life I surely changed." She felt that her tip would lead to Séguin's arrest and ultimately to the police "convincing Fritz to become an informant."[78] One thing we do know for sure: Séguin did flip.[79] The Keable Commission reports that "Fritz" provided the police with details of the dynamite thefts at the Demix Agregats quarry and in St. Paul-d'Abbotsford, as well as the names of the four men and two women who took part in the robbery of a credit union in Mascouche on September 24, 1971, during which the young *felquiste* Pierre-Louis Bourret was killed by a gunshot wound to the head.[80] Needless to say, Séguin was never charged in relation to his own activities.

The Keable Commission dwelt for some time on the "Poupette" operation, particularly on the preparation of FLQ communiqués. It was established that de Vault participated in the drafting of ten communiqués and in the distribution of six of them, between November 7, 1970, and November 19, 1971.[81] It should be noted that Detective Lieutenant Giguère was warned in advance of the arrival of all but one of these communiqués.[82] Curiously, the ten communiqués were issued in the name of seven different "cells."[83] In addition, there was a "joint communiqué" dated October 23, 1971, signed by no less than eight *felquiste* "cells," the purpose of which was apparently to authenticate all these cells as being truly part of the FLQ.[84] The question arises, however, as to how many of these so-called cells existed solely on paper, a question which unfortunately was not answered by the Keable Commission's report.

Moreover, source reports indicate that de Vault provided information about nineteen communiqués, while the informant denied during her testimony that she mentioned anything to police about two of these, as well as a host of other information attributed to her.[85] Who was telling the truth? What lay behind these contradictions? In her autobiography, de Vault mentions a theory that she heard from Mario Bilodeau, a prosecutor with the Keable Commission: that Giguère had an informant involved in the Cross kidnapping and that he hid the reports from this "hot" source behind the same source number as "Poupette," SAT 945-171. De Vault, who up to that point had trusted her controller completely, no longer knew what to think. "They were crazy! Or was I the one who was crazy?" she wrote.[86]

When the Keable Commission examined these questions in 1977, it criticized the police officers involved for their "systematic refusal to enlighten the Commission" on the thorny question of the origin of the paper used by the FLQ to produce its communiqués, thus preventing it from reaching "a firm conclusion" on this question.[87] The Commission's report reveals that de Vault provided the paper for the production of twelve communiqués.[88] In ten of these, this was the official paper used by the FLQ to authenticate its communiqués. RCMP Sergeant Raymond Langevin, who was the liaison officer with the CRS(SA) from May to November 1971, told the commission that Montreal police found FLQ letterhead during their searches on Des Récollets Street.[89] The paper was then photocopied and passed on to informants, who then used the photocopies of the paper to produce their own *"felquiste"* communiqués.

It was also established that de Vault played a role of some sort in the preparation and/or distribution of thirteen of the twenty-three FLQ communiqués deemed "official" by the Keable Commission. This is not a trivial detail, given that all of these communiqués were "widely reproduced and commented on in the press."[90] It is as if the police were trying, in 1971, to perpetuate the strategies of control and manipulation that they had developed during the October Crisis, by prioritizing communiqués with a clearly violent tone. Was the goal to discredit the sections of the independence movement that were pursuing their goals in other ways, by artificially sustaining an FLQ that was as belligerent as it was impotent due to police infiltration?

Of all the daily newspapers in Montreal at the time, the *Journal de Montréal* was probably the one that devoted the most coverage to the activities of the FLQ, which was "presented as a powerful and far-reaching organization," in particular by journalist Pierre Bouchard.[91] Bouchard, the Keable Commission wrote, "collaborated with various anti-subversive intelligence services during a period extending at least from 1969 to 1973."[92] The commission based this claim on the testimony of Montreal police Sergeant Réal Mailhot, according to whom Bouchard worked with the RCMP and carried a card identifying him as a Canadian Army officer.[93] Interviewed by Louis Fournier, author of the premier history of the FLQ, Bouchard denied the Keable Commission's assertions.[94]

Police reports from the time are equally troubling. A document entitled *Activités terroristes et révolutionnaires à l'intérieur des mouvements ou associations au Québec* [Terrorist and Revolutionary Activities within Movements or Associations in Quebec], produced by the SQ and dated June 7, 1971, refers to the existence of four FLQ cells in the Montreal area, and suggests that their "next step" might be "selective assassinations"—a recurring theme in FLQ communiqués.⁹⁵ Yet the report does not mention de Vault's involvement in many of the communiqués in question. Similarly, the *Front de libération du Québec 1960–1975* report, produced by the CAD for the Premier and Executive Council of Quebec, concluded from a study "based entirely on the analysis of FLQ communiqués" that "all the elements seem to be in place for a new violent confrontation" in 1971.⁹⁶

The Keable Commission also looked at an RCMP report entitled *Current FLQ Groups*, dated November 24, 1971.⁹⁷ This document stated that "it is becoming increasingly difficult to infiltrate" the new FLQ cells, which, according to the document, had "learned from the experiences of the Chénier and Libération Cells."⁹⁸ The commission did not hide its amazement when it noted that "the passage in *Current FLQ Groups* that describes the security system adopted by Mr. Comeau's group as 'relatively sophisticated' is almost entirely based on information from an undercover source in that group (i.e. De Vault)."⁹⁹

In an alarmist tone, the document claimed to identify four main terrorist groups, with an additional thirteen groups believed to be preparing for action, and a total of twenty-two cells believed to exist. However, only two networks were deemed to pose an immediate threat, namely the Comeau and Laliberté groups—two networks that had clearly been infiltrated and kept under police surveillance, one by "Poupette" and the other by a certain "cab driver" who had been providing information to the RCMP since 1968.¹⁰⁰

"To the extent of the access the police forces had to the plans of the known cells regarded as most active, the police were in a better position than they had been in October 1970," noted the McDonald Commission,¹⁰¹ contradicting the claims made in *Current FLQ Groups*. Curiously, this document was produced after the RCMP's Montreal bureau had advised the Ottawa headquarters that many of the communiqués attributed to the FLQ were the work of groups infiltrated by the police. However, it appears that this information never made it to the top of the federal police force. The McDonald Commission suggested that "The failure to advise senior management of the RCMP of the true facts left it open to senior management to believe, and to communicate to government, that the FLQ threat in 1971 was on a level of intensity somewhat higher than it actually was."¹⁰² The fact remains that Ottawa was wrong about the state of the *felquiste* movement in the year following the October Crisis.

3. ON THE TRAIL OF THE FLQ

In December 1971, after this document was released, Inspector Donald Cobb, who led the Montreal bureau of Section G of the RCMP's "C" Division Security Service (SS), launched an operation to determine the veracity of the information the federal police was receiving from "Poupette."[103] Cobb also stated that he did not see anything at all scandalous about a police informant being involved in writing FLQ communiqués, which he said were "genuine in the sense that they claimed responsibility for criminal acts that had actually occurred."[104] So Cobb did not feel he had been misled. Ironically, the McDonald Commission itself questioned the inspector's assessment of the *felquiste* threat as it approached the first anniversary of the October Crisis. For the RCMP, the robbery in Saint-Henri-de-Mascouche on September 24 and the news that veteran *felquiste* Pierre Vallières had gone into hiding were signs of an impending new terrorist offensive. "There was less objective foundation for the alarmist advice that was given to the government in October 1971 than was required to justify that advice," the commission observed.[105]

Still, FLQ attacks did seem to be on the rise. On September 3, for example, dynamite exploded causing more than $300,000 in damage to the Bell Canada telephone plant in Dorion, west of Montreal. The next day, another bomb was detonated, this time targeting the Sainte-Rita school in Ahuntsic, a French-language institution that had just been converted into an English school.[106] It appeared, as the McDonald Commission later noted, that "The presence of police informers in violence-prone groups does not altogether eliminate the danger which those groups may pose to the lives and property of innocent persons."[107]

In this regard, one of the commission's revelations was that "an RCMP human source, during the year 1971 wrote at least three communiqués in the name of two different cells of the FLQ." According to the commission's legal counsel, "it was the source who was the leader and instigator." The communiqués were unambiguously threatening, and the first, dated October 17, was addressed directly to Quebec Premier Robert Bourassa.[108] The officer handling the informant told the commission that he "never asked the source to issue communiqués," a dubious claim given that two messages sent by the source's contact were destroyed at RCMP headquarters.[109]

Section G's Montreal bureau even went so far as to publish a communiqué prepared from scratch by the RCMP. Communiqué #3 from the "Minerve Cell" was intended as a response to Pierre Vallières's long text published in *Le Devoir* on December 13, 1971, in which he disavowed the FLQ and called on those struggling for independence to join the ranks of the Parti Québécois. Vallières noted that "the three letters F-L-Q can be used by any agent provocateur in the pay of the RCMP and the CIA."[110] At the time, this lucid observation provoked many reactions, but that of the RCMP disguised as the FLQ was certainly one of the most hysterical.

Inspector Cobb entrusted the production of the fake communiqué to Staff Sergeant Marc Leduc, who assembled a small team to carry out the operation.[111] Hélène Vigeant, an analyst in D Section (counter-subversion) who had been with the RCMP for only two months, was charged with working with Inspector Cobb to develop the text of the communiqué, with a particular emphasis on giving it a "Maoist" flavour.[112] Seeking maximum media coverage, Cobb and Leduc agreed that the communiqué would have more impact in the Monday papers than in the weekend editions.[113] On Sunday, December 19, Corporal Dubuc and Constable Richard Daigle released the communiqué. The full text was published in the pages of the now defunct *Montréal-Matin*:

> The "La Minerve" cell does not agree with Pierre Vallières's new ideas. Vallières convinced us of the effectiveness of violent revolution to free us from capitalist tyrants. Now Vallières, the failed revolutionary, can only write words. Mao, the true revolutionary, teaches us that power comes from the barrel of the gun. [...] The FLQ is the only force to fight against the exploiters of the proletariat. [...] Fighting means sacrifice, and death is commonplace. As we have the interests of our people at heart, to die is to make death meaningful. Vallières endorses the Parti Québécois. We know this petty-bourgeois party all too well, at ease in the establishment, a collection of all the failures, all the pseudo-intellectuals and the false revolutionaries. This party is complicit with the fascists of authority. What is the point of infiltrating the PQ when we can achieve our goals with our own weapons? Together, the "La Minerve" cell and its supporters will continue to liberate the Québécois race from the oppression imposed by the Anglo-Saxon bourgeoisie and its puppets in government, as well as all other enemies of our people. We will win.[114]

"When I saw Communiqué #3, I couldn't believe I wrote it," Cobb later recalled.[115] He was certainly not alone. The *Montréal-Matin* article also mentioned that the Riel Cell had rallied to Vallières's position, leading the paper

3. ON THE TRAIL OF THE FLQ

to declare that there was "a real split in the FLQ."[116] The Montreal police and the SQ opened an investigation and conducted forensic tests to ascertain the authors of the communiqué; all of which proved unsuccessful.[117] It wasn't until the Keable Commission in 1978 that Cobb, who had since been promoted to the rank of chief superintendent, was publicly identified as the person responsible for the fake communiqué.[118] In his testimony, Cobb explained that he had interpreted Vallières's proposal as a maneuver to have extremists infiltrate the PQ. The RCMP officer further testified that he had hoped his fake communiqué would lead to *felquistes* joining the Maoist group *En Lutte!*, which he said was easier to spy on than the Parti Québécois.[119] "Surveillance of the PQ was extremely delicate," Cobb observed.[120]

Did the RCMP issue any other fake communiqués? The federal police deny it, but an expert report from the Institute of Forensic Science and Technology indicates that the three communiqués issued in the name of the "La Minerve" Cell, including Communiqué #3, can all be connected to "the same group of people." The federal authorities were not inclined to help the commission get to the bottom of the matter. For example, when the commission attempted to obtain a handwriting sample from Hélène Vigeant in its efforts to identify the author of the three communiqués, RCMP counsel objected strongly, stating that such handwriting samples might prove incriminating in possible criminal proceedings.[121]

Beyond its attempts to manipulate the FLQ, the RCMP was still trying to frame Jacques Désormeaux, the founding member of the newspaper *La Cognée* whom they had already tried to entrap in March 1968. Four years later, the RCMP was once again determined to use all available means to get Désormeaux. As Sergeant Bernard Dubuc explains:

> It was common knowledge that Staff Sergeant McCleery harbored a hatred and frustration towards the terrorist Jacques Desormeaux. So this supervisor planned to obtain explosive materials that would be needed to frame the subject in order to neutralize him.[122]

On the night of April 26–27, 1972, Sergeant Dubuc, accompanied by Corporal Normand Chamberland and Constable Rick Daigle, stole four cases of dynamite, containing fifty-six sticks and a box of one hundred detonators, from Richelieu Explosives in Saint-Grégoire.[123] The following month, Désormeaux was arrested by the RCMP for possession of explosives. Donald McInnis, a teacher, was also apprehended carrying a bag containing thirty-four sticks of dynamite and detonators. The explosives had been supplied by a former Canadian Army NCO who was never charged. Yet again, however, the case was a fiasco: Désormeaux was acquitted on November 14, 1975, while McInnis received a six-month suspended sentence.[124]

The RCMP was also implicated in a hijacking plot in the fall of 1972. In September, federal police informed the Solicitor General of Canada[125] that a "controlled" *felquiste* cell was planning to hijack an Air Canada DC-9 aircraft flying from Montreal to Ottawa. The demands were to be the release of various Québécois political prisoners, $500,000, and safe passage to Algeria or Cuba.[126] This was just before the second anniversary of the October Crisis and in the midst of a federal election campaign. The plan, dubbed "Operation Ronald," was never carried out. The cell cancelled their plans on October 25, five days before the federal election, after they found a business card from a Montreal police sergeant in the home of a new recruit, Robert Turcotte, who claimed to be a labour activist with the plumbers' union of the Fédération des travailleurs du Québec (FTQ).[127] Not only was Turcotte one of the ones who had initiated the hijacking plot, but he was also meant to provide the weapons and ammunition to carry it out. Turcotte suddenly disappeared into thin air, confirming the suspicions against him.[128]

On November 9, *felquiste* Reynald Lévesque was arrested by the SQ; he faced some thirty charges in connection with sixteen bombings. In an article published in the *Journal de Montréal* a few days after his arrest, he was presented as one of the alleged architects of the cancelled hijacking.[129] But neither Lévesque, nor anyone else, was ever charged in connection with the plan.[130] The whole thing would resurface in the media five years later, in the context of the Keable Commission. Faced with allegations linking the RCMP to the hijacking plot, Solicitor General Francis Fox was quick to assure Canadians that such claims were completely false, while Prime Minister Trudeau, whose possible resignation had been mooted as a result of the allegations, simply dismissed them as "garbage."[131]

1973 proved to be a quiet year in terms of political violence in Quebec— the most quiet in the ten years since the emergence of the FLQ.[132] According to Louis Fournier, credit for this respite does not go the police:

> It was not so much police repression, with its strategy of infiltration, that prevented the revival of the FLQ in late 1972. It was, much more, the reorganization of a fraction of the radical left within what

became known as the "Marxist-Leninist" movement, a phenomenon that channeled many young militants' hopes for change. It was also, to a very large extent, the rise of the "legal" independence movement, represented by the Parti Québécois, and the prospect of the PQ taking power.[133]

Ironically, all this took place while members of the RCMP-SS's G section were still heavily involved in illegal activities in their efforts to counter the Quebec independence movement. On May 8, 1972, RCMP agents burned down a barn at the Petit Québec Libre farm, a commune close to FLQ circles, in Sainte-Anne-de-la-Rochelle. Later that year, on the night of October 6–7, agents carried out "Operation Bricole," breaking into the offices shared by the Agence de presse libre du Québec (APLQ), the Mouvement pour la défense des prisonniers politiques du Québec (MDPPQ), and the Coopérative de déménagement du 1er Mai.[134] On January 9, 1973, they broke into the offices of the Parti Québécois, in what was dubbed "Operation Ham," stealing a computerized list of the names, addresses, and occupations of some 102,500 PQ party members.[135] It was also around this time that Section G agents began to kidnap people suspected of sympathizing with the FLQ, snatching them up off the street and holding them in an attempt to recruit them as informers, traumatizing some of them to the point that they withdrew entirely from political activism.[136]

And Carole de Vault? Despite the steady decline of the *felquiste* movement, she continued to practice her "profession" as an informant, joining the Communist Party of Quebec Marxist-Leninist (PCQ-ML) for a time.[137] As for the FLQ, the informant would later claim that she had participated "in its last stirrings, its last attempts to resurrect itself, by carrying out a kidnapping" in 1974, an obscure project that was called off when the "main conspirator," whom she never named, took his own life. That same year, "Poupette" would claim she got married and stopped collaborating with the Montreal police.[138] It might have been expected that with this she would have exited our story, though as we shall see, she would return again some years later.

4. An Agent Provocateur "Made in the USA"

The Quebec independence movement was not the only target of police dirty tricks in the 1970s. Activists in Canada's Black communities were also targeted. From the 1960s on, these communities had been becoming increasingly visible, with the arrival of several thousand people from the West Indies, largely due to much more restrictive immigration policies that the government of Great Britain had just imposed. Processes of politicization, and sometimes radicalization, were encouraged by the influence of anti-colonial and independence struggles in the Caribbean, and most especially by the new wave of the Black nationalist movement in the United States, commonly referred to as "Black Power," of which the Black Panther Party remains the best-known example.

The RCMP began to pay attention to the Black liberation movement as early as 1968, the year in which the assassination of the Reverend Martin Luther King, Jr. triggered a wave of riots across a hundred cities in the United States.[1] In Montreal, 1968 was the year of the Black Writers' Congress at McGill University, which provided an unprecedented forum for Black radical politics. The RCMP viewed this event with suspicion, making it their mission to obtain "any additional advance intelligence relative to the Congress of Black Writers [...] and the identities of representatives of that Congress" and to "ensure that all proceedings are given as thorough a coverage as possible."[2] The RCMP concluded that the Congress was "a deliberate attempt to further motivate dissension and subversion within the population."[3]

The RCMP was worried about the increasing number of Canadian connections with these activists, whom they referred to as "Negro Black nationalists in the United States."[4] In his testimony before the Keable Commission, RCMP Sergeant Claude Brodeur even stated that the sole purpose of the barn fire in Sainte-Anne-de-la-Rochelle was "to wreak havoc and prevent meetings between real revolutionaries from the Black Panthers and our local agitators."[5] Nor did the RCMP's Office of Special Investigations mince its words when it claimed, in a memo dated January 29, 1969, that Black Power supporters

4. AN AGENT PROVOCATEUR "MADE IN THE USA"

constitute an extreme threat to the national security and their influence in our educational institutions is presently being felt with strong consequences. If able to break down the educational area of our society within the following generation the Nation's Government could be destroyed.[6]

That same day marked the beginning of a student occupation of the computer centre at Sir George Williams University (later renamed Concordia University), located on the ninth floor of the Henry F. Hall building in downtown Montreal. The movement was triggered by the university's questionable handling of complaints by six West Indian students against a biology professor who gave lower grades to students of colour.[7] The occupation lasted two weeks, during which time the RCMP received information from a "source"—never identified—who had managed to infiltrate the computer centre.[8]

The occupation quickly became a rallying point, not only for radical activists but also for shady characters, such as George Sams, an agent provocateur from the FBI who would later be implicated in the torture and murder of a young Black Panther Party member in Connecticut.[9] At the time, police infiltration had become a major problem for the Black Panthers; one lawyer estimates that in 1969, between sixty and seventy informers were snitching on members of the organization.[10]

The occupation came to a spectacular end on February 11. As the police forced their way into the occupied premises, the computer centre caught fire for reasons that remain unclear to this day.[11] "Let the n----rs burn! Let the n----rs burn!" racist onlookers chanted from the street below, as smoke billowed from the building.[12] In all, ninety-seven people were arrested, in many cases with violence, and charged with four criminal offences, including mischief endangering human life, which alone carries a life sentence.[13] Author David Austin notes that "The rebellion at Sir George was not just the largest student occupation in Canadian history, but internationally the most destructive (to property) act of civil disobedience on a university campus. Damages were estimated at $2 to $5 million."[14]

The event, dubbed the "Computer Riot," dominated the headlines. In the pages of *Le Devoir*, the vandalism was described as an "unbelievable massacre," while in the House of Commons the Conservative opposition spoke of an "abominable demonstration."[15] To the police, it seemed like the time was right to beef up their surveillance of Black radicals.

This was easier said than done. At that time, there were no Black officers on the Montreal police force.[16] At the federal level, the first African-Canadian agent had just joined the RCMP in 1969.[17] This shortage of "qualified manpower" no doubt explains why the RCMP turned to the United States to recruit a civilian undercover officer. His name was Warren Hart, a veteran of the Korean War who had co-founded the Baltimore chapter of the Black Panther Party in 1968 while working for the FBI.[18] Elevated to the rank of defence captain, Hart had become the highest ranking Black Panther in Maryland before being expelled from the group for "improprieties" in the summer of 1969.[19]

In April 1971, the US Department of Justice arranged for a meeting between Hart and RCMP-SS Sergeant Ian Douglas Brown in Washington, DC. The RCMP offered Hart a monthly salary of $900, plus $100 in expenses, to infiltrate Black nationalist circles in Canada. On April 15, Hart landed in Toronto.

> I was paid $900 in advance and given a tour of the black spots in Toronto. My target was Horace Campbell and Rosie Douglas at that time. I was to report on any and every one attending any of the meetings or contributing money.[20]

A native of Dominica, Roosevelt ("Rosie") Douglas had lived in Canada since 1961. He had served as co-chair of the organizing committee for the Black Writers' Congress, but he was best known for having acted as a spokesperson for the activists during the computer centre occupation. Douglas was far from being an extremist, as evidenced by his friendship with John Diefenbaker, the former Prime Minister and leader of the Progressive Conservative Party of Canada.[21] But according to the university's lawyer, Claude Armand-Sheppard, he was a "dangerous agitator" who was "seen, observed and photographed at just about every demonstration involving colored people in Montreal. Police have been watching him for a considerable time. If it were not for Mr. Douglas, we might not be here today."[22] On April 22, 1970, Douglas was found guilty of mischief for blocking access to the computer centre.[23] "Long live Black Power," Douglas shouted as the court sentenced him to two years less a day in prison and a $5,000 fine, the highest sentence imposed in the case.[24] The sentence was suspended, however, pending appeal.

Introducing himself as a former Black Panther, Hart "came to me and

4. AN AGENT PROVOCATEUR "MADE IN THE USA"

told me that he was going to help me with my legal defences," Douglas would later recall.[25] Hart, who also went by the name Clay Heart, quickly integrated himself within Douglas's social circle, becoming "his chauffeur, his bodyguard and his confidant."[26] This was not the only way the secret agent was keeping busy, however—he also claimed that he had infiltrated Black and First Nations organizations, a Maoist group, the Socialist Party of Canada, and even a Rastafarian group. "Needless to say I was very successful in infiltrating the various black and white organizations," he would boast.[27]

One of Hart's main appeals was his flashy cars. Not many Black activists could afford a car at the time, and Hart was always on hand to drive Douglas and his comrades wherever they needed to go. As Gary Cristall, an activist with the Revolutionary Workers League, recounts:

> Hart drove a late-model Lincoln Continental, with license plates from an eastern U.S. state. He tried to give me and others the impression the car was stolen. He said he had picked it up for several hundred dollars and could get anyone a similar deal. He hinted he had links with a Black Panther 'auto theft ring' and said even the car registration would check out as valid.[28]

Hart would pick up the tab at restaurants and seemed happy to lend money to comrades in need. In short, Hart knew how to make himself useful. Furthermore, he claimed to have underworld connections, pre-empting any questions about his financial situation.[29] "You can't be an angelic person or a Boy Scout," Hart would say.[30] Ronald Joseph, a person close to Douglas, says Hart once told him he could get him counterfeit papers and passports.[31]

Known as "The General," Hart also tried to encourage activists to engage in violence. The RCMP even authorized him to pose as a demolitions and weapons expert to his targets.[32] As Ainsley Vaughan, a former Black student activist in Toronto, would recall, "He once suggested blowing up the South African embassy. It was like he was always testing us, seeing how far we'd go. But we never went very far."[33]

At a meeting to arrange for Angela Davis to speak at the University of Toronto, the "General" proposed that the famous activist should be protected by armed guards. He also suggested driving Davis in his car, while men armed with semi-automatic rifles would follow in a van, with snipers positioned behind Davis as she delivered her speech. Hart's plan fell through when Davis herself indicated that she would cancel if she saw a single weapon.³⁴ According to Vaughan, the agent's suggestions about weapons were not just empty words, since he had an impressive arsenal at his home:

> I saw them. There must have been a hundred of them: submachine guns, rifles, pistols—and hand grenades. And he kept them all right there in his bedroom, without even any curtains on the windows. He offered us guns around the time the Jamaican Canadian Association was burned down in 1972; no one knows who was responsible for that. When we were going to hold a rally there the General stockpiled the guns in the back of his car. But we never used them. We never felt the need. We saw the struggle in a different light from that. And we didn't want to be locked up in some jail.³⁵

Richard Atkinson was not so successful at avoiding prison. Atkinson met Hart in Toronto when he was only sixteen. "He used to give us books on military tactics and stuff like that. He taught us demolition and police avoidance and surveillance,"³⁶ he would recall. His first armed robbery, in 1972, was organized by the "General." It ended badly: Atkinson and his three young, inexperienced accomplices were arrested, and at the age of seventeen he was sentenced to four years in prison. After his stint in "crime school," Atkinson embarked on a long career of robberies that would eventually earn him a forty-seven-year prison sentence.³⁷

On December 8, 1971, Hart and Douglas were arrested in Toronto under the Immigration Act. Douglas's arrest was based on his conviction in the Computer Riot case, which made him eligible for deportation.³⁸ In its report, the McDonald Commission suggested that Hart's deportation was engineered by the RCMP to derail a conspiracy to kill both the president of Sir George Williams University and the biology professor behind the controversy.³⁹ However, no charges were ever laid in connection with this alleged plot, nor was the university president offered police protection.⁴⁰ Douglas maintains that the idea came from Hart himself: "His role was to train me to use violence … and he failed."⁴¹ Vaughan confirms that Douglas was not an advocate of such heavy-handed tactics—"[Douglas] used to say all the time that we should be educating people about who we are, not getting into trouble with the police."⁴²

It was also true that the RCMP wanted to reinforce Hart's "cover," so as to make him seem more credible to radical activists—an objective that was served by this mock deportation. The informant was therefore instructed to

4. AN AGENT PROVOCATEUR "MADE IN THE USA"

present himself to the immigration investigator in the worst possible light, in order to make sure that he was expelled. Hart informed the investigator that he had overstayed his welcome in Canada, was a former Black Panther, and had a criminal record in the United States for making threats, assault, and possession of firearms, all of which made him a prime candidate for deportation.[43] After five days in detention, Hart was sent back to the United States. But by January 1972, he was back in Canada.[44]

As for Rosie Douglas, he obviously did not cooperate in his own deportation. His lawyer, Clayton Ruby, was successful in having the proceedings postponed.[45] When a removal order was issued against him on October 16, 1972, Douglas lodged an appeal, preventing its enforcement.[46] While awaiting the final decision, Douglas made numerous public appearances across Canada, as well as in the United States and the Caribbean. On three occasions, Hart accompanied him on trips outside the country.[47] In 1972, the informant was with Douglas at an international meeting in St. Lucia, then a British colony in the Caribbean, taking the opportunity to provide information on the West Indian left to British intelligence.[48] During a trip to Grenada, Hart claimed to have foiled a plot to assassinate Prime Minister Eric Gairy.[49] RCMP agents also traveled with Hart to the islands of Antigua, Barbados, St. Vincent, Dominica, and to Guyana.[50] A lot of trips to the tropics at taxpayers' expense ...

But there was trouble in paradise: In 1972, Hart ended his association with the RCMP and moved back to Baltimore. His controllers, Sergeant Brown and Corporal Jim Laird, offered to increase his monthly salary to $1,300, plus insurance and benefits. The informant accepted the offer and returned to Canada to continue spying on and trying to entrap Black activists. Not everyone in the RCMP was happy to see the "General" return, however. Inspector James Worrell, who was in charge of "human sources," described Hart as nothing less than a "sand lot thug" and "an egomaniac" with an inflated sense of his own importance.[51] To the McDonald Commission, the RCMP said Hart was, "A most difficult source to handle and failed to follow direction and accept guidance [...] frequently becoming involved in activities he was told not to become involved in, and was not always truthful."[52]

The RCMP was also unhappy with Hart for accepting stolen checks and credit cards. Many of these problems arose subsequent to Hart becoming involved with a mobster he had met in custody while awaiting his pseudo-deportation. The RCMP had authorized this relationship to assist in his cover, but had also asked him to "refrain from becoming involved in criminal intelligence,"⁵³ meaning that he should stick to security intelligence. In its report, the McDonald Commission wrote of senior RCMP officers, that

> We are satisfied that their concern was not that he might be performing criminal acts, but that his coming into possession of evidence of crimes committed by others and his desire to deliver the evidence to the RCMP risked his true identity and thus his usefulness to the Security Service.⁵⁴

In reality, Hart was always allowed to play fast and loose with the law. In the spring of 1972, for example, the RCMP agreed that he could stash weapons on a farm in Tweed, halfway between Ottawa and Toronto, owned by a man they considered a "potentially dangerous radical."⁵⁵ The RCMP got a shock to learn that people on the farm were selling the arsenal to finance a trip to Europe. The undercover officer retrieved the remaining weapons and handed them over to his controllers, and the RCMP then staged a burglary to make it look like Hart had been the victim of a break-in.⁵⁶

In the spring of 1973, the Canadian government went to great lengths to secure the deportation of Rosie Douglas. Solicitor General Warren Allmand and Immigration Minister Robert Andreas filed a security certificate "based upon intelligence security reports" that it was "contrary to the national interest" for Douglas to remain in Canada.⁵⁷ In fact, the government was basing this on information provided by Hart about the alleged murder plot at Sir George.⁵⁸ A rarely used procedure, the security certificate had the effect of preventing the Immigration Appeal Division from hearing the appeal of the removal order issued the year previous. Douglas's lawyer immediately announced his intention to challenge the security certificate in court.

In July 1973, Douglas began serving his prison sentence for the Computer Riot. During his time in prison, he rubbed shoulders with FLQ activists and started a literacy course.⁵⁹ He also had a surprise meeting with Solicitor General Warren Allmand himself: learning that the Minister was visiting the detention wing where he was incarcerated, Douglas banged on the bars of his cell to get his attention.⁶⁰ The meeting apparently went well since Allmand would later agree to meet with Douglas after his release from prison in November 1974.⁶¹

News of this possible second meeting was met with concern by the RCMP, and Assistant Commissioner Howard Draper tried unsuccessfully

4. AN AGENT PROVOCATEUR "MADE IN THE USA"

to dissuade the Minister.[62] According to the RCMP-SS, any government support for Douglas would "only serve to legitimize his presence in Canada," a prospect they contemplated with dismay.[63] "I bet the S.O.B. will offer Douglas a job," Sergeant Jack Plummer said during a discussion with Hart and Sergeant Wayne McMorran.[64] As Hart would later explain, "Most of the RCMP was under the impression Mr. Allmand is a communist."[65]

On December 2, 1974, Douglas met with Allmand, to whom he presented a lengthy essay he had written detailing his ideas for prison reform.[66] Not only was Hart present at the meeting, with the blessing of RCMP headquarters, but he secretly recorded it. The question of whether the RCMP had authorized Hart to make this recording would be the subject of conflicting accounts during the McDonald Commission. The Commission did not believe Hart when he testified that the RCMP had not prohibited him from recording the meeting. Even if the informant had disobeyed RCMP instructions, this did not stop his two controllers, Sergeants Plummer and McMorran, from listening to the tape before it was destroyed by order of Assistant Commissioner Draper. Allmand would only learn much later, through the media, that he had been recorded by an RCMP mole. The McDonald Commission found that the RCMP's failure to inform Allmand of the tape was evidence that RCMP-SS head Michael Dare was "motivated by a desire to protect his subordinates."[67]

In 1975, Douglas embarked on a cross-Canada tour to campaign against his deportation. The "Rosie Douglas Tour," as it was called, made stops in many cities, including Vancouver, Regina, Winnipeg, and Thunder Bay.[68] Gary Cristall explains that "Douglas wanted to meet Native militants. He hoped to promote an alliance between Natives and Immigrants to fight racism and political repression."[69]

As more and more links were being forged between the Black Power movement and First Nations activists in Canada, such plans were obviously not going to go unnoticed by the RCMP. In Vancouver, for example, a group called the Native Alliance for Red Power drew directly on the Black Panthers to formulate its political agenda.[70] "There is no domestic situation which currently equals the Indian movement in terms of unpredictable volatility," the RCMP's Counter-Subversion Branch wrote in September 1973.[71] That was the year Wounded Knee, in South Dakota, was occupied by Oglala activists supported by the American Indian Movement (AIM).[72] A caravan of roughly fifty Indigenous activists from Canada travelled to the United States to offer their support during the occupation.⁷³ Soon after, AIM chapters appeared in southern Ontario and British Columbia.⁷⁴

Hart was present when Douglas visited Mount MacKay, on an Ojibway First Nation reserve near Thunder Bay, to take part in a pow-wow in the early summer of 1975. The informant did not make a particularly good impression, to put it mildly, as veteran Indigenous activist Vern Harper recounts: "He wanted to get a group of us and train us in explosives. He was always trying to get me to carry a gun. What would I want a gun for? No one was threatening me."⁷⁵

Louie Cameron, of the Ojibway Warrior Society, said of the help offered by the "General":

> He said that if we placed a bomb under a police car, the chemical would eat away at the metal for two or three days, so that when the bomb went off, we wouldn't be there to be identified. We were kind of surprised. We'd never heard of anything like that before.⁷⁶

In August 1975, Hart accompanied Douglas and Cristall to the Mount Currie reserve north of Vancouver to meet with members of the Lil'wat First Nation and AIM activists. During his testimony to the McDonald Commission, Hart acknowledged that he had offered to "train" the people there.⁷⁷ Cristall stated in an affidavit that the agent provocateur had offered to provide AK-47 assault rifles and suggested blowing up bridges and power lines.⁷⁸ Bill Wilson, president of the United Native Nations group, reports that the offer was rejected out of hand.⁷⁹ "They certainly weren't going to trust someone who had just showed up in a Lincoln Continental offering AK 47's," Cristall explained.⁸⁰ Things could have turned out differently: if, by some misfortune, a single Indigenous group had fallen into the trap, here's what Noel Starblanket, president of the National Indian Brotherhood, believes would have happened:

> The RCMP would have conducted a well publicized raid and uncovered the planted arms cache. Indian land, hunting and fishing claims would be set back 10 years in the public back-lash which would undoubtedly follow.⁸¹

On October 31, 1975, the RCMP decided to cut its ties with Hart. There were many reasons for this decision. There was pressure from the Department of Immigration, which had discovered in August that Hart was still in Canada

4. AN AGENT PROVOCATEUR "MADE IN THE USA"

despite having been deported four years earlier. In a memo, the department stressed "the seriousness of the case (i.e.—it is a case of great potential embarrassment for the Department and the Minister)."[82] The fact that the informant was not following his handlers' instructions also played into the decision. The RCMP had also noticed that the informant's targets were less active when Hart was out of the country. "It made us wonder whether this wasn't a self-perpetuating kind of thing," said Inspector Worrell—in other words, Hart was acting as an agent provocateur.[83]

The fact that Rosie Douglas's time in Canada was running out may also have helped convince the RCMP that it did not need Hart. Douglas's chances of staying in the country appeared slim after the Immigration Appeal Division upheld his removal order on April 28, 1975.[84] Abandoned by the RCMP and knowing that he being targeted by Immigration Canada, Hart returned to the United States on December 16, 1975. During his four and a half years in Canada, the RCMP paid him a total exceeding $70,000 in salary and expenses, tax-free.[85]

For his part, Douglas continued his legal fight to avoid deportation. When he lost again at the Federal Court of Appeal in April 1976, the Immigration Department informed him he would have to leave the country voluntarily or else be deported by force. Arrested by Montreal police on April 28 for failing to report to immigration officials, Douglas resigned himself to leaving to Jamaica the next day.[86] By the time Douglas returned to Canada for a brief visit in May 2000, he had been elected Prime Minister of Dominica.[87]

5. Moles Come Out of Their Holes

The duplicity of Carole de Vault and Warren Hart only came to light due to a rather unusual incident and the unlikely series of events that followed.

It all started in the Town of Mount Royal, an affluent suburb of Montreal, with the ill-timed explosion of a bomb planted behind the home of the owner of Steinberg Supermarkets on the night of July 26, 1974. The bomb had been planted by RCMP Constable Robert Samson, who was seriously injured in the blast.

Samson had apparently been acting on behalf of the mob.[1] As a result, he was not supported by his superiors at trial, where he was sentenced to seven years in prison. Samson decided if he was going down he wouldn't go alone, and so he disclosed to the court how he had participated in Operation Bricole: the 1972 burglarizing of the offices of far-left nationalist groups.[2]

At first, the media did not pay much attention to Samson's revelation. After all, this was coming from a cop who had lied repeatedly during his trial. Journalist John Sawatsky, however, decided to dig deeper. His investigation would eventually lead him to conclude that "the highest levels of the RCMP in Ottawa" had tried to cover up the Operation Bricole scandal.[3] And so it came to pass that three officials, one from each of the police forces involved, were charged with conducting a search without a warrant.[4] The three officers—Chief Superintendent Donald Cobb of the RCMP, Inspector Jean Coutellier of the SQ, and Captain Roger Cormier of the Montreal police— all pleaded guilty on May 26, 1977. Judge Roger Vincent then granted them an absolute discharge on June 16, which meant that they all walked away with no criminal record.[5]

For the three police forces concerned, these guilty pleas had the benefit of preempting a trial that would have afforded the public some insight into this "search without a warrant." But the PQ, which had been elected Quebec's provincial government for the first time in 1976, was not about to let the case be swept under the rug. Provincial Minister of Justice Jean-Marc Bédard immediately ordered a public commission of inquiry into the context around Operation Bricole, which he entrusted to the lawyer Jean-F. Keable, a former

Parti Québécois candidate who sat as a judge at the Court of Quebec until 2018.[6] The Keable Commission's mandate would eventually be extended to examine other controversial police operations.[7]

In Ottawa, the Progressive Conservative Opposition and the NDP were pressing the federal government to follow suit. On July 6, Solicitor General Francis Fox finally agreed and established a Royal Commission of Inquiry into the "extent and frequency" of illegal RCMP practices.[8] Justice David C. McDonald, former president of the Alberta Liberal Party, was given the mandate to head the commission along with two co-chairs: Donald S. Rickerd, a Toronto lawyer with close ties to Fox, and Guy Gilbert, a Montreal lawyer who was friends with Marc Lalonde, a pillar of the Pierre Elliott Trudeau government.[9] The McDonald Commission had been established.

Ottawa tried to block the Keable Commission by filing various legal motions in the higher courts.[10] These stall tactics would end up hemming in Keable's investigative powers. For example, Keable was denied the power to compel the federal government to provide documents whose disclosure would allegedly be injurious to "national security." The Supreme Court of Canada also prohibited Keable from making recommendations regarding the RCMP.[11] What's more, the Montreal Police Department filed a motion in Superior Court to prevent the Keable Commission from investigating "the preparation, drafting and distribution of a fake communiqué or communiqués" and "the recruitment of informants by illegal means."[12] This eventually failed, but as things dragged on the numerous interruptions caused by these various maneuvers succeeded in getting many journalists to lose interest.[13]

The Keable Commission also had to contend with a lack of cooperation from former *felquistes*, who often feared incriminating themselves if they provided details of their activities.[14] Robert Comeau, who had ended up in the Maoist group *En Lutte!*, went further still, refusing to testify at all, risking a contempt of court charge. During the hearing on November 27, 1979, he read a long statement, co-signed by François "Fritz" Séguin, also a member of *En Lutte!*, in which he denounced the Keable Commission as a court of exception whose political goal was to cast doubt on the "revolutionary integrity" of the FLQ.[15]

Keable was aware that Séguin had been a police informant for many years. As such, the statement read by Comeau looked like a police gambit aimed at torpedoing the work of the very Commission of Inquiry that had been set up in order to shine light on such dirty tricks. For Keable, "the untenable role played by Mr. Séguin before this Commission was in the process of becoming a rot that would have infected the entire future work of the Commission."[16] Refusing to silently give in to this ploy, Keable felt he had no choice but to reveal, in the midst of the hearings, that "Fritz" was an informant for the Montreal police, a revelation that provoked a certain amount of consternation.[17] Ironically, Séguin was known for having accused various comrades of working for the police in the past. Dropped by *En Lutte!*, who chose not to defend him publicly, "Fritz" continued to protest his innocence, but nobody was buying his stories any more.[18]

Carole de Vault took the opposite approach: "As soon as the Keable Commission was announced in June 1977, I said to myself, 'I have to go and speak out!'"[19] Julien Giguère, her former handler, did not see things the same way. "There's no way you're going to the Keable Commission or the McDonald Commission. You have no business there!"[20] But de Vault disagreed: "For the first time, his little Poupette wasn't listening!"[21] In fact, de Vault was eager to tell her story.

De Vault testified *in camera* (in private session) between April 1979 and February 1980, and then publicly, beginning on November 21, 1979, for a total of ten days. This was the first time someone who had acted as an informant would testify before a commission of inquiry, either federal or provincial.[22] That is how the public learned of the role played by "Poupette" in writing the FLQ communiqués.[23] For her part, de Vault learned what it was like to have people know one had been an informant. This was a painful discovery, judging by her letter to Justice Minister Bédard dated August 9, 1980:

> As a result of the public hearings, I lost my anonymity, my reputation and all of my friends, and perhaps my security. I do not dare return to Montreal where former Felquistes or others could want to see me dead.[24]

Agents provocateurs of her calibre cannot expect to be welcomed with open arms when their double game is revealed. In his report, Keable did not hold back when describing the role played by "Poupette," noting that "Far from decreasing the terrorist activities of the group she had infiltrated, the presence of de Vault had the effect of prolonging these activities by guaranteeing immunity to those who engaged in them."[25]

In other words, the police kept the October Crisis artificially on life support for a number of years. Or in the words of Detective Lieutenant Giguère:

5. MOLES COME OUT OF THEIR HOLES

"In 1972, the FLQ was us."[26] But Keable did not recommend laying charges against Giguère or de Vault, noting that their testimony was so contradictory that it was difficult to tell exactly how much was true.[27]

Warren Hart also chose to come out of the shadows at this time. After the McDonald Commission got going, he contacted an opposition MP, Progressive Conservative Elmer MacKay, and revealed that he had taped a conversation between Solicitor General Warren Allmand and Rosie Douglas. Beginning in February 1978, the former informant began giving interviews to the Canadian media in an effort to embarrass Ottawa. He explained that he wanted to immigrate to Canada, where he had met his second wife, and that the RCMP owed him.[28] In its report, however, the McDonald Commission concluded that "Hart was allowing himself to be misled" when he claimed that the RCMP had promised him a permanent job.[29]

When Noel Starblanket, president of the National Indian Brotherhood, learned that Hart had been working for the RCMP, he called for a criminal investigation into his activities, including his many trips to Indigenous communities.[30] But Hart was never charged, to nobody's surprise. The Indian Brotherhood also presented two affidavits to the McDonald Commission, one from Thunder Bay attorney Donald Colborne, the other from Gary Cristall, detailing how Hart had offered to supply weapons to Indigenous activists. The commission of inquiry showed no interest in pursuing the matter further, however. As Cristall would recount, "Everybody in the native movement just assumed I'd be called to testify. We were really surprised when I wasn't."[31]

This was all the more galling, as Hart used his testimony before the Commission to smear his targets. For example, he testified that Horace Campbell had confessed to him that he had stolen a case of guns from a sporting goods store in 1973. "I wasn't even in Canada in 1973. That's a blatant fabrication," Campbell protested in a media interview.[32] For his part, Rosie Douglas wrote to Prime Minister Trudeau requesting permission to return to Canada to refute Hart's allegations—Ottawa refused to issue him the visa required. Regarding the McDonald Commission's refusal to allow him to cross-examine Hart, Douglas's lawyer Clayton Ruby explained, "For the commission to give a public platform to these false allegations and then deny the victim even a few minutes of time to prove his innocence is contrary to all our standards of fair play."[33]

The McDonald Commission was apparently only interested in one side of the story, and it handled Hart with kid gloves. According to the commission, there was "nothing illegal" about the "General" offering weapons to the Indigenous activists he met at Mount Currie, or offering to train them in the use of explosives.[34] Similarly, when Hart asked lawyer Donald Colborne for a safe place to hide military-grade weapons he said he wanted to steal in Thunder Bay, the commission concluded that these words did "not amount to offences."[35] The commission seemed to be forgetting that according to the Criminal Code a person who counsels another to commit a criminal offence is himself a party to the offence.[36] Worse yet, the commission even stated that the agent provocateur had "performed laudable service for the people of Canada."[37] These obscene findings were certainly not unrelated to Ottawa's decision, a few years later, to pay Hart $56,000 as "compensation" for the way the RCMP had disposed of him.[38]

That said, the McDonald Commission's work was enlightening. The public learned that the RCMP-SS had conducted over 419 warrantless break-ins across Canada between 1970 and 1976.[39] RCMP agents also illegally opened the first class mail of Canadian citizens 865 times between 1970 and 1977.[40] In addition, the RCMP-SS was keeping files on more than 800,000 people living in Canada (out of a total population of approximately twenty-three million at the time), including members of the political class at both the provincial and federal levels, as well as union leaders, civil servants, diplomats, journalists, judges, professors, and leaders of various ethnic and Indigenous communities.[41] According to journalist Richard Cléroux, author of a major investigation into the Canadian secret services,

> Nearly two hundred thousand of these files were on potential or apprehended "subversive elements." Some files even contained accurate information. Others were a mix of rumour, gossip, and hearsay, occasionally spiced up with some fact that may or may not have been up to date or relevant.[42]

The McDonald Commission enjoyed greater cooperation from the RCMP than did the Keable Commission, and it was able to obtain documents that had been denied to Keable by lawyers representing the federal government.[43] However, the situation began to sour in October 1978 when the McDonald Commission sought access to "government documents": documents related to the Cabinet or its members.[44] Joseph Nuss and Michel Robert, attor-

5. MOLES COME OUT OF THEIR HOLES

neys representing Ottawa, argued before the commission that these documents should not be made public.[45] They also argued that the commission should leave it to the Solicitor General to decide what evidence was related to "national security"[46]—the catch-all term that frequently serves as a convenient excuse for government secrecy. But the commission rejected these claims, saying its report would be "incomplete" if it failed to investigate whether the RCMP's breaking the law occurred under the "Minister's express or tacit authority."[47] "Observers who expect that a commission of inquiry will be a mere instrument of the government that created it are wrong," the commissioners stated.[48]

What lay behind the objections of Ottawa's lawyers would soon become clear: the need to protect the government by suppressing evidence that various ministers were aware of the RCMP's illegal activities, leaving the federal police holding the bag. On October 26, for example, lawyers for the federal government objected strongly to RCMP lawyers using "government documents" during the testimony of William Higgitt, federal police commissioner from October 1969 to December 1973.[49] Higgitt had testified two days earlier that three former Solicitors General—George McIlraith, Jean-Pierre Goyer, and Warren Allmand—had all been informed that the RCMP was breaking the law. Allmand dismissed the allegation out of hand, saying Higgitt was contradicting his testimony to the Keable Commission.[50] In short, Ottawa and the RCMP were now openly at odds in a public spat, much to the delight of the opposition parties.

The Keable Commission's report was made public on March 6, 1981. During its hearings, Keable had heard from 171 witnesses, generating 20,000 pages of stenographic notes, while 600 exhibits were entered into evidence.[51] In his 450-page report, Keable recommended that undercover operations targeting a person or group be subject to an application for authorization from the Attorney General of Quebec or a judge, specifying what "type of activities the informant is supposed to engage in to gain the confidence of his targets and to preserve his relationship with the police."[52] Once granted, the authorization would be valid for a maximum of ninety days, with the possibility of being renewed. According to Keable:

> No informant should be undercover with a person or group for a continuous period of more than one year ... The Commission considers the duration of the undercover activity to be crucial. [...] The

degree of provocation and passive participation is very difficult to assess in the case of activities of sources who infiltrate a group for a considerable period of time.[53]

Ottawa would simply refuse to act on these recommendations.[54]

In June 1981, the Attorney General of Quebec responded to the Keable report by laying 44 criminal charges against seventeen current and former members of the RCMP.[55] Eleven were charged with breaking into the Parti Québécois's offices and stealing its membership list (Operation Ham); five others were charged for setting the barn on fire at Sainte-Anne-de-la-Rochelle; and four others for the theft of dynamite in Saint-Grégoire.[56] Then, in August, more charges were laid against four RCMP members, this time for the abduction and kidnapping of two men in Montreal in 1971 and 1972: André Chamard, a young lawyer close to the MDPPQ, and André Laforest, an unemployed machinist.[57]

On January 26, 1981, it was the McDonald Commission's turn to submit its report—over 2,400 pages long, 700 pages of which were redacted by the federal government, and including six volumes of *in camera* testimony.[58] The size of the document reflected the magnitude of the task assigned to the commission of inquiry, which cost a total of almost $12 million, with 169 public and 144 *in camera* sessions, during which 149 witnesses—including several federal ministers—were heard and 805 exhibits were filed.[59]

In its report, the commission deplored the existence of an "institutional acceptance of disregard of the law" in the RCMP, as well as the "willingness on the part of members of the RCMP to deceive those outside the Force who have some sort of constitutional authority or jurisdiction over them or their activities."[60] However, the Commission noted, "the problem of illegal acts was, to a certain extent, raised with Ministers and senior officials over the years."[61] In other words, it was not only the RCMP—the Liberal government was being implicated, too. Apparently commissions of inquiry, unless they resign themselves to doing nothing at all, constitute somewhat of a gamble to the powers that be.

The report contained some 285 recommendations, some of which directly addressed undercover work by informants and undercover cops. Unlike Keable, however, the McDonald Commission did not recommend that "judicial authorization be required for the use of undercover operatives."[62] Infiltration "involves human relationships whose defining character-

5. MOLES COME OUT OF THEIR HOLES

istics are more complex than those of mechanical devices" (such as wiretaps), the commission wrote to justify its position, adding that it wanted to avoid "involv[ing] the judiciary too closely in the investigative process."[63] Instead, it would be up to the Solicitor General to approve the use of "human sources" in cases where "the activities of a group inclined to violence pose a sufficient threat to the democratic institutions of the country."[64] Nonetheless, the commission did recognize the risks associated with undercover operations:

> Undercover operatives may go far beyond gathering information. They might endeavour to trap the group into carrying out incriminating actions—become, in effect, agents provocateurs—or carry out the kinds of disruptive tactics which have come under review by us.[65]

Rejecting the use of police provocation, the McDonald Commission instead proposed that undercover operations be used to try to "persuade group members to adopt more moderate methods of protest."[66] The commission completely rejected the idea of agents being allowed to carry out criminal offences as part of their undercover missions. "Premeditated criminal offences by security intelligence undercover operatives must not be permitted under any circumstances," the commission wrote. "The source's activities must be lawful."[67] The commission also ruled out authorizing a "limited range of permissible conduct," since "such an extension of investigative powers involves encroachment on civil liberty that would be a more serious evil than the damage to security resulting from the fact that the security intelligence agency lacks these powers."[68] (One can surmise that the Commissioners would not have been happy with Bills C-24 and C-51, which would have the effect of legalizing the commission of criminal acts when committed on behalf of the Canadian state ...) From its report, it would appear that the Commission took the time to consider various counter-arguments before stating its position:

> This policy means that the security intelligence agency's informants will not be able to penetrate cells of movements in which the commission of an offence is the passport to admission, and will find it difficult, and in some cases may find it impossible, to play any role in violence-prone groups. But neither our extensive review of Security Service experience to date nor our speculation about future security threats, especially the threat of terrorism, has convinced us that the

"evil" to be thwarted is great enough to justify the "evil" of secretly authorizing agents of the government to carry out a range of activities which would otherwise constitute criminal conduct, no matter how carefully and narrowly the criteria are drawn.[69]

The Commission did support amending federal laws to "permit the security intelligence agency sources not to declare as income payments received by them from the agency" and to "facilitate the obtaining of false identification documents in a lawful manner for undercover agents."[70] A similar recommendation was also made to streamline surveillance operations so that "there will no longer be a need for cover documentation to be manufactured by the RCMP themselves for individuals engaged in surveillance."[71] The commission also recommended the "amendment of trespass legislation to permit entry onto land or into buildings," adding that "the federal government should compensate those individuals who suffer damages as a result of a trespass by security intelligence surveillance team members."[72]

As with Keable, the McDonald Commission report also sought to set limits on the duration of investigations involving undercover agents, suggesting they should not exceed a "maximum of one year."[73] "[I]ndividuals and groups should not be subjected to indefinite investigation by the state's security agency," it insisted.[74] The commission also expressed concern about the consequences of "long-term undercover work by a regular member of the RCMP" that involved "simulation of the habits and manners of the milieu which he has penetrated."[75] It noted the possibility of a "decreased effectiveness while under cover," "personality disorders," and leaving the RCMP, which would constitute a "heavy cost both in human terms and in terms of the loss of the state's financial investment in his training as a policeman."[76] The commission therefore recommended "the use of a psychiatrist who meets the member regularly while he is under cover and afterward."[77]

When the report was released on August 25, 1981, Ottawa moved to publicly defend the RCMP. Canada's Solicitor General, Robert Kaplan, protested that the government "does not accept this broad criticism of the Mounties" and "is very concerned about the findings that the RCMP has an institutionalized mentality that places expediency above respect for the rule of law."[78]

According to *Le Devoir* editor Jean-Claude Leclerc, Ottawa's attempt at damage control wasn't fooling anyone:

5. MOLES COME OUT OF THEIR HOLES

Despite the salve applied to the "Mounties" ego by the Solicitor General of Canada, there was no avoiding the conclusion that the RCMP had come to pose a more serious threat to our democratic society than spies (which they were so hard pressed to find) or revolutionaries (which they tended to see in all opposition).[79]

But Kaplan was not content with trying to limit the damage to the federal police force's battered image; he argued that the RCMP had the "right" to act illegally because, in his view, the police cannot be subject to the law like everyone else.[80] He even admitted that he had personally authorized the RCMP to do "a lot of these things," referring to breaking laws.[81] The next day, he was at it again, this time before 200 members of the Canadian Association of Chiefs of Police, to whom he described the commission of illegal acts as an "essential part of police work."[82] The Minister further argued that both common law and the "common sense" of police officers trumped those laws passed by the Parliament of which he was himself a member.[83]

Kaplan's views did not appear to be shared by many of his provincial counterparts: Initially, the justice ministers of Quebec, British Columbia, Ontario, and Alberta all stated that they were studying the possibility of laying charges against RCMP officers involved in illegal activities in their respective provinces, based on documents provided to them by the McDonald Commission.[84] Two years after the report was tabled, however, none of the provinces had laid charges against the officers in question.[85] Ottawa similarly favoured impunity, concluding that to charge RCMP officers for the new offences uncovered by the McDonald Commission would require too much work and that in many cases too much time had elapsed anyway.[86] That left the charges laid by the Attorney General of Quebec—but there too, things would end up leading pretty much nowhere. In September 1982, once the dust had settled, the four police officers charged in the dynamite theft case were all acquitted due to insufficient evidence.[87] Only Superintendent Alcide Yelle was found guilty for his role in Operation Ham, receiving a suspended sentence with six months' probation in May 1983.[88] In May 1991, the Appeals Court cleared the other nine defendants in this case, citing unreasonable delays.[89] Finally, the last four defendants in the barn arson case would have to wait until September 1991 before being acquitted on similar grounds.[90]

While individual perpetrators of crimes who acted in the name of "national security" got off scot-free in the courts, the RCMP did not emerge similarly unscathed. On the same day that the McDonald Report was released, Ottawa announced the dismantling of the RCMP Security Service.[91] This may have been simple political payback from Ottawa, as the RCMP had gone after members of the government during the public hearings. One thing is certain: the decision was not popular with the RCMP. Retired Assistant Commissioner Weldon Fitzsimmons went so far as to complain that ending the Security Service posed a serious threat to Canada's national security.[92]

The discredited RCMP-SS was to be replaced by a new agency: the Canadian Security Intelligence Service (CSIS).

CSIS agents are not police, and therefore have no powers of arrest or detention, hence the otherwise questionable term "civilian agency." Broadly speaking, CSIS's mandate, which remains unchanged to this day, was to investigate four types of "threats to the security of Canada": espionage and sabotage, foreign interference, "political violence" and "terrorism," and revolutionary subversion, i.e., activities aimed at overthrowing the Canadian parliamentary system.[93] The purpose of these investigations is not to identify offenders, but to provide "security assessments to departments of the Government of Canada."[94] In other words, CSIS is the official source of security information for the federal government.

Born of a flurry of revelations of major police abuses and in the context of broad-based social movements, CSIS would soon prove to be nothing more than a new acronym behind which the same old illegal, dirty tricks would continue—the kind of acts which could lead to lengthy prison sentences if committed by private citizens …

6. The Birth of a Monster

The idea of transferring "security intelligence" to a civilian agency was nothing new. As far back as 1955, Mark McClung, an analyst with the RCMP's Special Branch, had made a similar proposal in a report that was shelved by Ottawa.[1] Over a decade later, the idea resurfaced with the Royal Commission on Security, chaired by Montreal lawyer Maxwell Mackenzie. In his report, published in June 1969, Mackenzie wrote:

> A security service will inevitably be involved in actions that may contravene the spirit if not the letter of the law, and with clandestine and other activities which may sometimes seem to infringe on individuals' rights; these are not appropriate police functions.[2]

The Mackenzie Commission therefore supported "the creation of a new non-police agency to perform the functions of a security service in Canada."[3]

If the law is going to be broken—as it seems destined to be—it is better that it be broken by a civilian agency than by a police force, the Mackenzie Commission seemed to be saying. It was not alone in this view: "The theory being advanced in some quarters was that breaking the law might somehow be easier for a civilian service than for the RCMP," John Starnes, Director of the RCMP-SS, had written in a document dated November 26, 1970.[4] Former Solicitor General Francis Fox testified before the McDonald Commission that it would be more difficult for a civilian security service to keep within the bounds of the law than for the RCMP, which was saying something.[5] The McDonald Commission itself seemed to be laying the groundwork for lowered expectations regarding whatever new agency would replace the RCMP-SS:

> We have no illusions that removing the Security Service from the RCMP will provide an iron-clad guarantee of future behaviour which is proper, legal, and effective.[6]

In fact, Bill C-157 establishing CSIS, presented by Solicitor General Kaplan on May 18, 1983, included a provision that would grant members of the future intelligence agency the power to break the law.[7] For example, when C-157 was introduced, a backgrounder provided to reporters stated that it was hard to say whether actions such as exceeding speed limits on roads, breaking and entering, or vandalizing private property were "violations of the law" when committed in the course of a national security investigation.[8] As the document explained, "To resolve legal doubt the legislation provides that a CSIS employee is justified in taking such actions, but only such actions which are reasonable and necessary for the performance of their duties." These actions "will therefore not be considered to be contraventions of the law."[9]

According to NDP MP Svend Robinson, this provision would give a "carte blanche" to CSIS agents: "The fact is any law can be broken."[10] According to Richard Cléroux, "The McDonald report called for the new Security Service to not be above the law, yet Kaplan's proposal allowed for CSIS officers to perform illegal acts whenever they thought it 'reasonably necessary,' provided they used 'reasonable methods.'"[11]

In a rare move, the Attorneys General of all the Canadian provinces came together and issued a joint communiqué to denounce Bill C-157. Marc-André Bédard, Attorney General of Quebec, went so far as to speak of "the birth of a monster."[12] According to Roy McMurtry, Ontario's Attorney General, "Members of the force would have powers far exceeding those granted to any police agency including the power to routinely and secretly break the law of the land."[13]

McMurtry said he had asked experts in constitutional law to look into the possibility of challenging Bill C-157 in court once it had passed.[14] Warren Allmand, Solicitor General of Canada from 1972 to 1976, also criticized the section of the bill that opened the door to illegal acts by the secret service:

> I call that the "justification for illegal acts section." The words are very subjective. The courts would have a difficult time putting limits on it. Not only do Canadian citizens want a section that isn't so wide open, but members of the security service also want to know what the limits are.[15]

Progressive Conservative MP Allan Lawrence, who briefly served as Canada's Solicitor General in 1979–80, also spoke out against the legal exemptions being prepared for CSIS agents by C-157. Such immunity "is simply abhorrent to us all," being far too broad, he argued.[16] Jack Ackroyd, Chief of the Metropolitan Toronto Police, agreed.[17] The Quebec Bar Association

6. THE BIRTH OF A MONSTER

explained that the provisions granting immunity to CSIS agents "could lead to even more serious abuses than those that led to the creation of the McDonald Commission."[18] The immunity conferred by the bill was an indication of how the federal government viewed the work of its intelligence agents. Is it possible to protect Canada's national security without breaking the law? Mission impossible, seemed to be Ottawa's answer.

Other criticisms included the fact that C-157 gave the Director of CSIS the final say as to determining national security objectives and the release of information, thereby depriving the Solicitor General of Canada of any operational role. This meant that neither the government nor Parliament, let alone the public, had any say about the objectives of the new agency. This led Toronto lawyer Edward Greenspan to refer to CSIS as a "Frankenstein monster that will have a life of its own."[19] There were also objections to the provision in C-157 that granted CSIS access to confidential census data, especially since the McDonald report had specifically recommended that such information not be made available to the security services.[20]

These criticisms of C-157 were echoed by the media and by the public. As Philip Rosen of the Parliamentary Research Branch of the House of Commons Library reported, "So vehement was public opposition that the government decided against proceeding to second reading, and instead referred the subject matter of the bill to a special committee of the Senate."[21]

This committee, chaired by Liberal Senator Michael Pitfield, held hearings throughout the summer of 1983, registering a wide range of opinion on the bill.[22] Its report, released in November 1983, recommended more than forty amendments to the original bill. The committee supported allowing CSIS members to commit what it called "technical breaches of the law or violation of minor criminal or regulatory law."[23] The committee also stated that there should be "no legalization in respect of more serious offenses," but added that "the line between serious and minor offences may be difficult to draw." Nonetheless, the committee did propose that CSIS agents caught in the act might benefit from "flexibility in the application of the law" that would recognize "mitigation" arising from the fact that the illegal act was committed in the course of their duties. Disconcertingly, the Pitfield Committee went no further than to say that there should be a presumption "that any employee of a security intelligence agency, when confronted with a situation in which he might act illegally in the performance of his or her duties, would be predisposed to act legally."[24] How could anyone be so naive after the Keable and

McDonald Commissions, with their flood of damning revelations about the RCMP's illegal conduct?

The Pitfield Committee also objected to the proposed creation of a new offence, carrying a maximum penalty of five years imprisonment, which would make it illegal to divulge information that would reveal the identity of a CSIS agent. In the committee's view, such a provision would "imped[e] freedom of expression" and "could make difficult the reporting of any CSIS wrongdoing."[25] The same might be said of the confidentiality of the identities of intelligence sources. At the same time, the Pitfield Committee stated that it fully endorsed the objective of protecting "covert employees and sources."[26] In other words, only the identity of CSIS agents and their informants acting under the cloak of secrecy deserved protection in the eyes of the committee.

On January 18, 1984, Solicitor General Kaplan introduced Bill C-9 to replace C-157.[27] The new bill contained almost all of the Pitfield Committee's recommendations, as well as many of the ideas set out in the McDonald Report, and no longer explicitly condoned breaking the law. Instead, C-9 replaced this controversial provision with Section 20, still in effect today, which gives CSIS agents the same protection afforded by law to the police.[28] Section 20 also stipulates that the CSIS Director must report to his or her responsible minister (the Solicitor General of Canada) any unlawful acts committed by CSIS agents. If the CSIS Director chooses to remain silent about offences committed by CSIS personnel, the Minister has no other way of knowing about them.

Unlike C-157, the new bill gave the Solicitor General the final say as to the specific objectives to be pursued by CSIS. The Minister was also given the authority to approve all warrant applications for a wide range of "investigative techniques"—from breaking and entering to intercepting communications—committed by CSIS agents against a designated target.[29] These warrants would also have to be authorized by the federal court; this new version of the bill thereby raised the bar for the conditions under which a warrant would be issued.[30]

Bill C-9, however, provided for the same penalty as in C-157 for the disclosure of information that would reveal the identity of a "person who is or was a confidential source of information or assistance to the Service" or a "person who is or was an employee engaged in covert operational activities of the Service."[31] Other controversial aspects of C-9 included the power of CSIS to access the offices of doctors and even Members of Parliament with

6. THE BIRTH OF A MONSTER

a judicial warrant.

In addition to CSIS, the bill also created two review bodies, the Security Intelligence Review Committee (SIRC) and the Office of the Inspector General of CSIS, both of which were to report to the minister responsible. Among other things, SIRC was mandated to review CSIS operations and to investigate complaints about the activities of the intelligence agency, while the Inspector General was made responsible for evaluating the legality and propriety of operations conducted by the secret service. In its report, the Pitfield Committee had emphasized the importance of CSIS being subject to "a close and thorough system of control," while maintaining that the "relationship between the government and the agency must be very close."[32] "Defects in these matters could render nugatory all the other proposed changes in the Bill, and potentially return us to the state of affairs that led to the creation of the McDonald Commission," it warned.[33]

Like C-157, the new bill established that these two oversight agencies would have access to all information in the possession of CSIS except Cabinet documents, despite the fact that the Pitfield Committee had clearly objected to such an exception.[34] According to journalist Richard Cléroux, "this meant that if the agency did not want the Committee to see a document, it could simply have it classified as a cabinet document."[35] These restrictions led to "extremely heated" deliberations in parliamentary committee, where NDP and Progressive Conservative MPs "vigorously opposed fundamental aspects" of the bill.[36] As many as 175 amendments were proposed to modify C-9;[37] yet on June 21, 1984, the version Parliament passed "remained essentially unchanged."[38] CSIS had been created.

"For all intents and purposes, the legislation that created CSIS simply legalized the tactics of the old system," explains Michel Juneau-Katsuya, who worked in Canadian intelligence for twenty-one years.[39] Cléroux agrees: "Apart from burning down barns and brutalizing people, CSIS can legally do everything the RCMP once did illegally."[40] The creation of CSIS was nothing but smoke and mirrors:

> In theory, the RCMP Security Service—organized in the old fashioned, biased, scandal-ridden way, with its undereducated detectives—was supposed to lose its police mentality and Cold War ideology overnight and be transformed into a new, impartial, forward-looking intelligence service with a well-educated staff. In

reality, the RCMP Security Service merely changed its name but not its personnel. For many in the RCMP Security Service, the immediate physical changes were not very apparent. Since the new CSIS headquarters was not ready, they did not even have to change their chairs. Their offices were still located in the RCMP's Ottawa headquarters on what was then called Alta Vista Drive. The officers continued to watch the same people as before. The only difference was that they were now watching them as intelligence officers rather than police officers.[41]

Twenty months after its creation, more than 98% of CSIS personnel were still being drawn from the ranks of the RCMP-SS.[42] As Juneau-Katsuya explains, "Those who in the 1970s had carried out the incidents investigated by the McDonald Royal Commission, as well as those who ordered them, were left in place to become the new ruling class of CSIS."[43]

Faced with this army of seasoned ex-cops, CSIS's so-called "watchdog," SIRC, has always seemed a bit out of its league. SIRC is an agency with five part-time members, mostly former Members of Parliament, supported by a staff of fourteen, whose main activity is to conduct investigations and research. In 1990–91, its budget was $1.5 million.[44] At that time, CSIS had a budget of $200 million and a staff of 2,700.[45] This stark disparity between the two agencies unfortunately remains unchanged today. This is a far cry from the Pitfield Committee's demand that "the extraordinary powers of the agency under the Bill must be balanced by a review body with broad powers."[46] Juneau-Katsuya notes that,

> The fact is that SIRC is not up to the task. SIRC's young analysts are left alone with the old CSIS intelligence officers who are responsible for "liaising" with SIRC. These intelligence officers have years of experience in source manipulation and the young analysts are no match for them.[47]

According to Cléroux, the Review Committee is a great help to CSIS, serving as a fig leaf shielding it from public accountability when allegations of abuse or criminal behaviour arise.[48] Juneau-Katsuya notes that "[SIRC] has bailed out CSIS so often that to acknowledge its failings would be to admit its own ineffectiveness. 'Protecting' CSIS has become an almost unconscious reflex in order to avoid facing the more difficult truth of its own incompetence."[49]

6. THE BIRTH OF A MONSTER

In the absence of adequate oversight, there is no reason to think that CSIS would act any different than its predecessor, the now-defunct RCMP-SS.

The story of how CSIS was created is the story of parliamentary institutions showing their utter disinterest in defending the interests of the society they claim to represent. Not only did members of civil society have no real say about Ottawa's creature, but they would find themselves to be both its targets and its main victims. The decision of Canadian legislators to give CSIS what basically amounts to free reign would have serious consequences. As we shall see in the next chapter, the Marc-André Boivin affair is testament to this excessive power, which laid the groundwork for abuses that were as predictable as they were inevitable, since they occurred not only without oversight, but without any real mechanism of accountability.

7. Paid by the CSN ... and CSIS

For fifteen years, Marc-André Boivin led a double life, earning a double salary: union consultant for the Confédération des syndicats nationaux (the CSN—Quebec's second-largest trade union federation), and informant for the RCMP-SS, then for CSIS. "All the ingredients for a *remake of* the criminal activities of the RCMP Security Service are there! Years after the creation of CSIS, nothing has changed. *Business as usual,*" in the words of Normand Lester, a former journalist at Radio-Canada who devoted several pages to this affair in his book on Canada's secret services.[1]

In a lengthy interview with Monique Giguère of *Le Soleil*, Marc-André Boivin recounted how it all began in 1972 when he was twenty-two years old and working as a clerk at the Enfant-Jésus Hospital in Quebec City. "We were on strike. Suddenly, a Volks approaches the picket line and the guy at the wheel says to my friend next to me: 'I have some gear for you, weapons and dynamite.'"[2] Marc-André Boivin—who had always dreamed of following in the footsteps of his father, a police officer in Beauport—decided to bring the incident to the attention of the RCMP, where he had previously applied for the position of constable. The tip got noticed by the RCMP-SS, who contacted Boivin soon after to recruit him as a "human source." "I wasn't sure what I was getting myself into. But I was willing to give it a try," he would later explain.[3]

In its report on the Marc-André Boivin case, SIRC explained that the mandate conferred by the federal police was "to report on labour organizations. The objective of the Service was to monitor suspected criminal and 'subversive' activities in the labour milieu."[4] Boivin summarized the broad outline of his mission as follows:

> I had to establish myself where things were moving, the *En Lutte!* group, the CPCML (Communist Party of Canada Marxist-Leninist). [...] The front groups set up multiple contacts in democratic organizations to get their anti-American message across. [...] I was working on foreign infiltration. Russians coming here to infiltrate our democratic organizations is not make-believe. It is a fact.

7. PAID BY THE CSN ... AND CSIS

> There are communists working here. [...] I am a family man. I am also a patriot and I am happy that Canada has a secret service. It's important, it's crucial to protect ourselves from outside infiltration. [...] In 15 years, none of my targets has ever been inconvenienced. The Canadian secret service does not make a mess, it carries out surveillance.[5]

In 1974, Marc-André Boivin became a union representative at the CSN. During his thirteen years with the union, Boivin held several important positions, including strike director and action coordinator for Eastern Quebec during the 1976, 1978, and 1982 common fronts.[6] In addition, the agent participated in almost all the major labour conflicts that occurred in the Quebec City region during that period.[7] Boivin himself admitted that he was not one to be trifled with:

> I've been through a lot. It's true that I wasn't always easy to deal with. I've threatened bosses. When I had to apply pressure, I did, even blocking roads, railroads, and blowing up a bridge. I'm a guy who does not back down. I made mistakes, but I never lost control of the situation and I never put lives at risk.[8]

In its report, SIRC recounts two incidents that led to Marc-André Boivin being arrested: a picket line in January 1973 and an action to block access to the Quebec City Coliseum, where the Quebec Liberal Party convention was to be held. In both cases, he had informed the RCMP beforehand, claiming to be acting to "avert anticipated violence between the police and [strikers]."[9] However, as the RCMP documents forwarded to CSIS reveal, the Security Service was extremely concerned that Boivin might be engaging in criminal activity while in the employ of the federal police: the agent was questioned and given "clear instructions regarding the RCMP Security Service's interests and limits."[10]

These "specific instructions" do not seem to have dampened Boivin's spirits, however, based on his "accomplishments," as listed in a letter from CSN President Gérald Larose to SIRC Chair Ron Atkey:

> Conflict at the Interprovincial Agency, a Quebec City distributor. Boivin proposes to someone to set fire to the company's warehouses.
>
> Conflict at Robin Hood in Montreal. Security guards fired on the

strikers and Boivin looks for someone to retaliate by firing a rifle into the company's grain silos. He claimed that this could lead to an explosion.

1978. Conflict at La Poulette Grise, in La Malbaie. Boivin looks for people to shoot rifles at the trucks as they leave the factory.

Direct Film Conflict. Boivin looks for people to shoot rifles at the company's trucks, and for volunteers to throw bottles of ether into the company's stores. [...]

1982. Boivin suggests to someone to kidnap, and then make disappear, a union leader. Also, he suggests to someone to kill (or arrange to have killed) a fellow worker.[11]

In the meantime, SIRC reports, the federal police had adjusted their focus in terms of what information to collect, presumably in response to the combined pressure of the Keable and McDonald inquiries:

In 1980 the RCMP Security Service started to reorient its efforts from the labour movement itself to what it believed to be subversive elements within the labour movement. That is to say, against communists or other individuals or entities which were thought to be manipulating or attempting to manipulate the labour movement in Canada on behalf of foreign agencies or countries. Despite this change in orientation, by 1982 Mr. Boivin was still assigned to report upon the labour movement.

However, by 1983, the RCMP Security Service had reduced its "labour desk" at Headquarters—which had previously been responsible for Mr. Boivin's overall direction—to a "passive collation stance." Accordingly, responsibility for Marc Boivin shifted to another counter-subversion desk. In June, 1983, a senior counter-subversion official at RCMP Security Service Headquarters summarized Marc Boivin's usefulness as follows:

"[He] enjoys a privileged position in the labour movement to give us informed assessments of what subversives are up to, even on a provincial basis, in their perpetual efforts to penetrate and influence labour to their Marxist ideologies."[12]

7. PAID BY THE CSN ... AND CSIS

The decision to target communists was somewhat anachronistic, given that the big Marxist-Leninist organizations had practically disappeared in Quebec by this point.[13] But it would seem that the Canadian secret service was still seeing "reds" everywhere. The fear of communism is hard to cure ...

SIRC also expressed concern about the decision to continue working with Boivin once intelligence activities had been transferred to CSIS:

> In this particular case, because of doubts within CSIS concerning his productivity as a source, and the potential for him to become involved in illegal activities which might lead to his exposure as a source, CSIS should have more seriously questioned the utility of continuing to use Mr. Boivin as a source shortly after separation.[14]

According to Gérald Larose's letter to the Review Committee, Boivin continued to break the law in the years following the creation of CSIS:

> Fall 1985. Conflict at the Sainte-Foy terminal. Boivin asks people to provide money for some hired muscle. [...]
>
> Summer 1986. Conflict at the Lauzon shipyard. Boivin proposes to burn down and blow up buildings on the shipyard grounds. He also suggested to the strategy committee a number of actions that were strongly rejected; among others, the possibility of derailing a train, setting fire to a paint warehouse, and setting fire to a car on the Pierre-Laporte Bridge. He incidentally proposed the occupation of Canadian Navy facilities classified as "Top Secret" as part of the destroyer refitting project (the TRUMP project).
>
> Spring 1987. Conflict at Valcartier Industries, which manufactures munitions for the Canadian Armed Forces. Boivin asks two people, on two different occasions, to supply him with grenades and priming powder. They refused. Boivin then looked for someone who would be willing to bring him these munitions. Incidentally, when developing negotiation strategies, he had suggested and planned the occupation of this arms factory. At the same time, Boivin was looking for hired muscle because he had, he said, "certain problems to deal with."
>
> During his clandestine career in the union movement, Boivin sought to obtain dynamite, to obtain a gun with a silencer, and to commit crimes of arson in houses in Sainte-Foy.[15]

Far from being discreet, Marc-André Boivin was also playing a leading role in the union movement. "We had seen him dozens of times in news clips, with a megaphone warming up his striking troops," Simon Durivage, a Radio-Canada television journalist, recalled.[16]

Infiltration by this agent provocateur extended beyond the labour movement: in 1987, the Communist Party of Quebec revealed that it too had been targeted. As Marianne Roy, a member of the Party's executive, explained, "Starting in September 1986, Marc Boivin attended at least five meetings of our party. He never played an important role in our activities, but it is clear that he was there to play a destabilizing role."[17]

Boivin was expelled from the party when his ties to CSIS were exposed.[18]

When he wasn't hunting communists, Marc-André Boivin enjoyed engaging in some curious pastimes … On March 13, 1987, the informant was arrested at the Terminus Voyageur bus station in Montreal by two cops from the Montreal police's youth squad for having "unlawfully and voluntarily committed an indecent act in a public place, in the presence of one or more persons […] contrary to section 169 of the *Criminal Code*."[19] On April 29, Boivin pleaded guilty to the charge before Judge Alexander Stalker of the Montreal Municipal Court. He was fined $300, which he paid on the spot.[20]

It should be noted that in the intelligence world, any form of so-called "deviant" sexual behaviour is viewed as an Achilles heel that can potentially be used by foreign interests for the purposes of blackmail.[21] Yet while Marc-André Boivin seems to have been caught quite literally with his pants down, CSIS continued to do business with him as if nothing had happened. It would seem that anything goes when you are an agent provocateur for the Canadian State!

Marc-André Boivin's clandestine activities would probably have remained secret forever, had it not been for the magnitude of the labour dispute at the Manoir Richelieu between businessman Raymond Malenfant and the CSN. After buying the Pointe-au-Pic luxury hotel from the Quebec government in December 1985, Malenfant refused to recognize the union certification of the 306 hotel workers who were represented by the CSN. Instead, he had them all replaced by non-unionized staff at reduced salaries. Faced with the bullheadedness of Malenfant, who was known as the "Tough Guy from Malbaie," the CSN committed itself to what would become one of the biggest labour battles in Quebec history, and the Universel hotel-motel chain owned by Malenfant became the object of numerous demonstrations and acts of sabotage.[22]

7. PAID BY THE CSN ... AND CSIS

The Manoir Richelieu strike was one of many labour conflicts in which Boivin pushed CSN members to commit acts of violence. According to Gérald Larose, the CSIS informant suggested to strikers that they blow up drinking water tanks with dynamite, fire .12 calibre bullets at Malenfant's residence, and assault a person in order to prevent a convention from being held at the Manoir.[23] Nor did the agent provocateur stop at verbal incitement: he even instructed his own younger brother, Richard Boivin, on how to carry out a bomb attack on October 7, 1986, in the parking lot of the Wandlyn Inn motel in Sainte-Foy, another property belonging to Malenfant. Richard Boivin, who worked in the kitchen at the Robert-Giffard hospital, was also a CSN union member. When his older brother Marc-André offered him $1,000 to carry out the bombing, Richard couldn't say no. "The subject identified himself strongly with his brother Marc," a probation officer would later note. "It was out of a need to prove that he could do something for the labour movement" that he agreed to the plan.[24]

Tensions rose sharply in the conflict when union activist Gaston Harvey died moments after being placed in a choke hold by SQ police officers during a demonstration by former Manoir Richelieu employees in Pointe-au-Pic on October 25, 1986.[25] But the undercover agent was not interested in de-escalating matters.

On May 23, 1987, at 4:10 a.m., the first bomb exploded in a food storage area in the cellar of the 120-room Le Bordelais restaurant in Chicoutimi.[26] No one was injured, but the bomb caused an estimated $10,000 in damage even though the blast's force was partially absorbed by an earth floor, to the point that there was virtually no damage to the concrete wall.[27] In media interviews following the incident, Marc-André Boivin would claim that he had not been happy about the attack:

> I was listening to the radio like everyone else, when suddenly I hear that there was an explosion in the kitchen of the Universal Motel. [...] I am very familiar with this hotel. Six feet from where the bomb exploded, there is a large propane tank. If shrapnel had hit the supply pipe, the building would have been lifted off the ground and everyone in it, and those passing by, would have been torn to pieces. Propane is worse than dynamite.[28]

Marc-André Boivin knew that two other bombs were about to be planted in establishments belonging to Malenfant, in Montreal and Drummondville. Referring to the establishment in Montreal, Boivin would later explain:

> The hotel is built on high ground. An explosion there would have been simply catastrophic. That time, we wouldn't have been able to get away with it, there would have been deaths. [...] In the end, I told myself that I, Marc Boivin, the individual, would not be able to live with deaths on my conscience. I decided that I would rather lose everything.[29]

The informant decided to raise the alarm with CSIS on May 30, 1987. He told his handler at the intelligence agency that he had hidden fuses used in the Chicoutimi bombing and that similar attacks were planned for two days later.[30] CSIS then made use of the legal provision that allows it to disclose information to police "where the information may be used in the investigation or prosecution of an alleged contravention of any law of Canada or a province,"[31] as was clearly the case in this instance. In its report, however, SIRC would criticize CSIS for being slow to contact the SQ:

> Late on Monday, June 1, after a further interview with Mr. Boivin, CSIS officials in the Quebec district finally brought this matter to the attention of the Sûreté du Québec. [...] CSIS' tardy response to Mr. Boivin's startling disclosures on Saturday, May 30, 1987 that specific and serious criminal offences might be imminent not only breached CSIS policy but also ordinary standards of common sense.[32]

The Solicitor General of Canada, James Kelleher, and the Director of CSIS would later state that the person responsible for the delay faced disciplinary action.[33] As we can see, Marc-André Boivin arranged to make himself look good in this story. But something in his version of events did not add up: it was on May 30 that the agent provocateur allegedly handed over two more fuses to an accomplice in preparation for the planned bombings in Montreal and Drummondville. However, Boivin claims that it was on that same day that he revealed everything to CSIS.[34] If the CSIS informant wanted to prevent further bombings, then why did he provide the two fuses knowing they would be used to assemble new bombs?

Marc-André Boivin claimed to have difficulty convincing the SQ that he was telling the truth:

> The police didn't believe me. They refused to believe that hotels were going to be blown up. They couldn't get it into their heads. They were so skeptical that they wanted me to submit to a lie detector test.[35]

7. PAID BY THE CSN ... AND CSIS

A Radio-Canada report later claimed that Boivin's handler at CSIS had intervened to try to shield the informant from facing charges. Fearing the loss of their most valuable "source," intelligence agency officials told the SQ that Boivin's arrest would jeopardize surveillance in an "important operation."[36] Subsequent events seem to suggest that SQ officials did not believe that this "important operation" actually existed. In Ottawa, the denial was not long in coming: "The agency did not interfere or attempt to interfere in any way with the police investigation or the indictment of Mr. Boivin," said Daryl Harker, Deputy Solicitor General of Canada.[37] In its report, SIRC would clear the intelligence agency of these allegations, claiming that "There is no indication whatsoever that CSIS or any of its officials at any time attempted to interfere in either the arrest or the prosecution of Mr. Boivin."[38]

On the night of June 4–5, the police went into action. Assisted by police officers from Quebec City, Montreal, and Chicoutimi, the SQ conducted some fifteen searches and arrested three CSN officials: Gérard Thériault, a member of the Shawinigan central council; Arsène Henry, strike director; and Guy Boisvert, the union advisor for the Manoir Richelieu conflict.[39] The timing of these arrests, however, points to another inconsistency in Boivin's account: since the arrests only took place on June 4, how to explain that no bombs went off on June 2, as planned? In other words, were the attacks that Boivin claimed to be preventing (despite having played a crucial role in their preparation) called off even though the police had failed to intervene?

All three union officials were charged with conspiracy to carry out bombings. There were also additional charges of possession of dynamite, possession of an unregistered firearm, and inciting the bombing at the Chicoutimi motel. Marc-André Boivin, whose name was mentioned in two of the eleven indictments, was conspicuously absent in court. During the appearance of the three CSN members, Jacques Larochelle, one of the lawyers for the union, asked the Crown prosecutor where Boivin was. He specified that he was asking at the request of Boivin's girlfriend, which implies that the informant had not even told her of his decision to work with the police.

At the time of the arrest of the three CSN staff members, rumours were already circulating that Marc-André Boivin had become an informant. In its June 6, 1987 edition, *Le Soleil* reported that it had information "from reliable sources" that Boivin had "sat down at the table."[40] Two days later, the same newspaper reported that SQ investigator Jean-Marc Fortin had confirmed to it that Boivin was neither charged, nor detained, nor accused, but was being held at a secret location for his own protection.⁴¹ The Solicitor General of Quebec, Gérard Latulippe, refused to "confirm or deny" that Boivin had become an informant.⁴² Boivin disappeared for twenty-five days. "I was kept *incommunicado* as a main witness by the SQ who had asked for my cooperation," he said.⁴³ The informant also claimed to have cut his ties with CSIS. "I have not seen anyone from CSIS since June 4, and I do not want to see anyone again," he said in his interview with *Le Soleil*.⁴⁴ As Alain Quirion, an investigator with the Sûreté du Québec, explained, "He was under 24-hour protection. He had no choice. He had to stay with the SQ. There could be four police officers, there were always at least two. All his communications were monitored."⁴⁵

Boivin was only allowed to communicate with certain people: his father, his three children, his spouse, his ex-wife, and ... his bank manager.⁴⁶

On June 9, the former CSIS informant signed an agreement with the SQ stipulating that the latter undertook to provide "for Boivin's financial needs to the same extent as prior to his revelations" and "to eventually help Mr. Boivin find an equivalent job [...] in order to help him reintegrate into a normal living and working environment."⁴⁷ The agreement provided for a guaranteed weekly income of $540 until he could find new employment.⁴⁸

That same day, some twenty-five SQ cops carried out raids at the CSN offices in Montreal and Quebec City. Their goal: to corroborate Marc-André Boivin's allegations that Gérald Larose himself had been aware of the bombing plot "for several weeks."⁴⁹ According to the *Journal de Montréal*, the former agent provocateur had told the SQ that "funds from the union central had been specially authorized by Mr. Larose for the campaign against Malenfant."⁵⁰

On June 10, journalist Michel Auger revealed that Marc-André Boivin was a "privileged informant" for CSIS: "According to the information obtained, the union representative had decided to collaborate with the justice system for personal reasons," he wrote.⁵¹ For his part, Gérald Larose already had a clear idea of what Boivin was:

> He is an RCMP officer who also works for other police forces.⁵² [...]
>
> I have become convinced that this is an agent who did work he was not hired to do at the CSN.⁵³

At first, CSIS had the gall to pretend that it had had no contact with Marc-André Boivin. "We know nothing about him," a Canadian intelligence official told *The Gazette*.⁵⁴ This crude lie did not last long. Based on a Radio-Canada investigation, *La Presse* reported that Boivin's CSIS handler had paid him $10,000 in cash every year.⁵⁵ The Radio-Canada report also claimed that Boivin was one of only thirty-eight people with a special social insurance number, beginning with the number 9, reserved for people with a very particular status.⁵⁶

Paule Gauthier, a lawyer and member of SIRC, was openly skeptical about these spectacular revelations. "It's practically impossible," she told a reporter from *Le Soleil*, adding that she "jumped" when she heard the news that Marc-André Boivin was employed by the intelligence services.⁵⁷ Robert Kaplan, a former Solicitor General of Canada who was at the time a simple Member of Parliament, reacted to Gauthier's comments by questioning whether SIRC was really doing its job.⁵⁸ Kaplan was ill-placed to complain about SIRC's toothlessness: he had only himself to blame for having presided over the creation of this paper tiger. The situation was not much better with the Inspector General of CSIS, Richard Gosse, who said he was "astonished by the Marc Boivin affair,"⁵⁹ which he learned about "from the newspapers."⁶⁰ Clearly, this was light years away from the Pitfield Committee's hope that "the Inspector General is not to be limited to after-the-fact review of operations."⁶¹

But CSIS was in no rush to clarify matters. Jean-Louis Gagnon, a spokesman for the agency, explained why the intelligence agency was so tight-lipped: "First, the case is before the courts," he said. "Secondly, the law prohibits us from revealing the identity of the service's human sources."⁶² It should be noted that, despite its stonewalling, CSIS was no longer claiming to know *nothing* about Marc-André Boivin ... For his part, the former agent provocateur did not seem particularly happy to see his double life now exposed in the media. As he would explain in an interview:

> I felt like the sky was falling. I had twice as many problems when the news spread that I was collaborating with [CSIS]. In the secret service, giving away a target is considered high treason. Burning an informant should be taken just as seriously.⁶³

On June 11, new charges were laid against Arsène Henry: this time, he was accused of having conspired with a certain Richard Boivin to plant a bomb at the Wandlyn Inn in October 1986. Boivin was not charged at the time, even though his name was listed in the indictment as a participant in the plot.⁶⁴ Like Marc-André Boivin, his brother Richard had left both his job and his home without explanation.⁶⁵ He was following in the footsteps of his older brother: "Richard confessed that his collaboration in the police investigation was like a release because he had felt guilty since October 7, 1986," a Crown prosecutor later claimed.⁶⁶ According to the Crown, it was Arsène Henry who had asked Marc-André Boivin to plant a bomb at the Wandlyn Inn. The informant then asked his brother Richard to plant the bomb. Then the agent provocateur apparently compensated his brother with an initial payment of $1,000, followed by another of $2,000, this one reimbursed by Henry.⁶⁷

On June 17, a fourth CSN staffer, Renald Tardif, was arrested and charged with both conspiracy to detonate a bomb at the Motel Universel in Chicoutimi and with planting the bomb.⁶⁸ Tardif's lawyer was able to convince the court to release his client, while the other three co-accused remained behind bars, awaiting trial.⁶⁹

On June 29, Marc-André Boivin pleaded guilty to six offences under Sections 79(1)(a) and 423 of the *Criminal Code*.⁷⁰ Richard Boivin followed suit, pleading guilty to conspiracy to bomb the Wandlyn Inn Motel and to actually detonating a bomb in the parking lot of that establishment on October 7, 1986.⁷¹ Justice Yvon Sirois of the Peace Sessions Court agreed to release the Boivin brothers, who were being watched over by the SQ "for their safety and the preservation of evidence," on $50,000 bail.⁷² The two brothers, who were not represented by a lawyer at the hearing, disclosed the value of their respective properties in order to demonstrate their solvency to the court.⁷³ It was discovered that Marc-André Boivin's annual salary at the CSN amounted to $35,000—equivalent to more than $75,000 in 2022 Canadian dollars. If we include the sums received by CSIS, the exact amount of which has never been made public, it is clear that the agent provocateur was not in dire straits financially.⁷⁴

Having entered his guilty plea, Marc-André Boivin took the witness stand. He then stated the following:

> I worked 15 years at the CSN, your honour, I stirred things up in strikes, I had quite a reputation. I stopped people from crossing picket lines. I smashed cars, I painted many cars, I took extreme measures […] but we were careful not to endanger lives.⁷⁵

Ten days later, Daniel Johnson Jr., the deputy leader of the government and future premier of Quebec, contradicted a Radio-Canada report in which it was stated that the province might take legal action against CSIS because of

7. PAID BY THE CSN ... AND CSIS

the actions of its informant:

> There is no file as such in the Department of Justice that would lead to prosecution. There is no investigation of any kind that I am aware of. I have no information leading me to believe that there is a need for proceedings, as rumours have it.[76]

The Marc-André Boivin case led to two federal investigations. First, on June 26, Solicitor General James Kelleher asked Inspector Gosse to investigate whether the former informant's activities were legal and to determine whether the intelligence agency had used its powers improperly or unnecessarily.[77] Inspector Gosse's interim report was submitted to the Solicitor General in October.[78] The document, which totals 240 pages, was never made public, unlike SIRC's much smaller twenty-four-page report, the result of an investigation initiated in July of the same year.[79]

On July 9, 1987, Marc-André Boivin began to testify at the preliminary hearing of three of the four CSN staff members charged. Escorted by two plainclothes SQ officers, the former agent provocateur entered the courtroom through the door usually reserved for cops, presumably to avoid any possible contact with the public and journalists.[80] Boivin's lengthy testimony stretched over four days of hearings, all under a publication ban.[81]

The presence of Philippe Bibeau, director of CSIS's Quebec section, outside the courtroom confirmed the interest of the Canadian secret service in the case, even though Boivin's status as a CSIS informant had yet to be confirmed by official sources. Laurent Hugo, deputy director of CSIS, even intervened during the testimony of the former secret agent to object to his answering certain questions, all in the name of "national security."[82] All four of the accused CSN staff members were brought to trial following this preliminary investigation.[83]

On October 2, Judge Sirois sentenced Marc-André Boivin to fifteen months in prison on each of the six counts on which a guilty plea had been entered, to be served concurrently.[84] It should be noted that these were offences that carried a maximum sentence of life imprisonment. In terms of mitigating circumstances, the judge took into account the fact that the former CSIS informant had "reversed direction" by warning the SQ about the impending bombings, as well as by cooperating in the criminal investigation.[85] The court portrayed Boivin as a person "driven by loyalty to the union who dissociated himself from a series of criminal acts that he saw would be carried out, though he acted a little late." As for the aggravating circumstances, the court noted the fact that the former informant held a position of authority at the CSN and that he had "bribed" his own brother to plant the bomb at the Wandlyn Motel.[86] Richard Boivin, who had no prior criminal record, was sentenced to ten months in prison.

In a decision rendered on November 18, 1987, in the case of union consultant Guy Boisvert in the Manoir Richelieu affair, Justice Claude Jourdain of the Quebec Superior Court took a different position, clearly viewing Marc-André Boivin as the real instigator behind the bombings:

> It appears from the evidence that it was Marc Boivin who first came up with the idea of using explosives or other means of intervention for the Manoir Richelieu. He was the one who brought it up; he made the suggestion to Boisvert during a conversation a year earlier, when the two men were taking stock and evaluating the situation. At that time, Boivin's suggestions were dismissed, put aside by Boisvert and, subsequently, Boivin spoke to Boisvert again a few times in the months that followed, but the defendant Boisvert refused to follow up, until June 2, 1987, when he decided to take action because, according to him, there was no alternative, unless he dropped everything, abandoned everything, which Boisvert was apparently not prepared to do.[87]

Three of the four union officials charged entered guilty pleas. Arsène Henry was sentenced to three years in prison, Gérard Thériault was sentenced to two years less a day in prison, and Guy Boisvert received a fifteen-month sentence. Rénald Tardif, the only defendant who did not plead guilty, was acquitted.[88]

It was not until September 15, 1987, that the federal government confirmed for the first time, through Solicitor General James Kelleher, that Marc-André Boivin had indeed been an informant for CSIS. Still, Kelleher took the opportunity to deny that the intelligence agency was targeting the labour movement.[89] A statement that was immediately disputed by NDP justice critic Svend Robinson:

> The reality is that Marc Boivin worked as a paid informant for CSIS in the Quebec labour movement. This takes us right back to the days of RCMP Security Service abuses … They don't understand the distinction between subversion and dissent.[90]

7. PAID BY THE CSN ... AND CSIS

A week later, Radio-Canada revealed that CSIS had infiltrated four other unions—the Centrale de l'enseignement du Québec, the BC Federation of Labour, the Canadian Union of Public Employees, and the United Auto Workers—under the pretext of monitoring "clandestine cells" formed by "communist groups."[91]

At a press conference held on January 21, 1988, Gérald Larose released a list of nineteen incidents in which Marc-André Boivin had been involved while working at the CSN. These were essentially proposals for acts of violence (arson, dynamiting, kidnapping, etc.) proposed by the agent provocateur to members of the trade union central. Larose claimed that the information came from union members who were willing to "testify in a free and serious investigation."[92] How could Boivin have advocated violence within the CSN for so many years without the CSN leadership ever knowing about it, asked Pierre Cayouette, a reporter for *Le Devoir*. To which Larose replied that "Boivin had been trained as a secret agent. He was trained to do this job covertly. He went after impressionable and compliant targets; he approached individuals, not general assemblies."[93]

The CSN leader also indicated that the informant had not been able to find any takers among the various people he had approached to commit the criminal acts listed in the nineteen incidents. Instead, these people had been "astonished or amazed or incredulous or simply embarrassed," Larose said.[94] Larose also took aim at SIRC: "We find it unfortunate that your investigation appears to be limited to internal procedures without hearing from those who were victims of CSIS's actions," wrote the CSN president in a letter to Ron Atkey, Chair of the Review Committee.[95] While SIRC was slow to respond to the November 19 letter from the president of the CSN, the Review Committee wasted no time in stepping up to defend its reputation.[96]

Solicitor General James Kelleher also responded to the CSN president's press conference. First, he stated that SIRC's investigation was now "over."[97] Kelleher then proceeded to clear CSIS, saying that Boivin was never encouraged by CSIS to do anything illegal, nor to take action against the CSN or any other Canadian labour organization. This did not convince Svend Robinson of the NDP, who asked, "How many more such revelations will it take before the Minister finally recognizes that he no longer has any kind of control over CSIS and makes the only honourable decision left and resigns?"[98]

Marc Laurendeau, a columnist for *La Presse*, agreed:

Let's face it. CSIS, even though it was set up as a civilian agency and taken away from the [RCMP], remains outside of effective government control. Moreover, in interpreting its mandate, the security Service continues to engage in the illegal behaviour and threats to individual liberties that the RCMP secret service was previously accused of.[99]

On March 2, 1988, Marc-André Boivin was released. Incarcerated at SQ headquarters in Quebec City since October 2, 1987, the former informant had served five months of the fifteen-month prison sentence imposed by the court, or one-third of his sentence. It should be noted that the conditions of his release stipulated that Boivin could not make any public statements until the end of his sentence.[100]

On March 29, SIRC's report was made public. It is immediately apparent that the document raises questions about the nature of the Review Committee's investigation. By the agency's own admission, "much of the information" in the report comes from the Inspector General's investigation, which, as we have seen, had already taken place. It is therefore information that the Solicitor General already had in its possession. The difference between the two documents is therefore purely formal: the SIRC report is intended to be made public, while the Inspector General's report is not.[101] The Review Committee's report provides a glimpse into the substance of the Inspector General's investigation: CSIS staff interviewed many of the Service's senior officers but did not question Boivin himself, as it was deemed inappropriate to do so while legal proceedings were ongoing.[102] It is therefore to be understood that the main witness and interested party in this case was never even questioned by SIRC.[103] Following this botched investigation, SIRC concluded that:

> There is no evidence to suggest that Mr. Boivin was at any time directed or encouraged by CSIS either to commit the illegal acts for which he was convicted or to act in any other way as an "agent provocateur" within the CSN. However, we have some concern as to whether CSIS exercised sufficient diligence in attempting to ensure that Mr. Boivin was not involved in unlawful activities or in detecting the possibility that such activities were occurring.

> Mr. Boivin was targeted, essentially, against communists. During the same period, much of the CSIS Counter-Subversion Branch's human resources were targeted against communists. [...]

7. PAID BY THE CSN ... AND CSIS

Such an emphasis on communists and unions does not lend itself to logical analysis by reference to specific provisions of the CSIS Act. The RCMP Security Service before 1984, and to a lesser extent CSIS since then have had an interest in left-of-centre activities, particularly when associated with unions or the labour movement, that has had more to do with attitudes of mind than provisions of the law. Clearly, the CSIS Act had very little effect on this situation until CSIS received direction from the Solicitor General in 1987.[104]

The Review Committee was referring to the Solicitor General's decision to dismantle CSIS's "Counter-Subversion" branch after it was revealed that it was keeping files on more than 30,000 individuals.[105] This does not mean that all of these files were to be destroyed: some were simply transferred to the Counter-Intelligence Division, others to the Counter-Terrorism Division.

While SIRC wrote that "Mr. Boivin apparently refrains from reporting on either union activities or on union members per se, as he does not have a mandate to do so," it nevertheless made an important qualification:

> Nevertheless, in reporting on the "non-union" targets against which he was directed, the information provided by Mr. Boivin at times touched upon certain activities of either his union or its members, or otherwise related to labour union activities generally.[106]

The Review Committee also criticized CSIS for casting too wide a net in its intelligence gathering. Noting that by 1983, "and up to the time of the formation of CSIS, unions were generally not considered by the RCMP as a subject of active investigation," the Committee found it difficult to understand why CSIS retained the RCMP's labour movement files, which contained a great deal of information on unions.[107] This is a significant amount of information that, in theory, could no longer have been collected under the *CSIS Act*, hence the admonition to the intelligence agency:

> Since the creation of CSIS in July 1984, investigative files inherited from the RCMP Security Service on unions have been maintained and added to in a manner which made them accessible on a day-to-day basis to CSIS officers. Since much of the pre-1984 information in these files could not have been collected under CSIS' investigative mandate, we must conclude that the maintenance of these files in

such a manner amounts to an unreasonable and unnecessary exercise of CSIS' powers.[108]

SIRC claimed that the tabling of the Inspector General's report had already prompted the Solicitor General to correct the situation. The fact remains that CSIS ignored the limits set out in the legislation by which it had been founded. The intelligence agency was making its own rules. Even Members of Parliament were no longer convinced by the "protections" laid out in the legislation creating CSIS. SIRC could talk about "abuses" until it was blue in the face, but as long as there were no consequences for those involved, these were empty words that did nothing to ensure that such "mistakes" would not be repeated in the future. SIRC stubbornly refused to draw the appropriate lessons from the recklessness of the very agency it was charged with reviewing. If CSIS didn't care about the *CSIS Act*, what was the point of SIRC suggesting the intelligence agency "ought to have had a policy to determine whether the use of a source such as Mr. Boivin associated or close to the labour movement in Canada was 'strictly necessary'"?[109]

As further evidence of the Review Committee's vacillation, despite its various criticisms it still presented CSIS as a victim: "We also believe that the public image of the Canadian Security Intelligence Service has been affected by speculation much of which has been found, in this inquiry, to be inaccurate."[110] The report did not elaborate on what "speculation" was "inaccurate," but one can guess that this was a reference to television reports and newspaper articles that had called into question the reputation of Canada's secret service.

Criticism of SIRC's report was not long in coming. So far as Gérald Larose was concerned, the report didn't solve anything:

> In the end, the Committee listened to the chiefs and underlings, heard from Boivin, but at no time did they approach the victims, that is, us and the activists, and this resulted in a limited report. We have no reason to believe that we are no longer being targeted by the security services or that they are following the law, and there is no indication to date that they have actually changed their methods in line with the Minister's directives.[111]

This would explain why SIRC found no evidence that Marc-André Boivin was acting on behalf of the Canadian secret service when he was breaking the

7. PAID BY THE CSN ... AND CSIS

law—it simply did not look for any! Clayton Ruby, the high-profile Toronto lawyer, was similarly unimpressed with SIRC's report:

> The committee, inexplicably, did not require Boivin to testify under oath and so was never able to cross-examine him. [...] CSIS did not inform the Quebec police of the Ste. Foy bombing which had occurred some seven months earlier. Nor did the report of the committee give any information as to whether they were ever asked "Why not?" [...] We are never told what it was that CSIS knew, nor what they did about it. And one suspects that if we knew the truth, we'd conclude that there was more than mere negligence by CSIS. What were the facts?[112]

As the CSN president explained, no matter how you look at it, CSIS was at fault, one way or another:

> Boivin could not have done what he did alone. I would be very surprised that CSIS does not closely monitor its agents. If they were not watching him, they are a gang of incompetents. And if they were, CSIS was in agreement and giving Boivin orders.[113]

For his part, parliamentary analyst Raymond Giroux took to the editorial page of *Le Soleil* to underscore the glaring deficiencies in the Minister's directives:

> The dismantling of the anti-subversive squad is nothing more than a smokescreen as long as CSIS remains in the hands of "ex-RCMPs" who have been recycled into civilian life. The mentality of those who burned down barns or wrote communiqués attributed to the FLQ still persists.[114]

Having simply relied on the word of CSIS, SIRC's Paule Gauthier acknowledged that the Review Committee did not check for itself whether the old RCMP files had been destroyed, as claimed by the intelligence agency.[115]

The story did not end there. Marc-André Boivin proved once again that he was not lacking in chutzpah, as he went to court to get his job back at the CSN, filing a motion to this effect in the Superior Court.[116] During the hearings, union leaders testified that it was clear to them that Boivin "had found another job with the SQ for $545 a week."[117] The court found against Boivin, concluding that he had indeed taken "actions that could be taken as a resignation" from his position at the CSN.[118]

In early 1989, Marc-André Boivin went on the offensive and publicly attacked CSIS in a series of media interviews.[119] The former secret service mole denied having spied on the CSN: "My targets," he said, "were not just at the CSN. They were everywhere there were communists, they were everywhere there were targets. Me, my job, was to go and monitor that."[120]

On March 23, 1989, Boivin filed a motion for damages in which he claimed half a million dollars from CSIS, SIRC, and the Solicitor General of Canada.[121] The former informant blamed the intelligence agency for leaving him out to dry and, by the same token, for getting him kicked out of the labour movement by unnecessarily revealing his role as a "source" to the SQ. Boivin said he "lived in fear of reprisals" and "lost all credibility with the general public."[122] He said CSIS could have simply informed the SQ that CSN members were preparing to carry out bombings. "Boivin would have been arrested and convicted along with the others and would have benefited from the CSN's insurance policy," he claimed.[123] The lawsuit alleged that SIRC had made Boivin a pariah in the labour movement by publishing a report containing both false and secret information about him, without giving him an opportunity to present his side of the story. "[Boivin] always acted with the understanding, just like any other person who acts as a source, that the rules of confidentiality would be respected," the lawsuit stated.[124] As such, Boivin sought $250,000 in compensation for damage to his honour and reputation and for the inconvenience and disruption he suffered as a result of these revelations, and $250,000 for unlawful and intentional infringement of his "fundamental rights." The federal government countered by saying that "the rule of confidentiality of the identity of police informants is not absolute" and that the former secret agent "owes the problems he is complaining about to his turpitude and his turpitude alone."[125] Boivin withdrew his civil suit in November 1998, after the case was "settled out of court."[126]

In 1991, the former informant founded a labour relations consulting firm in which he represented bosses in negotiations with union organizations. The metamorphosis seemed complete for this former agent provocateur, now openly selling his services to the highest bidder. The skills Boivin had acquired during his long career as a snitch could now be put to work for management. "No one can afford the luxury of a confrontation anymore," he explained. "The business world has changed. The unions are resisting. Those who will not change will die."[127]

7. PAID BY THE CSN ... AND CSIS

Although Marc-André Boivin's days of breaking the law in the name of national security were a thing of the past, his legal troubles were not over yet. In 2007, Boivin pleaded guilty before Judge Jean-Paul Aubin to a charge of receiving stolen vehicles, a case that dated back to January 2003. Boivin wrote a check for $32,000 to reimburse the insurance company, and got away with a conditional discharge and a $3,000 donation to the *Le Pignon bleu* charity.[128]

Looking back on the turbulent years when Marc-André Boivin was living his double life, he clearly got off lightly. Yes, he served a prison sentence, but only for bombing Malenfant's properties. The agent provocateur therefore went unpunished for the many other "armed actions" that the CSN denounced at its press conference—all of which contravene the *Criminal Code*—none of which were ever denied by Boivin himself. Let's not forget that simply advising someone to commit a criminal act—which Boivin did on multiple occasions—constitutes a serious offence.[129]

The state clearly chose to turn a blind eye. The media itself could have done more, could have conducted its own investigation into Boivin's repeated provocations, but it held back from doing so. As for those who had been snared in the agent's various traps—presumably more than a few—they likely concluded that it was in their best interest to remain silent. If they had publicly denounced Boivin, wouldn't they also risk incriminating themselves? What crime could be more perfect than one where the victim feels their best option is to remain silent?

The fight against subversion, and especially against "communists," served as a convenient alibi for CSIS to engage in terrorism, just as the crusade against Quebec separatism served as an excuse for its ancestor the RCMP-SS to keep the FLQ on life support. Despite pretensions about Canada being a "free country" (whatever that means), the fact remains that being on the political left can lead to one being targeted by the likes of a Marc-André Boivin.

But as the Cold War drew to a close at the end of the 1980s, CSIS was forced to look for other threats to national security. As it turned out, it was in the world of the neo-Nazi far right, which was booming following the fall of the Soviet bloc and German reunification, that CSIS would find its new playground for provocation and manipulation.

8. A Big Thank You from the Neo-Nazis

As we saw with the Marc-André Boivin affair, the Canadian secret services are not averse to using agents to exacerbate already tense situations. One might think they were in the business of creating conflict. Things get even more dangerous when agents begin to puff up far-right groups, many of whose members already have a penchant for violence. In this chapter, we will look at how informants from CSIS and its predecessor, the RCMP Security Service (RCMP-SS), played with fire by infiltrating Toronto's far-right milieu.

The Canadian secret services have long been interested in the Toronto-area far right. In the mid-1970s, the RCMP-SS decided to target the Western Guard Party, a Toronto group that had previously been known as the Edmund Burke Society (EBS). The EBS was fiercely anti-communist and its membership included many people from Eastern European countries that were at the time one-party systems claiming to be socialist.

Whenever a far-left group would take to the streets, the EBS would organize its own counter-demonstration.[1] Scuffles were not uncommon, and the Burkers (as they were known) were not shy about fighting. But it was when EBS member Geza Matrai attacked Soviet Prime Minister Alexei Kosygin during his visit to Ottawa in October 1971, trying to tackle him before himself being brought to the ground by RCMP and security police, that the group received its greatest media exposure.[2] On October 24, within hours of Kosygin's arrival in Toronto, Metro police and the RCMP raided the homes of several EBS members, seizing ammunition and firearms, including a machine pistol and an anti-tank weapon.[3] The police said they had uncovered a plot to assassinate the Soviet leader. But only Matrai was charged, receiving three months in prison.[4]

Don C. Andrews, one of the founders of the EBS, dismissed the conspiracy allegations as the work of an informant under police pressure.[5] He did admit, however, that he was encouraging his group's members to train in marksmanship to defend Canada in the event of a "foreign invasion."[6] Andrews made this statement while on trial for making death threats against Margaret Best, a former member of the EBS—a charge for which he was acquitted.

8. A BIG THANK YOU FROM THE NEO-NAZIS

Best was at the time secretary of the Ontario branch of Social Credit Canada, a right-wing political organization that the Burkers were trying to infiltrate. Andrews became the leader of the EBS when it was renamed the Western Guard Party (WGP) in February 1972. With a mission to "preserve and promote the basic social and spiritual values of the White people," the Western Guard adopted a white supremacist discourse that was openly antisemitic and hostile to Black communities.[7] This shift to open racial hatred could only make the group appear more pernicious.

Although the neo-fascist movement had a much higher propensity for violence than Black Power or First Nations activists, the RCMP considered it less dangerous than either of these movements. In 1973, the RCMP-SS argued that "the Western Guard poses no threat to national security or to the government."[8] Perhaps the reason for the federal police's leniency towards the far right was that the RCMP shared a similar anti-communist paranoia. Just as there was no shortage of Mounties who suspected Solicitor General Warren Allmand of being a communist, the Burkers would accuse Prime Minister Pierre Trudeau of being a socialist.[9]

It was the advent of the 1976 Summer Olympics in Montreal that led the RCMP to launch an extensive investigation into the WGP. Four years earlier, the Munich games had resulted in a hostage-taking that left eleven Israeli Olympic team members, a West German police officer, and five militants from the Palestinian group Black September dead; the attack had been carried out with logistical assistance from German neo-Nazis,[10] while also being supported by sections of the far left.[11] Four years later, Canada would have no excuse to act surprised if a similar tragedy were to occur. Hence the RCMP investigation, which was more interested in protecting Canada's image than the victims of the Western Guard.

In May 1975, Robert Toope, a Newfoundland house painter known for his anti-communist views, was recruited by the RCMP to infiltrate the WGP. At the time, Andrews's group was engaged in a campaign of vandalism in Toronto. Racist graffiti was appearing all over the city, with slogans like "Hitler was right," "Keep Canada white," and "Juden Raus" (German for "Jews out").[12] Paid $300 to $500 a month, Toope would admit to being involved in about 200 incidents, ranging from distributing racist literature to acting as a driver on nocturnal outings where synagogues, Jewish and Afro-Canadian businesses, and leftist hang-outs were vandalized and daubed with swastikas.[13] In court testimony, Toope stated that "I knew I was breaking the law on every incident. But you had to prove yourself. The more active you were, the more information you got." Toope could rest easy: his controller, Corporal George Duggan, had assured him of his support were he ever to be arrested. The informant appeared so "credible" to the white supremacists that he ended up becoming one of the leaders of the then forty-member WGP during his fourteen-month undercover mission.[14]

The operation came to an end on July 19, 1976, with the arrest of Don Andrews and two other party members: Dawyd Zarytshansky (nicknamed "Tarzan") and Wayne Elliott.[15] Both Andrews and Zarytshansky were charged with possession of explosives for illegal purposes, conspiracy to commit arson, criminal mischief, and disrupting a soccer match between Israel and Guatemala at Varsity Stadium in Toronto by throwing smoke bombs onto the field. The three defendants were also charged with conspiracy to burn down the home of a woman whose ex-husband had reported her to the Western Guard as a communist sympathizer. The defendants were released on various conditions, including that they no longer associate with the WGP.[16]

At trial, Toope testified that Andrews ordered the vandalism, which was to be claimed by fictitious groups to cover their tracks. While Andrews had admitted to providing paint for some of the graffiti and participating in some of the nighttime expeditions, he also described the informant as a zealous man of action.[17] Zarytshansky testified that Toope was by far the "most radical" of the group, even initiating several plots, including the disruption of the soccer game.[18] In other words, the RCMP mole clearly appeared to be acting as an agent provocateur.

After a three-month trial, on February 1, 1978, Andrews was sentenced to serve two years in prison, and Zarytshansky, who was also found guilty of selling stolen cigars, was sentenced to eighteen months.[19] The case dealt a fatal blow to the WGP, but not to Andrews's right-wing activism. He subsequently founded the Nationalist Party of Canada, which remains active to this day. Ten years later, Andrews's group would once again encounter an agent provocateur—this time one working for CSIS—in the person of Grant Bristow.

Grant Bristow's association with CSIS began on March 6, 1986, when he was twenty-eight years old. Bristow was earning a living as a private security consultant when a South African diplomat in Toronto tried to recruit him to spy on the anti-apartheid movement in Canada; CSIS then approached Bristow and asked him to spy on the activities of South African consular staff.

8. A BIG THANK YOU FROM THE NEO-NAZIS

The diplomat in question cut ties with Bristow after Ottawa expelled one of the members of the South African diplomatic mission in August 1986.[20]

When CSIS contacted Bristow again on February 26, 1987, he had just landed a job as an investigator with the multinational company Kuehne and Nagel International. Bristow informed the intelligence agency that he knew an ex-cop, one of whose co-workers was a right-wing extremist. He offered to infiltrate the white supremacist milieu, an offer that was accepted by CSIS.[21] But just a week later, on March 5, the CSIS Toronto regional office was dismayed to learn that Grant Bristow was bragging about his ties to Canadian intelligence. CSIS headquarters wrote that "The source appears to be somewhat overzealous, which may have compromised his confidentiality. Security precautions should be reinforced and his progression in this field should be carefully monitored and directed."[22]

On June 11, the agency's senior management advised Bristow that his services were no longer required.[23] But on November 4, 1988, Bristow again took it upon himself to contact the CSIS Toronto regional office to offer information he had obtained on white supremacists. At the time, he was part of the scene around Don Andrews.[24] Bristow said he was ready to "identify as many of the individual cell members as possible."[25] His controller then asked that he keep him informed of any further contact with right-wing extremist circles. At the time, CSIS considered this movement to be in its "embryonic stage" in Toronto.[26] It was the beginning of Operation Governor.[27]

On December 12, another police force informed the Canadian secret service that Bristow was claiming to have "contacts at CSIS." This time, the intelligence agency decided to turn a blind eye. His controller was developing a good relationship with Bristow, whom he described as friendly and easy to get along with.[28]

Operation Governor took a new turn when Bristow met Wolfgang Droege in 1989. Droege was no small fry in the neo-Nazi scene. Born in Germany in 1949, he had immigrated to Canada in 1963. In the 1970s, he became a member of the WGP and then of the Toronto chapter of the Ku Klux Klan. Droege was imprisoned in the United States from April 1981 to June 1983 for his involvement in Operation Red Dog, a plot involving mercenaries, neo-Nazis, and the American mob attempting to overthrow the government of the Caribbean nation of Dominica.[29] Then, in November 1984, Droege was once again arrested in the United States, this time for possession of a knife and four-and-a-half ounces of cocaine. Sentenced to thirteen years in prison, he was released on April 21, 1989, and returned to live in Canada.[30] In a federal court affidavit, Droege recounted the following:

> I first met Grant Bristow within a week of returning to Canada at a meeting at the Nationalist Party in the house of its leader Don Andrews. [...] No one knew him but he volunteered to do investigative work for Andrews and the party and train people. Bristow took an immediate interest in me and we subsequently became close friends.[31]

Soon after, Droege got a job as a bailiff at Accurate Bailiff Services, a Scarborough company owned by former WGP member Alan Overfield, the man who had also compiled the list of weapons needed to carry out Operation Red Dog.[32] The CSIS informant did not pass up the opportunity to make himself useful to Droege:

> Bristow helped me in locating automobiles which had been missing for quite some time. That in turn provided me with extra bonuses which helped get me back on my feet financially. This helped me tremendously.[33]

Not all was going so well, however, for the CSIS mole: rumours were circulating within the Nationalist Party that Grant Bristow was an RCMP informant. These rumours did not stop the party leader from inviting Bristow, along with Droege and sixteen others, to travel to Libya to commemorate the twentieth anniversary celebrations of Colonel Muammar Gaddafi's rise to power, to take place from August 26 to September 4, 1989.[34] The trip was fully paid for by the Libyan government, which was willing to work with any group opposed to Zionism.[35] The trip led to tensions within the Nationalist Party, however, which eventually resulted in a split.[36] According to Droege,

> Bristow and I spent a large amount of time together tracking cars during which time the ideas were discussed of forming an organization fighting for white rights. Bristow was instrumental in urging me to seek an alternative to Don Andrews' Nationalist Party. He said that Andrews wasn't even white and never seemed to get anywhere with his white racialist message. He said that an organization needed to be founded which would take the racialist movement into the 1990s by using videotapes, seminars to upgrade people's speak-

ing skills, use of computers, and techniques that are used by major political parties in attracting the masses to our cause."[37]

The Heritage Front was founded shortly thereafter, on September 25, 1989.[38] According to Droege, the Heritage Front "was not a 'white supremacist' organization. [...] We are racial nationalists whose eventual goal would be the creation of an exclusively white state for those wishing to live in an area among their own kind."[39]

Grant Bristow was present at the founding meeting of the Heritage Front, along with Droege and Gerald Lincoln.[40] At that time, the group had only twelve to fifteen members.[41] The start-up costs of the organization amounted to $1,350, half of which was paid by Droege, with Lincoln and the CSIS informant splitting the difference. Droege made Bristow his right-hand man "because he could take it."[42] Moreover, "as Droege's confidant, Bristow was part of the internal leadership of the Heritage Front."[43] The mole was also entrusted with taking care of all legal matters, because of his "paralegal" training. Droege stated that

> Bristow would try to arrange bail, and help the lawyers in preparing the cases. He was heavily involved in the Canadian Human Rights Tribunal case by doing legal research and even represented me at a Ministry of Consumer Affairs tribunal review of my bailiff license. He would also represent some supporters in traffic cases for free.[44]

Bristow was also appointed office manager to oversee the various administrative requirements of the organization, as well as being in charge of security for the first three years of the Heritage Front's existence, a responsibility he shared with Eric Fischer, a former sergeant in the Canadian Forces Airborne Regiment.[45] In short, the informant quickly became indispensable to the organization, even having his own faction that supported him, a sign of how skilled he was at manipulation.[46]

On October 4, 1989, the CSIS Regional Director responded to these new developments by authorizing a six-month undercover operation within the Heritage Front. Droege became a Level 2 target, which entailed the use of investigative methods such as "limited tailing" and "personal interviews."[47] In fact, Droege himself had learned that he was being monitored by the Canadian secret service after a Canada Post inspector working with CSIS made the mistake of sending three envelopes intended for him to the Heritage

Front's post office box. As Droege explained in an interview, the blunder was not without educational value: "It really was amateur hour. Sending the mail addressed to my home to my P.O. box confirmed that CSIS was my main adversary and that I had nothing to worry about."[48]

Meanwhile, Grant Bristow was assigned a more senior controller: Al Treddenick, a former RCMP-SS agent.[49] CSIS seemed excited at the prospect of having "a source in on the ground floor" of an organization headed by Droege, who was becoming "the leading Aryan movement personality in Canada."[50] However, the higher ups at the intelligence agency stressed that it was important that the "Source's association with Droege did not become a matter of police responsibility."[51] Clearly, CSIS was concerned that its investigation might be taken over by a police force, not a far-fetched prospect given Droege's criminal record.

Rumours that Grant Bristow was a mole persisted within the Heritage Front, but Droege's trust in him made him virtually untouchable within the organization, as well as putting him in a position to act as a contact for other like-minded groups.[52] For example, in January 1991, Droege arranged for Bristow to meet with two racist leaders—Al Hooper, leader of the Aryan Resistance Movement in British Columbia, and Terry Long, head of the Canadian chapter of the Aryan Nations in Alberta—to discuss plans to unify the far right in Canada. The informant also travelled to Montreal in January 1992 to sound out the terrain.[53]

Then, in March 1991, Canada's Solicitor General, Pierre Cadieux, approved a CSIS request to allow Grant Bristow to travel to Munich, Germany, with Droege and other Heritage Front members, to attend an international meeting of some three hundred neo-Nazis and Holocaust deniers. It should be noted that Ottawa did not bother to inform the German government of this decision.[54] The event was sponsored by veteran Holocaust denier Ernst Zündel, who had been found guilty of spreading false information about the Holocaust, and it ended with the intervention of German police.[55] The informant also attended an annual convention of the KKK in Alabama and a meeting of the Aryan Nations in Idaho in July 1991.[56] Droege was barred from entering the United States, but Bristow had no trouble crossing the border to meet with leading American neo-Nazis.[57]

These contacts appear to have paid off, as in the fall of 1991 the informant briefly hosted Sean Maguire, a US citizen and member of the Aryan Nations who was visiting Toronto.[58] On September 20, Bristow and Maguire

8. A BIG THANK YOU FROM THE NEO-NAZIS

were arrested and taken to Metropolitan Toronto Police Station 41. Maguire was the subject of an immigration warrant, while Bristow was charged with transporting two weapons in the trunk of his car: a .12-gauge shotgun and a non-functional semi-automatic rifle. "Bristow always carried these guns in the trunk. I'd seen them several times before," Droege said.[59] But the police decided not to charge Bristow, claiming this was because the guns were holstered.[60] "Some people in the movement were surprised he was not charged with unsafe storage of firearms," Droege commented.[61] In fact, Harold Musetescu, a former immigration officer at the scene, told SIRC that there was a "heated discussion" at Station 41 about whether Bristow should be charged with possession of dangerous weapons and negligent storage of firearms. He said the cops were anxious to lay charges, but the informant was saved when CSIS intervened.[62]

Bristow also served as one of the Heritage Front's main spokespeople. The SIRC report notes that he spoke at the group's first public meeting, to which the media were invited, in September 1991. He also arranged for a room for journalists to interview speakers at the meeting.[63] In testimony before the House Subcommittee on National Security, Elisse Hategan, who joined the Heritage Front in the fall of 1991 when she was only sixteen years old, recounted the following:

> [Bristow] spoke at almost every rally, but it was edited from the tapes. His job was mainly fund-raising and getting people stirred up. Grant didn't want his recordings to be distributed. They used to sell the tapes for $20. Grant didn't want to be on tape, so Gerry [Lincoln] would edit them.[64]

However, it was later learned that video recordings of some of the CSIS informant's speeches were indeed retained, and some videos can even be viewed on YouTube to this day.[65] In the videos one can see that Bristow was an effective public speaker. In fact, he was probably a better speaker than many Members of Parliament. He was able to make his audience laugh, with occasional cries of "White Power" breaking out as he spoke. According to CSIS, Bristow initially tried to avoid speaking publicly but "was obligated to do so to maintain his credibility within the movement."[66]

In its report, SIRC acknowledged that the agent provocateur made "crude, abrasive, and probably racist statements in the presence of his racist associates in order to maintain his position in the group."[67] This was corroborated by Droege. "He always expressed very anti-Jewish sentiments and went so far as to say that the Holocaust wouldn't have been a bad idea," he stated.⁶⁸ Gerry Lincoln, editor of *Up Front*, the Heritage Front magazine, testified that:

> I believe that he was quite sincere in fighting along with the rest of us for "equal rights for whites." Grant Bristow was fortunate enough to get paid for doing something he enjoyed and believed in.⁶⁹

In addition, Droege told SIRC that Grant Bristow was in charge of collecting information on Jewish groups for the Heritage Front. This information consisted primarily of personal addresses, positions in organizations, travel plans, and sources of funds.⁷⁰ According to the secret agent, this information on the "Jewish lobby" came from television shows and subscriptions to Jewish publications.⁷¹

These facts show how Bristow did not pursue his mission by remaining in the shadows—quite the contrary! As such, a "police letter" quoted in the SIRC report, to the effect that the unidentified police source "considered the Source to be an information gatherer. He was known but not seen as an integral member of the Heritage Front," must be taken as not credible.⁷² Bristow's leadership position in the far-right group was confirmed by numerous sources. According to Lincoln, the video record "clearly shows that Grant was the co-founder of the organization, and active within it. The government contends he was a passive guy, sitting around gathering information."⁷³ Elisse Hategan also argued that Bristow was an important charismatic leader within the Heritage Front:

> He makes people feel as if they're taking part in this big activity; they're defending their race by doing this sort of thing. He did order, but he didn't put it in a military way. He made it friendlier, as if we were doing a good thing. [...] He was very good at manipulating a conversation. He was very amicable. He was friendly, made jokes of it. [...] Everybody looked at him as the all-knowing figure when it came to the enemies, the opponents, the left wing. So if he said this person is the leader, then everybody went after that person. His word was pretty much law when it came to the intelligence. [...] He never took orders. Giving orders ... on some occasions he did.⁷⁴

In the spring of 1991, Grant Bristow and other members of the Heritage Front began volunteering to provide security at various meetings of the

8. A BIG THANK YOU FROM THE NEO-NAZIS

Reform Party, a right-wing political party led by Preston Manning, son of the 1943–1968 premier of Alberta, Ernest Manning.[75] In addition to opposing bilingualism and multiculturalism, the Reform Party proposed an end to immigration policies "designed to radically or suddenly alter the ethnic makeup of Canada," a position that was viewed with obvious favour in white supremacist circles.[76]

In April 1991, the Reform Party decided to beef up its presence in Ontario and the Maritimes in preparation for the next federal general election. The Heritage Front found itself providing security for Reform Party events through Alan Overfield, a local party organizer who, as we have seen, was also a former Western Guard member who owned the bailiff agency that employed Droege. It should be noted that Overfield told SIRC that he never hid his background from the Reform Party. He even claimed that one Stephen Harper, a Reform Party activist working for MP Deborah Grey at the time, was aware of his political past. For his part, Harper, who would be Canada's prime minister from 2006 to 2015, would claim to SIRC that he did not remember ever meeting Overfield.[77]

Whatever the truth may be, Preston Manning's party accepted Overfield's offer to provide security. The Ontario Reform Party was financially strapped, and any offer of free services from small businesses was welcome.[78] On May 27, 1991, Heritage Front members, including Grant Bristow and Droege, provided security for the Reform Party for the first time at a small meeting in a Toronto church. That same month, Overfield and two Heritage Front associates were appointed to the leadership of Reform's Beaches-Woodbine County Association in the Toronto area. In early June, the CSIS informant was present at a security planning meeting with Overfield and Andrew Flint, the party's Ontario regional coordinator, in preparation for a major rally at the International Centre in Mississauga, Ontario. CSIS's Toronto regional office informed its senior management that one of its informants, along with other members of the Heritage Front, would be providing security for a Reform Party meeting. In fact, Bristow would act as the security coordinator for the event, and even as Preston Manning's main bodyguard during the rally, which attracted more than 6,000 people.[79] Bristow was also on hand on July 9, when the Heritage Front once again provided security, this time at the founding meeting of the Beaches-Woodbine County Association.[80]

In its report, SIRC wrote that the intelligence agency instructed Grant Bristow to "continue to participate in the security duties to allow CSIS to monitor the White Supremacist infiltration and disruption activity within the Reform Party." However, discussions were also taking place higher up within CSIS, where the "political sensitivities associated with the Source operation" were noted.[81] Senior staff at the intelligence agency were aware of the risk that "There might have been some attempt to imply that the Service was investigating the Reform Party although they thought that unlikely since the Party would not want its association with Droege publicized."[82]

While CSIS has always insisted that it never investigated the Reform Party, the SIRC report reveals that "there were a few instances where Service investigations on mandated targets had surfaced peripheral information regarding the Reform Party."[83] For his part, Bristow did not deny encouraging Heritage Front members to join Reform. "The Source could not remember making a speech encouraging people to join the Reform Party, but might have done so after Droege asked him to do it," according to SIRC.[84] In August 1991, the head of CSIS's Counter-Terrorism Branch concluded that Droege's involvement with the Reform Party was not central to the CSIS investigation.[85]

Then, on August 8, the Human Sources Branch at CSIS headquarters issued instructions to the Toronto regional office: "Please direct the Source to avoid Reform Party activities."[86] In its report, the Review Committee criticized CSIS for having been slow to issue such instructions. The Committee also concluded that the directive was "not sufficiently precise. The message reiterated that there was to be no reporting on the Reform Party, but it did not explicitly state that the Source was to leave the security group."[87]

Specific or not, the instructions appear to have had no effect: despite the CSIS directive, Bristow would again provide security for Preston Manning, this time at a Reform Party meeting in Pickering, Ontario, on January 22, 1992, one of the largest gatherings in the party's history.[88] On August 23, 1991, the CSIS Toronto regional office suggested headquarters should debrief

> the leader of the Reform Party of the Service's interest in individual(s) who support the White Supremacist movement that may have connections to the Reform Party but at the same time assure the leader that we are not/not (sic!) investigating the Party.[89]

Five days later, three CSIS officials lodged their disagreement with this recommendation, stating they believed that

8. A BIG THANK YOU FROM THE NEO-NAZIS

> A certain threshold of danger would have to present itself before it would be feasible to consider debriefing the leader of the Reform Party, regarding certain white supremacists connections within. The present circumstances would not seem to warrant this action.[90]

CSIS interpreted the Heritage Front's infiltration of the Reform Party as being motivated by the Front's quest for visibility.[91] The initiative was clearly part of an effort by far-right activists to leave the margins, much as the EBS had once attempted to infiltrate the Social Credit Party of Canada. This quest for visibility was all part of the Front's strategy to expand its activist base.

In late February 1992, the media revealed that the Ontario branch of the Reform Party had been infiltrated by the Heritage Front.[92] The controversy risked having major political repercussions on the federal scene, potentially undermining the party's chances of making inroads in Ontario. As a result, Reform set up a special committee of its Executive Council to investigate the allegations. Five people, including Droege and Overfield, would eventually be expelled from the party, but the damage had already been done.[93]

Despite these expulsions, the Heritage Front was on a roll. Since the fall of 1991, the group had been successfully operating a "hate line" (a phone number one could dial to hear pre-recorded racist messages) despite various lawsuits from Jewish and First Nations organizations.[94] Beginning in late 1992, right-wing activists attempted to recruit minors by distributing leaflets in dozens of high schools in southern Ontario.[95] By 1993, the Heritage Front claimed to have nearly 700 members spread throughout Toronto, Hamilton, Ottawa, Kitchener-Waterloo, and London.[96] Its public meetings attracted between fifty and one hundred people, the majority of whom were under twenty-five years of age.[97] According to the Jewish organization B'nai Brith, the Heritage Front was the "most organized, the most active and the most pervasive" far-right group in Canada at the time.[98] A sorry "success" for which much of the "credit" was due to CSIS's agent provocateur.

In the meantime, a response to the ominous growth of the Heritage Front was beginning to take shape. In February 1992, the group Anti-Racist Action (ARA) was formed in Toronto. ARA members would mobilize whenever the Heritage Front held a public event. The two groups also began to gather information on each other. That same year, Klanbusters, another anti-racist group, was also established in Toronto.[99] It was in this context that the Heritage Front began a full-scale campaign of harassment targeting anti-racist activists. Grant Bristow's key role in this campaign would become one of the most controversial aspects of Operation Governor.

In a book published in 2014, Elisse Hategan explains how it all began: in the winter of 1992, at a meeting of about thirty Heritage Front members, Droege announced the creation of an "intelligence unit" within the organization, to be under Bristow's control.[100] The agent provocateur then spoke: "Time to ramp up the fight against those who want to shut us down. Time to fuck with heads and make them shit their pants."[101] Bristow went on to say that a campaign of psychological warfare was intended to "push their opponents over the edge" until they would "self-destruct."[102]

CSIS viewed the Heritage Front's harassment campaign as a welcome development, in that it appeared to resolve a dilemma. According to the SIRC report, the intelligence agency wanted to continue its infiltration without its informant becoming directly involved in street fights with anti-racists, a position that was becoming increasingly difficult due to the escalating tensions between the neo-Nazis and their opponents. "In order to avoid, where possible, taking part in confrontational activities between the Heritage Front and others, the Source chose to become the 'information gathering' expert within the group," according to SIRC.[103]

In his testimony to SIRC, Bristow explained that targets of the harassment campaign would receive a message: "[Y]ou have been selected to be 'IT'. I am to become your closest personal friend; if you don't want to be 'IT', give me the names and telephone numbers of someone else and they can be IT."[104]

In a sworn statement dated September 23, 1993, Elisse Hategan described the harassment campaign:

> When someone was made IT that person's life would be made miserable. More precisely, the person would be reminded of the fact 24-hours a day; one would not be able to eat or sleep in peace. Calls would be made at home, at work, constantly, the goal being to make IT's life miserable, get IT fired from IT's job and made to fear one's own shadow, until IT felt IT was never alone for even a second, that IT was always watched. There could only be one IT. The only way one could get out of being IT was to give the name and phone number of another person in the ARA, so that that person would take the place of IT.[105]

8. A BIG THANK YOU FROM THE NEO-NAZIS

In its report, SIRC cites the cases of three anti-racist activists who were victims of this psychological warfare.[106] One of them was Ruth MacKenzie, a former ARA member who was singled out by the Heritage Front. From January to April 1993, this activist

> received 25 to 30 calls every day, at all hours of the day and night. [...] the calls involved increasing threats of violence. In early March, she was told that her house would be fire-bombed. [...] the activist said there was also some "stalking."[107]

In her sworn deposition cited above, Elisse Hategan confirmed Bristow's significant role in harassing this activist:

> [Grant] said [she] had been under a lot of stress lately, and she was on temporary leave from work. He said the fact that [she] had been IT caused her a lot of stress, and he seemed to take credit for it. He said that [she] was not getting a moment in peace—people were calling her in the middle of the night, at all times of day and night, they'd also been doing it at work, and the pressure was too much for her to handle, that she had to take a leave of absence. He said he thought she'd had a breakdown—in fact, he was sure of it. By this time, Grant was laughing really hard and was almost in tears—he said she had tried very hard to hold onto sanity and not given any names as of yet, but he was confident she'd break soon. He said she even had people move in with her, because she was so scared.[108]

Rodney Bobiwash, an activist with the anti-racist group Klanbusters, also testified as to the negative impacts of the campaign targeting him: "I've had my personal life disrupted, I've had my professional life disrupted and I have suffered as a result of a dirty-tricks campaign orchestrated by Grant Bristow and the Heritage Front."[109] The agent provocateur participated personally in the campaign, making hateful phone calls, explicit threats, and engaging in other forms of harassment. Bristow was responsible for gathering information for the campaign and illegally obtained codes to access the targets' phone messages. He was the mastermind behind the campaign, instructing other Heritage Front members to participate in the systematic harassment of anti-racists.[110]

> Grant Bristow provided the information and the knowledge to develop this campaign. [...] On several occasions I personally wit-

nessed his role in providing personal information on "enemies of freedom," as he used to refer to anti-racists and members of Jewish organizations, to members of the Heritage Front. [...] He also showed members techniques of intelligence gathering against anti-racists and also how to effectively harass someone.[...] Grant was the only one who instructed me regarding that. [...] He told me about certain psychological texts he had read about how to effectively harass someone [...] like letting them know that they're always watched, making them feel very paranoid so that they will turn on themselves.[111]

To the Review Committee, the CSIS informant only admitted to making telephone calls to two anti-racists.[112] In its report, however, SIRC conceded the obvious:

> The Source did engage in individual acts of intimidation or harassment. [...] They elicited concern or fear from those who experienced the oral attacks. [...] We consider that the campaign did have a substantial detrimental impact on those who were its targets. [...] The Source was involved in a campaign which tested the limits of what we believe Canadian society considers to be acceptable and appropriate behaviour from someone acting on behalf of the government.[113]

In her book, Elisse Hategan explains how enthusiastically Bristow took to this task, how he "delighted in tormenting people arbitrarily."[114] The CSIS mole burst out laughing when she informed him that Kevin Thomas, an ARA spokesperson, had lost his home after Bristow called his landlord to slander him as a child molester and HIV-positive heroin addict. "Man, I wish I was a fly on the wall when our boy gets his eviction notice," exclaimed Bristow.[115] Playing on the theme of bestiality, the informant had a box of live gerbils delivered to the workplace of another of his targets. He also asked Hategan to place a personal ad using the name and phone number of an anti-racist activist, portraying her as a fan of "real hard-core masochism, that you'd love to be raped by blacks and beaten with chains."[116]

SIRC concluded that "Bristow instructed Heritage Front members about security and counter intelligence methods."[117] SIRC further confirmed that Bristow was indeed the one behind the harassment campaign:[118]

> Droege wanted to involve other people and the Source was trying to control the process. He thought that by having everyone work

8. A BIG THANK YOU FROM THE NEO-NAZIS

through him on the "IT" campaign, he could retain the numbers that the Heritage Front members collected. He could also restrict, to some extent, the participation of others. To dissuade others from becoming involved, he would say that he had the whole thing under control.[119]

It was claimed that Grant Bristow himself ordered Heritage Front members to stop attacking Ruth MacKenzie, as CSIS became concerned about the harassment targeting the activist.[120] However, Hategan contradicts this claim: "it was totally the opposite. People were supposed to call even further. He wanted to really drive her …."[121] In any event, the SIRC report makes it clear that CSIS was well aware of the harassment campaign and of Bristow's active participation in it:

> The Toronto Region Investigator said that Droege authorized the telephone harassment campaign, and the Source controlled it. One call to the activist's employer was made by Bristow, as a conference call with Mitrevski also on the line. The Investigator told the Source to try to avoid getting into that sort of situation.[122]

SIRC also criticized the lackadaisical attitude of CSIS officials regarding the harassment campaign:

> CSIS senior management should have been sufficiently alert to ask what was going on behind the scenes; the harassment program would then have been brought to their attention. We saw no evidence that this was the case. […] Had CSIS management been engaged in assessing the best possible options, less harassment and intimidation might have occurred.[123]

The Heritage Front's telephone harassment campaign tapered off in June 1993 and finally came to an end the November following. The organization considered the campaign a major success.[124] The Canadian secret service was also very pleased, as SIRC would note: "CSIS believes that its work with the Source during this period was very successful in that a potentially explosive situation, with a great deal of anger on all sides, was defused without any physical violence occurring."[125]

But in her testimony before a parliamentary committee, Hategan drew an entirely different conclusion:

> In December 1992 the only progress the Heritage Front was making was pretty much getting new members. It was very contained and very self-absorbed. Grant is the one who made it expand into targeting the left wing. [...] He increased its capacity by teaching a lot of people who didn't know anything. [...] He taught us how to get intelligence, how to be effective, how to intimidate these people into not coming after us any more, how to do all those sort of things. It kind of grew. [...] A lot of people were unsure about the Heritage Front, but the excitement of being involved in this big spy operation, with intelligence and everything, made them even more active. It was exciting to go after people, threaten them and phone them with death threats and that sort of thing. He involved them in that, and in that sense it made it even bigger. [...] Most of the people didn't know what to do if they were ever stopped by a police officer. They didn't know any of those things. They didn't know what CSIS meant [...] or what the RCMP's or the OPP's mandates are. They didn't know any of that. Grant stepped in. He taught us the skills and how to take care of ourselves and how to make sure that our group was secure. It really helped build, more than anything else, the youth wing.[126]

In a lengthy interview with journalist Andrew Mitrovica in 2004, Grant Bristow tried to justify the harassment campaign: "I was trying to find a response that didn't include out-of-control, escalating violence."[127] Yet, by late 1992, the "uncontrollable violence" that the informant claimed to want to avoid at all costs finally erupted. The first incident occurred in November 1992, when ARA activists threw eggs at about fifty Heritage Front skinheads at Toronto's Ristorante Roma. The SIRC report portrayed Grant Bristow as de-escalating matters during the incident.[128]

Then, on January 25, 1993, four people were injured when a crowd of five hundred people responded to ARA's call to protest against the Heritage Front, some of whose members were appearing before the Human Rights Tribunal in Toronto that day. A heavy police cordon prevented any physical contact between the anti-racists and neo-Nazis, so the clashes were between ARA members and police, who used horses to push back and terrorize the protesters.[129]

On May 29, 1993, approximately fifty anti-racist activists engaged in a series of skirmishes with a roughly equal number of Heritage Front mem-

8. A BIG THANK YOU FROM THE NEO-NAZIS

bers over a period of more than two hours on the streets of Ottawa, where the far-right group was trying to establish a chapter.[130] Four Heritage Front members were charged with assault following the incident. Notably, SIRC's report reveals that Grant Bristow provided information to CSIS about the anti-racists involved:

> The Source was not present in Ottawa at the time. He had, however, been able to pass along "inside" information about the Anti-Racist Action group forming in Ottawa, and its support from Toronto. He told CSIS that the ARA would be sending two carloads of supporters from Toronto to participate in the Ottawa demonstrations.[131]

Then, on June 11, a crowd of two hundred anti-racists smashed the windows of Heritage Front spokesperson Gary Schipper's house and covered the front of the building with paint and feces, all in front of a dozen cops who found themselves outnumbered and outmaneuvered.[132] During her testimony to the parliamentary committee, Elisse Hategan recounted how Bristow was using a radio scanner that day to monitor the anti-racist protest. She also explained how the agent provocateur almost escalated the hostilities:

> He's the one who directed everybody. He said, okay, that's where they're going. Everybody jumped into cars and followed them to the demonstration. [...] Afterwards the HF got together in Allan Gardens in Toronto and they were very angry about what had happened. They wanted to do something. It was Grant on one end, and then there was George Burdi, who is also a Church of the Creator member, on the other. He got up on a table with a megaphone and said, let's go to Sneaky Dees and get those lefties. Grant, on the other hand, suggested a number of home addresses of people—I knew who those people were—and also a workplace to go and smear excrement on and break the windows, fire-bomb the place. What happened was there were more followers who were led by George Burdi, because he was young. He was a skinhead. He was totally paramilitary. So they decided to go with him, and they went to Sneaky Dees, which is why I said it was very close. If they had followed Grant, some people's homes would have been destroyed.[133]

While Grant Bristow's words did not do any harm that night, the same cannot be said of another incident that occurred around the same time. On June 5, a computer belonging to the Church of the Creator (COTC) was stolen.[134] The computer contained sensitive information, including a list of COTC and Heritage Front members who were also members of the Canadian Armed Forces. What's more, the theft occurred in a politically charged environment, with a broad range of political and civil society organizations calling for an investigation into the presence of neo-Nazis in the military after the media had revealed that former Airborne Regiment member Eric Fischer was providing paramilitary training to COTC members.[135] What's more, the robbery occurred on the same night that the Heritage Front was holding a "white power" concert. As Droege explained,

> The day after the theft, Bristow made accusations against Tyrone Mason who had left the concert early that evening. Bristow claimed that Mason had a record for computer theft and had previously been charged with possession of stolen goods. The Fisher brothers informed me that Bristow suggested to them that they had to retrieve the computer. Bristow agitated what was already a very volatile situation at the time.[136]

Accused of the theft by Bristow, Tyrone Mason tells what happened next:

> On June 8, 1993 I was approached by Eric Fischer on my street on my way to work and he offered me a ride in a white van. I was subsequently attacked by Eric and Elkar Fischer in the van which was being driven by Drew Maynard. I was handcuffed, my legs were bound and I was blindfolded. I was beaten while being questioned by Elkar about the computer theft. They placed plastic bags over my head in an attempt to suffocate me and threatened me with a syringe filled with Windex window cleaner. The attack continued over a period of about three hours until they became convinced that I knew nothing about the computer theft. At that point I was released.[137]

Mason reported the incident to the police and Maynard and the Fischer brothers were arrested and charged with kidnapping, false imprisonment, assault causing bodily harm, and threatening to kill. But, as Mason explained, his ordeal was just beginning:

> Several weeks later, I was invited by Grant Bristow to have lunch with him and James Dawson. Grant paid. He told me I should say it

was just an "initiation" into the White Berets[138] and no one could say anything to the contrary. He said it would make me look better in the Heritage Front. [...] In September and October of 1993, I was the target of a telephone harassment campaign by James Dawson and Paul Graham. It consisted of handcuffs being clicked into the receiver and death threats.[139]

Yet worse was yet to come.

On the night of June 6, 1993, Sivarajah Vinasithamby, a Tamil refugee from Sri Lanka, was savagely attacked in the back of the restaurant where he worked as a dishwasher. Jason Hoolans, a skinhead with ties to the Heritage Front and COTC, kicked him in the head with his steel-toed boots.[140] As one witness put it, it was as if he were kicking a soccer ball.[141] A father of three, Vinasithamby fell into a coma, the blows having caused a blood clot to form in his brain. When he regained consciousness, he was paralyzed on his left side.[142] The beating also left him with brain damage.[143] Unable to work, Vinasithamby had to support his family with a monthly workers' compensation payment of $1,000, while his rent alone amounted to $800.[144] "I am proud of my accomplishments and proud of my country," Hoolans would boast in court, where he was supported by Droege and nearly a dozen other Heritage Front and COTC associates. "I am proud of my race."[145] After pleading guilty to aggravated assault, he nonetheless expressed remorse to the court. Judge Hugh Locke sentenced him to four years in prison.[146]

Other violent attacks occurred in Toronto during the same period: on June 10, thirty-two-year-old Gunalan Muthulingam, also from Sri Lanka, died after being hit on the head with a beer bottle on the street; ten days later, another Sri Lankan immigrant, Ganeshamoorthy Vigenswaramoorthy, was seriously injured after being hit with broken beer bottles by two unidentified white men.[147] In both cases, witnesses attributed the attacks to racism, and Toronto Constable Luciano Zeni admitted that hate crimes were on the rise due to the growth of groups like the Heritage Front and COTC.[148] Operation Governor was useless in preventing this series of racist attacks, and never did anything to identify or apprehend the perpetrators.

During this same period, Elisse Hategan began to have doubts about what Grant Bristow was doing. One day, she asked him why his harassment campaign was targeting women. "They're the easiest targets, the first to break. They're more emotional, much more likely to totally lose it," he said.[149]

Hategan, who was still a teenager at the time, also began to question the Heritage Front's ideology when she found herself being pressured to have sex with men in the movement. At the same time, the organization had begun harassing members of the LGBTQ community.[150] Bristow, she wrote, "often called male ARA activists faggot as a rule of thumb no matter what their sexual orientation."[151] Yet at age 17, Hategan realized that she was a lesbian. "One of the activists they targeted was someone that I had a crush on. And it was a woman," she would explain many years later.[152]

According to Droege, Hategan only wanted to withdraw from the harassment campaign after her voice was recognized by anti-racist activist Ruth MacKenzie. "Hategan told me that Bristow was pressuring her into continuing the harassment activities against her will and he threatened her with a 'white van ride' in the summer of 1993,"[153] he recounted, a direct reference to what had transpired with Tyrone Mason. By this time, Hategan had begun taking notes about Bristow and was trying to dig into his past. When the informant learned of this, he asked Droege to deal with the young woman. Droege recounts the exchange he had with Bristow:

> Bristow sought me out and asked me to organize a party to break into and ransack her residence to retrieve her notes on him. I declined. This was the first time that Bristow was ever agitated with a decision of mine. Bristow was a person who was frequently at odds with people but this was the first time he had become visibly angry with me. He said he had done a lot for the movement and individuals, and gone to a lot of expense in doing so, but all people ever did was question his motives and character.[154]

In the summer of 1993, Hategan began secretly working with certain anti-racist groups. "I spied on the Heritage Front for four months," the young woman would explain.[155] She would later inform the police and the justice system of the criminal activities of a number of members of the organization. "Despite these meetings and affidavits, no real investigation or prosecution took place," she said.[156] Worse still:

> After repeated appeals to the OPP (Ontario Provincial Police) and the [RCMP] were ignored, I was officially denied admission into the Witness Protection Program. [...] I would later find out from an insider [...] that a CSIS mandate had circulated advising police

forces to deny me protection and ignore my information, even at the risk of Canadian taxpayers and the threat to my own life.[157]

According to a report on CBC's *The Fifth Estate*, "When Elisse came out and said she was going to tell the truth, CSIS was saying they were going to get out and discredit her because at least Hategan was pointing the finger at Grant Bristow ... 'we'll tear her to shreds.'"[158] Bristow's handler would acknowledge to SIRC that he had "probably told" police agencies that Hategan could not be trusted.[159] As Elisse Hategan explains, her whistleblowing still had some results:

> On November 24, 1993, my defection from the Heritage Front became public. In March of 1994, I testified in the Federal Court against Wolfgang Droege, Garry Schipper and Ken Barker in a contempt of court proceeding. Despite the sometimes vicious cross-examination, Judge Tremblay-Lamer found my testimony credible, pronounced these individuals guilty and sentenced them to prison terms. [...] During these proceedings two incidents were somewhat disturbing, to say the least. Grant Bristow was providing audiotapes and elements to feed the lawyers representing the Heritage Front in a failed attempt to discredit me. [...] Bristow was leading the charge to ensure that neo-Nazis would not be sent to jail.[160]

The informant also had to contend with a new development: Droege was now facing a lengthy prison sentence after being brought to trial on aggravated assault charges in Toronto.[161] If the Heritage Front leader was found guilty, Bristow would have been the obvious choice to succeed him as head of the organization, a prospect that did not sit well with the CSIS informant, who was apparently beginning to look for a way to return to "normal life."[162] By then, Bristow had lost his job at Kuehne and Nagel after the media identified him as a member of the Heritage Front. CSIS stepped in to compensate for the loss in salary, paying its agent provocateur $30,000 a year for fifteen months.[163]

In March 1994, Grant Bristow left the Heritage Front. The CSIS informant could "no longer abide the stress of living two separate lives," according to SIRC. CSIS and Bristow fabricated an excuse for the informant to leave the group on good terms: Bristow told Droege that he had reluctantly accepted a job in eastern Canada, which was obviously not true.[164] After five years, Operation Governor had run its course.¹⁶⁵ When Elisse Hategan appeared before the parliamentary committee, she was unimpressed with Grant Bristow's service record:

> Not only should he be charged for some of his criminal activities, but he did not reduce the effectiveness of the Heritage Front. He increased its capacity. I was there and I saw what he did. He never testified against any of these individuals, and his work led to no arrests of neo-Nazis. I repeat—zero arrests.¹⁶⁶

On August 12, 1994, Grant Bristow received a phone call from *Toronto Sun* reporter Bill Dunphy, who informed him that he was about to reveal his role as a CSIS informant and invited him to give his side of the story. By the time the *Sun* ran a front-page story on the case two days later, CSIS had stashed Bristow and his immediate family away in a Toronto hotel.¹⁶⁷ The revelation of Grant Bristow's dual membership in the Heritage Front and the Canadian Secret Intelligence Service created a huge media-political storm that raged from coast to coast for several months. The *Globe and Mail*'s Kirk Martin was outraged and placed the Bristow case in the context of previous RCMP scandals: "It was never meant to happen again. The barn burning and political dirty tricks that turned Canada's security service into a national disgrace were supposed to have ended in the mid-1970s."¹⁶⁸

The *Toronto Star* took advantage of the storm to paint a compelling portrait:

> Grant Bristow stood 6 feet 2 inches, smoked five packs of Du Mauriers a day and loudly announced his hatred for Jews, blacks, East Indians, Indians, gays and liberals of any kind. [...] Bristow always drank coffee with lots of sugar, and never touched alcohol; he told people he was a recovering alcoholic. The slightest taste of alcohol, Bristow would say, could knock him off the wagon. [...] Those who knew him in the Heritage Front now wonder if this was all part of the careful maintenance of Bristow's facade—he never revealed details of his life, and never allowed his tongue to be loosened. [...] Droege would request information on an anti-racist agitator and within a day or two, Bristow would come back with files that could include such confidential documents as criminal records, credit histories and even FBI files.¹⁶⁹

8. A BIG THANK YOU FROM THE NEO-NAZIS

With the media spotlight now upon them, members of the Heritage Front had a field day making shocking statements about Bristow. One of these, Ken Barker, did not hesitate to say that "Grant provided the wood, the fire starter, the matches, and gave the order to start the fire."[170] Holocaust denier Ernst Zündel recall how

> [Bristow] constantly discussed harassment campaigns against the left. Bristow would laugh uproariously when he picked up some juicy bit of information. Whenever a person talks about violence or illegality, I smell an agent. This was a man who hated the left. He was not a professional.[171]

The *Globe and Mail* reported that one of the agent provocateur's favourite tactics was to break into the voicemail systems of anti-racist activists. Taking down the names and phone numbers of recruits who left messages, he would then delete the message and call the recruit himself, posing as the anti-racist activist. On the phone, he would ask the recruit to make up a flyer with the names and phone numbers of apparent "white supremacists" who the public was called on to target with whatever action they thought was appropriate. In reality, they were the names of anti-racist activists who Bristow was targeting for harassment.[172] Gary Schipper, a Heritage Front leader, said Bristow provided the names, addresses, and phone numbers of roughly sixty anti-racists.[173]

What's more, the *Globe and Mail* reported that Bristow was also involved in producing propaganda for the far-right group.[174] The informant also allegedly provided neo-Nazi Tony McAleer with the phone number and address of Dr Michael Elterman, a Vancouver psychologist who was also president of the Canadian Jewish Congress's Pacific Chapter in 1992. One summer day, Elterman found blood poured on the doorstep to his home. While it was never ascertained who had carried out this act of harassment, the incident coincided with Bristow taking a trip to Vancouver.[175] Doug Christie, a BC lawyer and Holocaust denier who defended several far-right activists in court, also claimed that the agent provocateur offered to provide him with the names and addresses of prominent members of the Vancouver-area Jewish community. "He said we should take the war to the enemy."[176]

Heritage Front members also spoke of Bristow's generosity. "He never seemed to have any problem coming up with $100 or $200 whenever somebody needed it," said one of the group's leaders. Other members recalled that the CSIS informant often picked up the tab at restaurants, even when there were a dozen people at the table.[177] Although his annual salary at Kuehne and Nagel was only $30,000, Bristow never seemed short on money. All in all, Gerry Lincoln, one of the organization's leaders, had a very positive assessment of Bristow's time with the Heritage Front: "The positive things he did for us outweigh any negative things. I'd like to have 10 more (men) like him. […] With his money and his knowledge he was a big help."[178]

It wasn't just Heritage Front members who felt the informant made a huge difference to the far-right group: "The Heritage Front would not have come to be the group that it was without his knowledge," according to Rodney Bobiwash of Klanbusters.[179]

It was with a growing sense of shock and dismay that members of minority communities targeted by the far right followed the ongoing series of allegations, each more dramatic than the last. An anxiety that Bernie Farber, spokesperson for the Canadian Jewish Congress, summed up as follows: "I think there are many of us, both within the Jewish community and other ethnic communities, that have now a level of concern as to whether or not the possibility exists that there are other Grant Bristows."[180]

B'nai Brith even went so far as to suggest that CSIS be disbanded altogether if the allegations against Bristow proved true. According to Frank Dimant, the organization's executive vice president, the intelligence agency endangered a significant number of people by disseminating their personal information within the "international hate network," adding:

> I feel a sense of betrayal. I feel a government agency that was entrusted with a tremendous amount of responsibility in terms of intelligence gathering, may have turned into an instrument which has helped to promote hatred and racism in this country.[181]

While CSIS and its informant were being pilloried in the media, the intelligence agency was focused on caring for Bristow's mental health. CSIS went so far as to dispatch a crisis management team to the hotel where "the source" was holed up with his immediate family. A doctor, a psychologist, and a public relations expert were on hand to help Bristow make it through the ordeal. The agent provocateur didn't seem to find it so funny being in the spotlight. "The media assassinated me," he would complain a few years later.[182]

As usual, CSIS refused to confirm anything about Operation Governor, saying only that it had not broken any laws.[183] On the political front, the

8. A BIG THANK YOU FROM THE NEO-NAZIS

federal government could not ignore the growing controversy. Herb Gray, the Solicitor General of Canada, lost no time in asking SIRC to investigate the Grant Bristow affair … and then remained silent.[184] It should be noted that SIRC was at that time headed by Michel Robert, a former president of the then-governing federal Liberal Party. A lawyer for the federal government during the 1970s, Mr. Robert had also played a leading role in Ottawa's stalling tactics to limit the scope of the Keable Commission and to impede the McDonald Commission.[185] One should not be surprised that such an energetic opponent of "government transparency" should end up being handed the reins at CSIS's supposed watchdog.

The Reform Party, which was directly implicated in the affair, was the political party that reacted most strongly to the controversy. As Reform spokesperson Val Meredith pointed out, "It is often a fine line between a highly placed source and an agent provocateur. […] If we're talking about someone who organized the group, then what we have is the taxpayer paying for an individual to organize a subversive group."[186] He added that, "The big question here is: Would the organization have existed and would it have been founded without this guy?"[187]

The party's regional coordinator for central Ontario, Andrew Flint, for whom it would appear the entire affair had some educational value, agreed:

> I'm not sure what would scare me more—knowing he was in the Heritage Front or knowing he was a CSIS agent. […] If we have that sort of thing happening here, it says a great deal about our freedoms. Our system may not be what we think it is.[188]

The Heritage Front was quick to throw in its two cents' worth. Peter Mitrevski, a member of the group, claimed that Bristow had insisted on standing next to Preston Manning at Reform rallies and that he was very enthusiastic about infiltrating the political party.[189] Referring to the Grant Bristow affair as "Canada's Watergate," Preston Manning raised the possibility that the damage done to Reform's image by the infiltration of Heritage Front members might have resulted in his party failing to become the Official Opposition in the House of Commons in the October 25, 1993 federal election that brought Jean Chrétien's Liberal Party to power.[190] Leading figures in Reform alleged that CSIS passed on personal information about its members to other political parties, most notably the then-governing Progressive Conservative Party of Canada.[191] "CSIS, knowingly or unknowingly, may have abused the democratic process in this country," Meredith argued.¹⁹²

Unsurprisingly, those implicated by these allegations were quick to deny them: "CSIS never asked for or received any information about any political party," insisted Doug Lewis.¹⁹³ As the crisis unfolded, Prime Minister Jean Chrétien was even forced to respond publicly:

> I have been in politics for some time and I have never known of any spying. I am the leader of this government and the accusations come from the Reform Party. We don't need that. We don't need spies to know what they are saying. We don't need to know more. We have enough to eliminate them.¹⁹⁴

In its report, SIRC cleared CSIS by concluding that the intelligence service had not spied on the Reform Party, having apparently found no evidence to that effect.¹⁹⁵ The Review Committee, however, acknowledged the limitations of its investigation, confirming its remarkable impotence: "Though we did not conduct an intrusive investigation of people unconnected to CSIS, Bristow, or the Heritage Front, we did follow every lead we discovered regarding the infiltration of the Reform Party."¹⁹⁶

The Grant Bristow affair took on a new dimension when the *Toronto Star* quoted a classified document—a CSIS memo to federal government ministers—on the front page of its August 19, 1994 edition, suggesting that CSIS had spied on the CBC in the spring of 1993.¹⁹⁷ At the time, CSIS had learned "from a reliable source" that researchers for the television program *The Fifth Estate* were trying to obtain information about the presence of neo-Nazis in the Canadian Armed Forces. The "reliable source"—obviously Bristow—told CSIS that researcher Howard Goldenthal was trying to obtain information from Wolfgang Droege about whether any members of the Airborne Regiment had links to racist organizations in Canada.¹⁹⁸

On August 23, 1994, CSIS wrote to the *Toronto Star* requesting that it return the classified document. Thomas J. Bradley, Director General of the CSIS Secretariat, stated that he had "reasonable grounds to believe" that the newspaper "may retain certain official documents in violation of Section 4 of the Official Secrets Act."¹⁹⁹ Note that this law (which was replaced by the Security of Information Act in 2001) provided for a maximum penalty of fourteen years in prison for such a "violation." Two RCMP agents also visited the *Toronto Star* offices to request the return of the document. RCMP Sgt. Fraser Fiegenwald even warned the newspaper's lawyer, Gord Cameron, that he could be charged under the Official Secrets Act if he advised the *Toronto Star* not to return the document.[200] "I do find some irony in the fact that after *The Star* discovers and reports that CSIS is spying on the CBC, it finds itself part of a police investigation," observed Lou Clancy, editor of the paper.[201] Instead of complying with CSIS and RCMP requests, the paper put the disputed document in a sealed envelope before filing it in court.

On August 25, Brian McInnis, former press secretary to Solicitor General Doug Lewis, was arrested by the RCMP, as federal police also searched his home, seizing various documents. McInnis, himself a former journalist, now also faced charges under the Official Secrets Act.[202] Feeling the police pressure closing in on him, shortly prior to his arrest McInnis had admitted to a CTV reporter that he was the one who had leaked the information about Bristow to the media.[203] CTV's Bill Rodgers explained why McInnis wanted to go public with his version of events: "Trials under the [Official Secrets] act are carried out in secret. He wanted the public to know why he did what he did—that it wasn't for money, or anything like that."[204]

McInnis told CTV that he was deeply "disgusted" that a CSIS informant helped create the Heritage Front.[205] "The law was broken twice. Once by them and once by me," he explained.[206] On September 2, the RCMP were at CTV's offices with a warrant authorizing them to seize all documents related to the McInnis interview, but the TV station had, like the *Toronto Star*, already turned over all its tapes and notes to the legal authorities.[207]

In an article published in the *Ottawa Citizen*, David Harris, former head of strategic planning at CSIS, set out to put the media on trial by outlining the possible consequences of exposing state secrets:

> In Canada, emphasis on leaks will undermine agent recruitment by CSIS. Terrorist informers recognize that exposure on CBC Prime Time News inhibits life expectancy. There are probably lives in danger now—something to recall when leakers complain that investigations hamper their lifestyle. At a dangerous crossroads in the history of political violence, established operations may dry up if agents-in-place get cold feet.[208]

The unverifiable "lives at risk" argument being made by the former CSIS official was just crude moral blackmail to get the media to fall in line. The intelligence agency was probably banking on the fact that journalists would likely have more scruples than CSIS officials, who, as we have seen, went to great lengths to deprive Elisse Hategan of much-needed protection after she turned her back on the Heritage Front. The real purpose of Harris's media foray was not to protect lives but to protect CSIS secrets—and perhaps his own interests as a former CSIS official—and perhaps a few careers as well ...

In its report, SIRC concluded that CSIS "did not spy on the CBC, its journalists, or any of its other staff," before making this important qualification:

> We are of the opinion that some of the information collected and reported was not "strictly-necessary." If the Service wanted to update the Minister on the threat to national security presented by white supremacists in the Canadian Armed Forces, it could have done so without reference to a CBC program.[209]

In the end, no charges were brought against McInnis, as we would learn much later.[210] The whole story looked like an attempt to muzzle the media—which for once was doing its job—through legal intimidation.

SIRC's effectiveness was called into question again in the wake of the *Toronto Star*'s revelations that the Review Committee had written to Solicitor General Doug Lewis in 1992, warning him that Bristow's activities could "generate controversy."[211] Liberal MP Derek Lee, who chaired the House of Commons Subcommittee on National Security, observed:

> Hypothetically, if SIRC reported on an issue two or three years ago and there was no response inside government or inside CSIS, it raises the issue of whether or not SIRC is effective in what it's doing, whether we're getting value for our money.[212]

The same parliamentary committee held hearings, beginning in September 1994, to try to get to the bottom of the "assortment of allegations" about Operation Governor.[213] Reform MP Val Meredith, also a member of the parliamentary committee, prepared a list of 149 questions she wanted to ask Bristow. But there was a catch: as Lee was forced to admit, the parliamentary committee had no idea where the former CSIS informant was at the time. It was difficult to see how the subcommittee could issue him with a subpoena.[214]

The work of the House of Commons subcommittee was complemented by the launch of two investigations by CSIS Inspector General David Peel. The first looked at the intelligence agency's use of "human sources" and the second at the handling of "sensitive" national security documents in the office of former Solicitor General Doug Lewis during the final months of the

Progressive Conservative government.[215] Several organizations, including the Canadian Civil Liberties Association, the Canadian Labour Congress, the Canadian Union of Postal Workers, and the Simon Wiesenthal Centre, also called on Ottawa to launch an independent inquiry into the Grant Bristow affair, which could have potentially taken the form of a "mini-McDonald Commission."[216]

SIRC's report was released on December 15, 1994. According to Michel Robert, Chair of the Review Committee, it was probably the most extensive report ever produced by the organization since its creation ten years earlier. Robert said that SIRC consulted more than 25,000 documents and interviewed at least eighty-seven witnesses to produce the 200-page document.[217] In its report, SIRC revealed that CSIS had paid Grant Bristow nearly $80,000 over a seven-year period, not including expenses incurred by "the source" in connection with Operation Governor, averaging $260 a month, all of which was reimbursed by CSIS.[218] SIRC estimated that Bristow funded various Heritage Front activities to the tune of nearly $1,000, including helping pay for office expenses and the movement's legal defence fund.[219] Adding up all the money CSIS paid to the agent provocateur during Operation Governor—including the $30,000 compensation paid for the informant's loss of employment—the total came out to over $127,000. "There is no way of determining objectively if the Source was overpaid," SIRC admitted.[220] However, the Review Committee seemed to believe that CSIS "received value for money."[221] At least that is what the committee's admiring account of Bristow's various contributions to white supremacist surveillance in Canada and elsewhere suggests:

> Between the Years 1989 and 1994, Human source coverage has provided the Service with a high volume of quality-information concerning white supremacist activities in Canada, the United States and, to some extent, Europe. This coverage enabled the Service to monitor developing trends within the violent racist movement as well as to warn of potential public confrontations involving violence ... CSIS information primarily from [the Source] led to the arrest and deportation of a number of leading international white supremacists.[222]

Yet SIRC was unable to say whether Bristow's intelligence led to even one arrest.[223] Nonetheless, SIRC insisted that Bristow's work on Operation

Governor "deserves praise," and concluded

> We are satisfied that both the Source and his handlers in this "affair" discharged their duties in a competent and responsible manner. Both men, throughout this period, believed that they were doing valuable work helping to protect Canadian society from a cancer growing within. They deserve our thanks.[224]

SIRC also commented on guidelines issued by the Solicitor General of Canada on October 30, 1989, concerning the use of "human sources." The guidelines stated that CSIS informants "should be instructed not to act as 'agents provocateurs' or in any way incite or encourage illegal activity."[225] In short: do not do what Marc-André Boivin did ... The level of guidance provided to CSIS agents was initially described by the Review Committee as "seriously deficient," failing to clearly address a number of important questions, such as,

> What kind of a proactive role is acceptable for a source in an organization targeted by CSIS?
>
> Is it appropriate to have a source direct or be a leader within an organization or movement?
>
> Should sources be engaged in counter measures which would serve to destroy, rather than maintain terrorist groups or movements?
>
> Do the benefits of maintaining a source outweigh the benefits to be gained by taking measures (i.e. with Police Forces) to destroy the group?[226]

To these questions, SIRC offered its own answers:

> If CSIS were to use only "passive" sources in the racist right, then the quality of the information available to the intelligence community and to police forces would be considerably less useful at best or useless at worst. Most good sources are active. [...] We are also cognizant of the danger that in destroying one group, as opposed to watching it, another one which is worse may be created. [...] We realize that the best way to avoid criticism is to do nothing. Therefore, we do not advocate detailed rules that would unduly limit CSIS in its duty

8. A BIG THANK YOU FROM THE NEO-NAZIS

to protect the Canadian public and State. We recommend, rather, Ministerial guidelines that require CSIS management to carefully weigh the benefits and the dangers of each human source operation on a regular basis; taking due account of the special circumstances of each case.[227]

As such, the Review Committee seemed to hold that the Canadian secret service acted wisely in not destroying the Heritage Front. While recommending the preservation of "right-wing racist groups" according to the logic of "better the devil you know," SIRC might as well have suggested that CSIS give itself a new name better suited to the true nature of its mission: the "National Security Threat Maintenance Service"!

SIRC even had the gall to criticize certain media outlets in its report, even though its mandate is limited to reviewing the activities of Canada's secret services. In particular, the Review Committee singled out the CBC for having broadcast "confusing and ultimately misleading information" from a former immigration officer, which allegedly "discredited CSIS, the Government of Canada, and the various Police Forces and other agencies involved in opposing the racist groups in Canada."[228]

In the end, the Review Committee's report lined up with the highly positive assessment of Operation Governor by CSIS senior officials. Just a week after the SIRC report was tabled, Ward Elcock, Director of CSIS, went on the record saying that, "We at CSIS have considered our investigation of the Heritage Front a success."[229] Driving this point home, he reiterated that "We got a good human source, under control, in a high level in the organization. Did Canadians get the best bang for their buck? Sure."[230]

Elcock was being modest. After all, Grant Bristow did more than just gather intelligence on the far right; he also spied on and harassed anti-racist activists and got involved with an opposition party with seats in Parliament. In short, this hyperactive "human source" was doing the work of three informants, all for the price of one!

The CSIS Director also signaled that the Review Committee's findings did not necessitate any significant changes in the way CSIS operates. But while Elcock chose to maintain this denial, the same could not be said for many of those directly affected by Grant Bristow's activities, who did not mince words about the SIRC report. B'nai Brith, for example, denounced the "inadequate management by CSIS of Bristow's activities, particularly with respect to the harassment campaign against anti-racists."[231] Preston Manning of the Reform Party launched a full-throttle attack on the oversight committee's report:

> It is clear from reading the report that the members of SIRC lack both the competence and the objectivity required to safeguard Canadian internal security interests or to provide effective review of an agency such as CSIS. In our view, they should be removed from their positions immediately, without compensation.[232]

According to constitutional and civil rights lawyer Clayton Ruby, "It seems that SIRC has not yet figured out the exact difference between a watchdog and a cheerleader."[233] Mr. Ruby also explained why ARA activists were never heard by SIRC:

> When SIRC approached Hategan and the Anti-Racist Action group for information, they were delighted to be asked. But because they had no money and feared criminal charges might be laid against them out of their clashes with the Heritage Front, they made a simple request. Would SIRC, whose annual budget is $1,409,000, please be good enough to pay a few hundred dollars for Paul Copeland, their lawyer, to attend with them when they were questioned? No, they would not. […] Was SIRC pleased to avoid information that might put CSIS in a bad light?[234]

Bernie Farber of the Canadian Jewish Congress was stunned to learn from the SIRC report that a member of the Heritage Front was planning to make an attempt on his and his colleagues' lives. In its report, the Review Committee noted that Bristow learned on October 26, 1993, that a member of the group was planning to "take out some people" at the Canadian Jewish Congress offices in Toronto.[235] CSIS forwarded the tip to the Metropolitan Toronto Police three days later. The white supremacist in question, whom Bristow considered to be unstable, never carried out his "plan"—he was arrested for an armed robbery at a Donut Shop shortly thereafter.[236] There was no indication in SIRC's report that the individual in question was arrested by police for planning an antisemitic massacre, but the oversight committee wrote that "Source's efforts ultimately worked to enhance the protection of the Jewish community against the racists."[237] Yet, as noted by Canadian Jewish Congress president Irving Abella, "They had information of a plot to assassinate individuals by name and we were not told. We were not able to take precautions, increase security or deviate from our usual day-to-day activities to protect ourselves."[238] As he explained, "That was quite scary, to find out that they had ignored the target because they were concerned about keeping their mole secret."[239]

Responding to the controversy, SIRC's Michel Robert argued that the law prevents CSIS from notifying individuals that they are being targeted.[240] In fact, as seen in the Marc-André Boivin case, the law allows CSIS to disclose information to the police "where the information may be used in the investigation or prosecution of an alleged contravention of any law of Canada."[241] In this case, however, Toronto police Sergeant Wayne Cotgreave stated that he had concluded that the risk to the targeted individuals was minimal. "I suppose that in hindsight the fact that nothing occurred proved us right," he said.[242] In short, it was only *after the fact* that the authorities had confirmation that there was not necessarily a real threat—but the risk to several people's lives was not taken seriously prior to that, either.

The SIRC report continued to attract attention when Elisse Hategan appeared before the House of Commons Subcommittee on National Security in June 1995. The former Heritage Front member called the report "a cover-up" and called for a public inquiry into the Grant Bristow affair.[243] During her testimony, Hategan listed the many inaccuracies she had identified in the SIRC report, starting with statements about the harassment campaign against anti-racists:

> Despite the claims made in the SIRC report, this campaign was not a defensive measure or an information-gathering exercise. It was a concerted effort to harass individuals, have them fired from their jobs, and put their personal safety in jeopardy. [...] It said in the SIRC report that he would change certain telephone numbers or addresses, except for really well-known ... that didn't happen. All the names that I checked out, addresses—the people were there. [...] It says in there that he admits he called people, but pretty much only two. He called more than that. He called tons of people. I was on the line. He broke into answering machines a lot.[244]

In short, SIRC failed to live up to its mandate. It was not the first time this had happened—nor would it be the last ... In fact, the Parliamentary Committee's report was not as kind to CSIS as the SIRC had been, noting that "SIRC was supposed to be the watchdog of the security agency but failed to report accurately, it failed to be that watchdog and it failed to act independently. The whole process was flawed."[245]

The Parliamentary Committee also criticized SIRC for being too accommodating to CSIS and for failing to look into important aspects of Operation Governor. However, the committee, which was dominated by the governing Liberal Party, was unable to reach a consensus as to their recommendations. Reform and Bloc members felt that the law should be amended to allow CSIS to notify third parties of impending danger or of the infiltration of political organizations. As for the Liberals, they were more focused on the recommendation that CSIS no longer be able to use informants involved in illegal or improper activities.[246] But the intelligence service was unmoved by the various options proposed. "The checks and balances that govern CSIS are comprehensive and complete," CSIS Director Ward Elcock smugly concluded.[247]

In the summer of 1995, David Peel, the Inspector General of CSIS, finally admitted that Canada's secret service did not seem to have fully appreciated the damage to civil liberties caused by its handling of moles. According to the Inspector, "Effectiveness appeared to be their primary concern."[248] The notion of effectiveness must be understood here solely in terms of the collection of security intelligence by the Canadian secret service. But how many anti-racist and minority activists had their lives destroyed in the name of CSIS's effectiveness? Didn't Bristow's effectiveness go hand in hand with the effectiveness of the Heritage Front, to which he had devoted his heart and soul?

Like Marc-Andre Boivin, Grant Bristow's name would reappear in the Canadian news on several occasions after the storm had passed. First, in the spring of 1995, the *Toronto Star* finally managed to track him down. The former CSIS informant had put on weight, shaved off his legendary moustache, and was living with his family in Erin Ridge, a quiet suburban Alberta town, under the name Nathan Black, his new identity provided by the Canadian secret service. The family had taken up residence in a 2,000-square-foot house with a triple garage containing two vehicles, courtesy of the taxpayers. The *Star* further revealed that the state was paying Bristow and his family $3,000 a month to buy their silence. His wife was even able to enjoy unlimited long-distance phone calls and several trips a year—all expenses paid—to visit her family in Mississauga, Ontario—all thanks to the intelligence agency.[249]

Grant Bristow's name surfaced again in the media after a court ruled on the fate of the kidnappers and torturers of Tyrone Mason, the Heritage

8. A BIG THANK YOU FROM THE NEO-NAZIS

Front member that the CSIS agent provocateur had so kindly pointed out. Like Elisse Hategan, Mason had reported Bristow to the police and, at their request, had agreed to set a trap for him. He had invited the CSIS informant, along with Paul Graham and James Dawson, two Heritage Front members who had been harassing him, to come and discuss his potential court testimony in his apartment, which had been bugged by the police. Only Graham and Dawson showed up, but Detective McPherson told him that he already had enough evidence to charge Bristow without needing an audio recording. The Canadian intelligence mole was never charged, of course.[250]

As the trial approached in November 1995, Mason's assailants, the Fischer brothers and Drew Maynard, attempted to compel Grant Bristow, his handler Al Treddenick, and Canada's top intelligence official Ward Elcock, to testify. Ontario Court Justice Ted Wren refused to hear them, but said, "Mr. Bristow could very well be the subject of charges of attempting to obstruct the cause of justice."[251] A suggestion that was never acted upon. In fact, the trial itself never took place: the charges against Maynard were withdrawn due to unreasonable delays, while the Fischer brothers each got off with thirty days in jail after pleading guilty. One could say that the story was hushed up—especially given that Mason was never interviewed by SIRC, which devoted only five short lines to the incident in its report on Operation Governor.[252] Case closed!

While the controversy surrounding the Bristow affair seemed to have receded, CSIS continued to keep tabs on some of Canada's most prominent far-right figures, such as the notorious Holocaust denier Ernst Zündel, who was monitored under a top-secret program called Operation Vulva.[253] Zündel had long been the target of anti-fascists due to his prominent role in international antisemitic and Holocaust denial circles; at one point one group even sent him a home-made letter-bomb. In May 1995, the Toronto police bomb squad detonated one of these packages, creating a large crater in the porch of his home. Unperturbed by this incident, CSIS continued to send Zündel's packages to Ottawa for inspection, using regular flights to do so. "So what do you think was likely to happen if a bomb went off while we were transporting his mail by commercial jet?" asked John Farrell, a former Canada Post auxiliary inspector who was involved in Operation Vulva. "Farrell rang the alarm, but no one at CSIS bothered to listen," commented journalist Andrew Mitrovica.[254] And to think, this agency is responsible for Canada's "national security" ...

By 1997, the Heritage Front was a shadow of what it had been under Grant Bristow. The parcel bombs may have instilled fear in some white supremacists,[255] but it was first and foremost the grassroots efforts of Anti-Racist Action and other antifascists, who were able to mobilize hundreds of people to come out to militant demonstrations against the Front, that spelled the end of the organization.[256] This was of course exacerbated by several of the most important members being sentenced to prison, creating a leadership vacuum. "The people attracted to white supremacist groups tend to be sheep, and right now they are leaderless, rudderless," said Bernie Farber of the Canadian Jewish Congress.[257] One tangible result was a significant drop in the number of hate crimes, from 302 in 1995 to 175 in 1996—a decrease of 43%.[258]

In 2004, more than a decade after the scandal had broken, Grant Bristow spoke out for the first time, in a lengthy interview with journalist Andrew Mitrovica for *The Walrus* magazine. "Now is the time that I can say, 'Not guilty,'" said Bristow, who insisted that he never stopped wanting to make the world "a less hateful place."[259] In April 2005, the *Globe and Mail* reported that Bristow was living somewhere in Western Canada, supporting himself by teaching part-time, working as a tax accountant, and lecturing to police and security organizations on undercover work.[260]

More than twenty years after the end of Operation Governor, the far right is on the rise again across Canada. This time, much of the hate is fuelled by Islamophobia. It is not known how many of today's racist activists are also in the employ of CSIS or various law enforcement bodies. In the next chapter, however, we will see how one CSIS agent provocateur did his part to help fuel prejudice and fear against the Muslim community.

9. Terror Threats, Courtesy of CSIS

Long before the emergence of Daesh, the Paris attacks, and the subsequent spike of racism in the West, a curious figure had emerged in Quebec as the leader of "radical Islam"—even though he was actually employed by CSIS all the while. Like honey attracts flies, CSIS seems to attract shady snitches, the kind of overzealous informants who deliver more than their client has ordered. This was true of Grant Bristow, and it was just as true of Joseph Gilles Breault, aka "Dr Youssef Mouammar," aka "Abou Jihad."

Born in 1942 in the north of Montreal, Joseph Gilles Breault adopted the name Youssef Mouammar after converting to Islam around 1984. He subsequently became active in the Al-Oumma Al-Islamiah mosque, located on St. Laurent Boulevard in Montreal. Breault first worked as an informant for the Montreal police anti-terrorist squad in the 1980s. All we know about this collaboration is that the informant helped the police during an investigation about arms trafficking.

It should be noted, however, that SIRC's 1997–1998 Annual Report states that Joseph Gilles Breault "was a controversial figure before he was recruited by [CSIS]," without providing further details.[1] The date of his first collaboration with CSIS has never been made public, but the information available would tend to indicate that everything began in the mid-1980s.[2] It should be noted that even before he delivered his first tip, Breault was viewed with suspicion by members of the Canadian intelligence community, similar to how many within CSIS had initially doubted that Grant Bristow could be trusted. Yet CSIS eventually put these qualms about Breault aside, just as they had done with Bristow. Because CSIS apparently had big plans for Breault—the agency would work to make this informant a key figure in Montreal's Muslim community, as journalist André Noël explains:

> CSIS took him under its wing. The federal agency was in need of Muslim informants. CSIS rolled out the red carpet, while helping "Youssef" increase his influence in his new religious community. Breault rose to the top of several organizations.[3]

In an intervention before the National Assembly's Standing Committee on Public Finance, Liberal MNA Fatima Houda-Pépin, Quebec's first Muslim woman MNA and a staunch opponent of Muslim fundamentalism, presented a summary of the research she had conducted on the various organizations headed by Joseph Gilles Breault. The MP revealed that between 1986 and 1991, Breault created and dissolved no less than fifteen numbered companies, corporations, and foundations with unclear corporate names, of which he was the sole proprietor. These companies, which had highly variable lifespans (between three months and sixteen years), had impressive names—such as the International Islamic Foundation of Quebec, the Community of the Muslim Nation of Greater Montreal, or the International Muslim Foundation of Canada—and were officially intended to provide representation to the media, among other things.[4]

Even though all these organizations were artificial creations, with no real influence or importance, they helped to position Joseph Gilles Breault as one of the main media figures with whom the general public in Quebec would associate the Montreal Muslim community from the late 1980s to the early 1990s. This role was attested to by journalist Richard Hétu of *La Presse*:

> In recent years, this native Quebecker has become one of the leading spokespersons for the Muslim community here. Making good use of his own instinct for self-promotion and the ignorance of the media, he has been quoted about the coup in Algeria, the Gulf War, the death of Ayatollah Khomeini, the Salman Rushdie affair.[5]

In all, research in the archives of Quebec and Canadian newspapers has identified no less than forty-seven articles published in major newspapers—including the *National Post* in Toronto, the *Vancouver Sun*, and the *Montreal Gazette*—between 1987 and 1995 in which Joseph Gilles Breault was quoted as a spokesperson for Islamic organizations, most frequently the Canadian Muslim International Foundation (CMIF). But the informant's media profile was not limited to the major newspapers. In 1991, Joseph Gilles Breault had his own radio show, having purchased airtime on CJMS to "promote Islam." Breault was also the editor of a monthly magazine called *Le Monde islamique*, which once published a text arguing that "AIDS is a punishment for modern society at a time when homosexuality [and] drug addiction have become the norm."[6]

Ironically, many of Breault's public interventions were putatively aimed

9. TERROR THREATS, COURTESY OF CSIS

at defending the image of members of the Muslim community in the media. The CMIF—of which Breault was both president and spokesperson—was dedicated to educating the public about Islam, particularly in the French-speaking world. By the late 1980s, CMIF was actively cementing its own legitimacy by presenting itself as a lobby group dedicated to defending the interests of the Muslim community. For example, in March 1988, when Radio-Canada television broadcast a report alleging an Iranian connection to Montreal drug traffickers, Breault was among the spokespersons for Muslim organizations who demanded an apology from the public broadcaster, which was accused of having displayed a lack of judgment as to the choice of images accompanying the story.[7]

A talented actor, Joseph Gilles Breault seemed so well suited to play the role of defender of the Muslim community that the Quebec government adopted, on September 26, 1990, a decree authorizing him to exercise responsibility for keeping civil registers of births, marriages, and deaths of Muslims in Montreal, on behalf of his religious corporation, the Community of the Muslim Nation of Greater Montreal.[8] The informant was now sitting on a veritable gold mine of personal information about members of the Montreal Muslim community, much to the delight of CSIS. The Quebec government's decision was all the more surprising given that Breault was a controversial figure within the Muslim community itself. The year previous, the "spokesperson" had been publicly disavowed by nine Quebec mosques and Muslim organizations, which had issued a press release to make it clear that he was not authorized to speak on their behalf: "The statements, information and interviews that he gives to the media about Islam and Muslims represent only his personal opinion and that of his foundation, whose executive members are unknown."[9]

This public disavowal came in the context of statements Breault was making regarding the controversy around Salman Rushdie, the British author who had provoked outrage throughout the Muslim world with the publication of his famous novel, *The Satanic Verses*.[10] In March 1989, Breault's CMIF had made threatening remarks about the Salman Rushdie Support Committee that had formed in Montreal. Commenting on news of a demonstration being planned by the committee, the CMIF wrote that the organizers "must be held wholly responsible for any event that may occur during this provocative demonstration," adding that one cannot "provoke and scorn Muslims with impunity without creating problems for the provocateurs."[11]

Breault responded to being disavowed by so many Muslim organizations by presenting the media with a long list of organizations offering him their support. "The problem is that many of these [organizations] owe their existence to him," noted journalist Richard Hétu.[12] The media could not be unaware that Joseph Gilles Breault was far from enjoying universal support within Montreal's Arab and Muslim communities. As we shall see, this did not stop certain journalists from referring to the CSIS informant as an established Muslim leader.

A few months before the Quebec decree was passed, Breault found himself in the midst of another controversy, when links were revealed between the CMIF and Jamaat Al Muslimeen, a Muslim paramilitary group based in Trinidad and Tobago in the Caribbean and led by Yasin Abu Bakr, a former police officer who had converted to Islam during his studies in Toronto. In the summer of 1990, Abu Bakr and about one hundred armed rebels stormed the Trinidad and Tobago parliament and took Prime Minister Arthur Robinson and his entire cabinet hostage.[13] The attempted insurrection left thirty people dead and 150 injured, with about $400 million in property damage. Shortly thereafter, Breault admitted to the *Toronto Star* that the CMIF had paid $7,000 to Jamaat Al Muslimeen.[14]

Given this, the blessing that the Quebec government bestowed on Breault's religious corporation is all the more surprising. It makes one wonder what kind of vetting—if any—had been done before such a responsibility was placed in the hands of a person who had himself been disavowed by members of the community he claimed to represent.[15] Perhaps there were bureaucrats who did not pay attention to the daily news … In any case, Breault would soon be the subject of more bad press.

In November 1990, *The Gazette* revealed that "Youssef Mouammar" (i.e., Joseph Gilles Breault) was distributing a reprint of the infamous antisemitic tract *The Protocols of the Elders of Zion*.[16] First published in Russia in the early 1900s, this pamphlet purports to be an account of secret meetings of Jewish leaders aspiring to world domination. In reality, these so-called "protocols" were nothing but a forgery fabricated by Matvei Golovinski, an agent in the pay of the Okhrana, the secret police of Tsarist Russia. As if, from one century to the next, one state agent was passing the torch to another …

The controversies around the self-proclaimed "Muslim leader" would continue after the adoption of the decree. On January 13, 1992, *La Presse* published an article entitled "Algerian political crisis divides Montreal

9. TERROR THREATS, COURTESY OF CSIS

Algerians."[17] The crisis in question stemmed from the results of the first round of the first multi-party legislative elections since Algeria's independence: with the Islamic Salvation Front (FIS) having obtained nearly fifty percent of the vote, Algeria now appeared to be on its way to being governed by an Islamist party. To explain what divided "the Algerians of Montreal," journalist Raymond Gervais gave a platform to two local personalities, Ali Haouchine and ... Joseph Gilles Breault. The article quoted a communiqué issued by the CMIF, which argued that the Algerian people should "confirm their [electoral] decision by inflicting a crushing defeat on the enemies of Islam united behind the FLN [National Liberation Front] and the Socialist Forces Front (FFS),"[18] the two most important secular political parties in Algeria. One week later, *La Presse* published a letter from Amar Overdane, a reader of Algerian origin who was upset that the article "does not at all reflect the reality of our community, which is predominantly democratic." Overdane also deplored the fact that the article "largely quoted" the words of "the fundamentalist Youssef Mouammar," who, it should be remembered, "is not an Algerian." According to Overdane, Breault did not know what he was talking about since "his denunciation of the FFS as an 'enemy of Islam'—the FIS itself has never gone that far—displays an incredible ignorance of Algerian realities and an unbridled fanaticism."[19]

Beginning in 1992, Joseph Gilles Breault's communiqués took on a decidedly violent tone, as the CSIS informant began an international campaign of threats and intimidation, with targets in Algeria, France, Germany, Italy, the United Kingdom, and other countries.[20] Some of these communiqués found an echo in Quebec's print media. For example, on December 14, 1994, *La Presse* reported on communiqués in support of the Armed Islamic Group (GIA), an Algerian clandestine organization renowned for its brutality and violence against civilians.[21] Designated as a terrorist entity since 2002, the GIA had emerged in 1992 after the cancellation of the second round of legislative elections in the North African country. The Montreal daily revealed that the communiqués were written on CMIF letterhead and signed by "Dr Youssef Mouammar."[22] One of these communiqués, which included the CMIF's old fax number, urged the

> International and Algerian Muslim Community in particular [to] fight on the path of Allah, by all means possible, to eliminate the members of the High State Committee, the prefects, the police com-

missioners, the generals, the colonels, their families and their collaborators, who unconstitutionally and illegally oppose by force the freely expressed will of the Algerian people."²³

In another communiqué, dated February 9, 1994, "Dr Youssef Mouammar" invited "all our fighters to strike with all their strength to rid the country of these despots in power," as well as "foreigners who refuse to leave Algeria."²⁴ When questioned by *La Presse*, Breault denied everything, explaining to anyone who would listen that it was possible to fax a document using the number of another fax machine.²⁵ The matter bounced back to the National Assembly, where MNA Houda-Pépin questioned the Minister of Justice, Paul Bégin, asking him what measures he intended to take "to put an end to these incitements to terrorism and political assassination that are being disseminated in Quebec and abroad from the territory of Quebec." The Minister was unable to answer the question, nor did he seem to have any interest in doing anything about the situation.²⁶ Indeed, as journalist André Noël would reveal in 2001, it was CSIS that was responsible for translating from Arabic to French the GIA statements that its informant was receiving ... ²⁷

Breault found himself in the news again in the fall of 1994, following his dissemination of virulently anti-Israel messages, the latest chapter in his international intimidation campaign. First, on October 29, *The Gazette* reported that a letter on CMIF letterhead had been intercepted in France by the Simon Wiesenthal Centre, saying "We must declare a war without pity on the Zionists and on their allies until the flag of Islam flies over Jerusalem."²⁸ The letter also urged all followers of Islam to "torpedo and sabotage" the Oslo accords and to not stop until "Israel is finally wiped off the map."²⁹ Although the document bore the signature of "Dr Youssef Mouammar," Breault once again claimed that it was a forgery, even stating that it was the work of people who wanted to do harm to the CMIF and himself. "Extremists on any side could have done this to discredit me," he said.³⁰ *The Gazette* reported, however, that the position of Breault's group was that the use of violence to achieve the destruction of Israel and the creation of a Palestinian state was legitimate, but that the violence should remain confined within the borders of Israel and the Occupied Territories.³¹

On December 15, the CSIS informant found himself at the centre of a new anti-Israel controversy: this time, the case concerned a threatening message that the CMIF leader had left on the answering machine of the Canada-

Israel Committee two months earlier. Two days later, a member of the CIC brought the recording to the Montreal police, who showed little interest in the case, as Daniel Amar would recount:

> When I asked them if there would be a follow-up, one of them told me that this did not warrant an investigation. I said, "That's what you think?" He then told me that if I was not happy, I should contact this person (Mr. Mouammar).[32]

Contacted by telephone by *La Presse*, Breault admitted that he was "perhaps" the person who had left the message.[33] Despite this near admission, the case went no further. "According to our guidelines, this is not a hate crime," said the Montreal police. A view that Amar did not share, as he understandably felt there was a hateful implication in the desire expressed by Breault, "to get the Israelis out of Israel but also out of elsewhere, implying Quebec and Canada."[34]

In February 1995, *La Presse* reported that Breault had targeted another victim, a British journalist who was later identified as Gillian Lusk. Shortly after Lusk had criticized the government of Sudan, at the time controlled by Hassan al-Turabi's National Islamic Front, on a European radio program on January 2, 1994, the radio station received a communiqué signed "Dr. Youssef Mouammar" describing the journalist as an "enemy of Islam": "The Muslim People must eliminate all enemies of Islam and Mrs. Lusk is one of them," the communiqué proclaimed.[35] Not taking this threat lightly and no longer feeling safe at home, the journalist moved in with a friend, changed her locks, and had an alarm system installed, and also lodged a complaint with the British police, who contacted the RCMP and CSIS. On January 11, an RCMP representative met with Lusk in Europe and sought to reassure her. On January 20, CSIS contacted Lusk, explaining to the journalist that "Mr. Mouammar might not be as dangerous as he looks," that "these threats of his are a habit," and that he was "well known to the authorities."[36] It was learned much later that the RCMP had wanted charges laid against Breault, but that the file was closed after a Crown prosecutor concluded that there was insufficient evidence.[37]

By going to ridiculous lengths to trivialize Breault's activities, CSIS was not simply protecting one informant among many, but rather was becoming an accomplice to the excesses of an agent provocateur. With his campaign of threats, Breault had clearly crossed the line from informant to provocateur. But it took months before the authorities decided to wake up and smell the coffee. In 1996, the Solicitor General of Canada finally ordered CSIS to sever all ties with Breault. At the time, SIRC felt that Breault's actions were "too controversial."[38] But CSIS apparently could not do without its mole, so the intelligence agency continued to work with Breault, paying him through a "small slush fund."[39] In its 1997–98 annual report, SIRC commented on CSIS's refusal to part with its agent provocateur:

> Based on our assessment both of the source's controversial actions and the intelligence generated, the Committee was troubled by the Service's decision. The Service's comment to us in this regard was that its decision to resume contact was based primarily on his potential to provide important information in the future.[40]

"The scandal was hushed up," explains journalist Normand Lester, noting that SIRC "only issued a mild rebuke to CSIS."[41] The intelligence agency had clearly "disobeyed" government directives, yet another example of the lack of any effective institutional control over the secret services.

Breault was thus able to continue faxing his death threats to the four corners of the world, albeit with some adjustments. The agent provocateur had to make some effort to cover his tracks, since he no longer officially had a relationship with CSIS. Until this point, the informant had signed his communiqués "Dr. Youssef Mouammar" on CMIF letterhead. From 1996 on, the threatening communiqués would be signed "Abu Jihad" from the "World Islamic Front."[42] Thus, on July 24, 1996, the "World Islamic Front" sent a particularly threatening fax to the Washington offices of Agence France-Presse (AFP):

> American and French civilian populations must expect important actions, mainly in the USA and France, so the men, women and children of those countries can also know the horror of bombs and the pain of losing loved ones.[43]

CSIS may have a long reach, but there were limits to the protection the intelligence agency could offer when Breault went after targets outside of Canada, where the Canadian intelligence services hold less sway. It was only a matter of time before authorities in a foreign country sought to crack down on this agent provocateur with his penchant for making threats.

Breault's inflammatory communiqués came to the attention of the French judge Jean-Louis Bruguière, who was in charge of investigating

9. TERROR THREATS, COURTESY OF CSIS

attacks attributed to the GIA in France. During a search in the Paris suburb of Sartrouville at the home of Boualem Chibani, a man of Algerian origin suspected of being linked to an Islamist arms trafficking network, French national police discovered twenty-one communiqués signed by "Dr. Mouammar Youssef." There were also documents suggesting that Breault had previously solicited funds from Chibani.[44] When Bruguière sent investigators to Montreal to look into "Dr. Mouammar Youssef," CSIS made various excuses to not cooperate in the case, while keeping its own connection to Breault quiet.[45] But in November 1997, the informant targeted Judge Bruguière himself, threatening him with "merciless and exemplary vengeance" in a communiqué faxed to French journalists in Paris and Montreal.[46] CSIS intervened to prevent the RCMP from revealing to Judge Bruguière that the author of the threats was working for them.[47] Once again, the RCMP meekly gave in to the intelligence service.

Bruguière was not intimidated, and so Breault doubled down. On June 15, 1998, the agent provocateur issued a communiqué in which he demanded that Judge Bruguière cease his investigations, cancel trials against "his brothers in arms," and stop proceedings against four suspects, including himself. He also invited the French magistrate to ask "the CIA and the RCMP" about his ability to attack city transit networks, international airports, trains, sports stadiums, large buildings, and major headquarters in France with "chemical, biological and bacteriological weapons and high-powered bombs."[48] Following this advice, Judge Bruguière contacted the RCMP to request an explanation, and the matter even reached the office of Lawrence MacAulay, the Solicitor General of Canada. When asked to explain, CSIS officials swore they had cut off all contact with Breault.[49] However, when Bruguière visited Montreal in October 1999, the intelligence agency went so far as to help Breault hide out at the Motel Universel, near the Olympic Stadium, in order to ensure that the French magistrate would not be able to meet with its firebrand informant.[50]

Unconvinced by CSIS's protestations, in April 1999 Minister MacAulay asked the RCMP to open an investigation to determine if there were any ties between the intelligence agency and Breault. The secret RCMP investigation would be known as Project Shawl and was led by Inspector Yves Roussel; it was successful, with the RCMP even managing to photograph Breault without his knowledge while he was meeting with CSIS agents.[51] Like something from a thriller, one secret police force was spying on another that had clearly gotten out of control.

Meanwhile, not realizing he was under intense surveillance, Joseph Gilles Breault continued his daily provocations. Between March and June 1999, he sent between forty and fifty "subversive communiqués" to American and European newspapers, as well as to Lebanon, from an Internet café next to his home, on Sherbrooke Street in Westmount. He also used the computers at the Westmount Public Library, where he had become somewhat of a regular.[52] In sixteen of these communiqués, Breault claimed responsibility for the contamination of Coca-Cola products in France and Belgium, a mysterious incident that had occurred in June 1999, forcing the American soft drink giant to organize the largest product recall in its history: 160 million bottles and cans had to be taken off the market. But as the French newspaper *Le Figaro* reported a few years later, the agent provocateur never provided any proof as to his claims in this regard.[53]

On June 19, 1999, Breault attended the 100th anniversary of the founding of the Westmount Public Library. The self-styled Muslim fundamentalist downed a few glasses of alcohol before attempting to steal six flutes of champagne and an apron. The attempted robbery was noted by an undercover RCMP officer who had him under surveillance. The theft was reported to a library security guard who had Breault empty his bag, and the informant was arrested and charged with theft. Among his belongings was an Islamic Jihad communiqué which was strikingly similar to eighteen other communiqués sent to the media and public figures. The document was sent to a laboratory for analysis.[54] As journalist Michel Auger—who was largely responsible for the "scoop" in the Breault case, as he had been with Marc-André Boivin—would report, this was a crucial turning point in the RCMP's investigation:

> The results of the handwriting analysis soon confirmed the RCMP's suspicions. Not only did the majority of the communiqués come from the same computer and printer, but DNA analysis and fingerprint comparisons linked the suspect to the envelopes in which the communiqués had been sent.
>
> This discovery was to provoke a full-scale war between the RCMP and CSIS. Because the civilian officers were not responding quickly enough or were hiding too much from the RCMP, the latter even drafted a search warrant application to go through the federal security service's files.[55]

9. TERROR THREATS, COURTESY OF CSIS

Now CSIS had no choice but to actually end its relationship with Breault. A senior official from the intelligence agency even had to travel to Paris to make a formal apology to Judge Bruguière.[56] The was the height of irony, as CSIS—which had been created to make amends for the RCMP's antics in the 1970s—was brought to heel by the RCMP, after proving to be just as out of control as the Mounties had been.

As for Breault, he never had to answer in court for all the threats he made over the years. According to André Noël, "Once again, CSIS asked the RCMP to hush things up. Discussions took place in high places, in Ottawa."[57] The impunity enjoyed by the CSIS agent provocateur indicates that Breault had been acting with the full blessing of his powerful intelligence agency patrons.

Despite ties finally being severed with the informant, one of Breault's threatening communiqués would continue to make waves in the years to come. Dated March 4, 1998, and signed by the "World Islamic Front to Promote the Internationalization of Armed Struggle," it threatened to detonate a "biochemical bomb" at the Beaubien metro station in Montreal.[58] This was followed by another communiqué on March 23, this one signed "Abu Jihad, Islamic World Front," which referred to a "holy war" against Jewish and Western populations and threatened to detonate bombs filled with "chemical or bacteriological products" that could kill "more than 1,000 people" in a large building or in the ventilation system of underground Montreal.[59] Then, on March 28, a third communiqué found in a St. Catherine Street bar warned that chemical bombs supposedly tested in Iraq were to be detonated at the Molson Centre during a hockey game.[60]

The Gazette was the first newspaper to break the story, reporting at the end of March 1998 that a mysterious threat of a poison gas attack was looming over Montreal. The rumour had even spread to the Quebec government, the English-language daily reported.[61] Montreal police commander Normand Bernier responded to the threats by summoning executives from the Montreal-Centre Regional Health Authority and Urgences Santé (the public emergency medical service for the islands of Montreal and Laval) to two meetings at the municipal police headquarters on March 26 and 27. The next day, the Health Authority instructed Montreal's largest seven hospitals to go on "alert" and replenish their stock of Atropine, an antidote against sarin poison gas. Hospital officials were asked to contact their off-duty staff and advise them to prepare to report for work in case of emergency.[62] It should be noted that all these measures resulted in unanticipated costs, including

$6,500 in overtime for nurses at Notre Dame and St. Luc hospitals, at a time when the health care system was facing budget cuts.[63]

Once Montreal newspapers began reporting on the threats, however, the police began downplaying the whole affair. "There was never a concrete threat," insisted public relations officer Pierre Houbart.[64] Since no one wanted to take responsibility for this costly exercise, the heads of the police and the Regional Health Authority spent a few days passing the buck back and forth between themselves in the media. According to Constable Houbart, the RHA "took it too seriously and alerted the hospitals for nothing," while calling the meeting at headquarters "a routine meeting."[65] Contradicting the police, Health Authority Director Marcel Villeneuve replied that Major Bernier "did not intervene to signal that this was only a vague long-term plan" when talk turned to acquiring 5,000 doses of Atropine to treat sarin gas poisoning.[66]

As for CSIS, it did not hesitate to exploit the false threats made by its own informant, using them for "educational" purposes to convince the authorities and the general public that the terrorist threat should be taken seriously. In a text entitled *Chemical, biological, radiological and nuclear terrorism*, the intelligence agency wrote that

> unsubstantiated threats of "chemical or biological" use in Montreal, made in the name of the "Word Islamic Front," caused brief disturbances in that city in March 1998. [...] Canada remains vulnerable to this type of nightmarish chemical, biological, radiological or nuclear terrorism.[67]

This alarmist statement was sent to the Canadian Press and *La Presse*, and was quoted in an AFP dispatch.[68] The fact that they had been made by a CSIS informant did not prevent the threats from causing quite a commotion and being used to justify reinforcing the repressive apparatus. On March 28, 2000, the RCMP announced that a simulated terrorist attack using biochemical weapons would take place in Montreal in early June.[69] According to a report in *Le Soleil*, the reason for the simulation was the threat of terrorist attacks in March 1998. It even stated that these threats "were taken seriously by CSIS."[70]

Michel Auger's revelations about the links between the Abu Jihad communiqués and CSIS in his book *L'Attentat* ended up being overshadowed by an event with global repercussions, as the book was scheduled for release on September 11, 2001. From that point on, a sense of collective paranoia would

9. TERROR THREATS, COURTESY OF CSIS

grip North America, the result being that fear of terrorist attacks would come to dominate the minds of millions.

"These people could be your neighbours," said Prime Minister Jean Chrétien, referring to the al-Qaeda "sleeper agents" who had allegedly infiltrated the Western heartland. "They have cells all over the world, it seems," Chrétien continued. "Maybe even in Canada."[71] But it would take more than such vague and alarmist words from the Canadian prime minister to overcome the skepticism of a section of the population. What was missing in the arguments insisting Ottawa must adopt new anti-terrorist legislation, was any specific credible terrorist threat against Canada.

This missing link was provided by a document that made its appearance at the end of September 2001 in France, during the mega-trial of twenty-four people accused of "criminal association in relation to a terrorist enterprise," held before the 16th correctional chamber in Paris.[72] A brief accompanying *Le Monde*'s lead article on the trial reported that French police had found a "technical file" in a Marseille apartment.[73] The document was "signed by the 'World Islamic Front to Promote the Internationalization of Armed Struggle'—an unknown organization whose name sounds like something Bin Laden would use."[74] In fact, it was the communiqué produced by Breault, using the name "Abu Jihad," on March 4, 1998.

This short text fired the imagination of Montreal's journalistic community. The *Journal de Montréal* was the first daily to take up the story. "Islamic terrorists targeted the Montreal metro," read the front page of its October 1st edition, which reported that "in 1999, an Islamic terrorist cell associated with Osama bin Laden's group had planned to carry out several bombings in the Montreal metro."[75]

The news sent shockwaves through the Quebec metropolis, so much so that the Montreal police had no choice but to call a press conference that very day, in an attempt to reassure the public. "The person who made this manifesto was looking for attention. There are a lot of hoaxes," said Major André Durocher, explaining the motives of the suspect, who he said had never been charged because of a "technicality."[76] Several journalists left unsatisfied, most of their questions unanswered. Brian Myles of *Le Devoir* described the press briefing as "a public relations exercise designed to allay public fears and refute the information in *Le Monde*," before concluding on the following note: "The threat of chemical or biological terrorism is very real in Canada, as indicated in a public report by [CSIS]."[77] Everything had come full circle!

The police press briefing was well attended, with Montreal's four major dailies all sending reporters. *Le Devoir* alone devoted no less than three articles to the case in its October 2nd edition.[78] In addition, the Canadian Press dispatch reporting on the press conference was picked up by most of the major French-language dailies and by four major English-language newspapers across the country.[79] As proof that Major Durocher had failed to get his message across, the front page of *La Presse* carried an article with the headline "It was not a hoax: a bin Laden group threatened Montreal." Éric Clément wrote that "Montreal was indeed the object of threats made in March 1998 by the 'Islamic World Front,' an organization led by Osama bin Laden who had issued a fatwa against 'the Americans and their allies' a few days earlier."[80]

In *Le Devoir*, Jean-Robert Sansfaçon wrote a dramatic editorial:

> A terrible tragedy could have occurred on that March 4, 1999, if a handful of militants from an Islamist organization, whose existence no one here even suspected, had carried out their plan to place explosives on three Montreal subway lines. These people must have known Montreal and lived there, even if it was in Marseille that the "technical file" of the attack was found, that same year of 1999.[81]

Later that day, Radio-Canada released what should have been a bombshell, broadcasting a report by Normand Lester revealing that the author of the violent communiqués found in Marseille was in fact a CSIS informant. "Radio-Canada learned that Mouammar was already meeting with CSIS agents at the time of the Gulf War in 1991," the journalist stated bluntly.[82] Normally, such news should have dominated the headlines; but while some papers had rushed to use their front pages to spread the (false) news that Montreal had been threatened by the West's public enemy number one, Osama bin Laden, none of them saw fit to use their front pages to issue the necessary *mea culpa*, or even to inform their readers that a CSIS agent provocateur was behind the threats.

There were no editorials on the Joseph Gilles Breault case. Nor did any political party hold the federal government to account or call for a public inquiry, unlike in the Grant Bristow affair. In fact, for the next two months, Breault's name disappeared from the news as if the story had never existed.[83] This huge scandal went unnoticed by most of the public in Quebec, who probably felt more worried about the Montreal population being threatened by Al Qaeda than by a CSIS agent provocateur. After all, the media space

9. TERROR THREATS, COURTESY OF CSIS

devoted to shedding light on the provocations of "Abu Jihad" really doesn't compare to the mass psychosis that accompanied the false threats. Unlike Operation Governor, where the media played a central role in publicizing the affair, in the Breault affair the media seems to have been content to act as a conduit for the CSIS set-up, parroting the intelligence agency's fear campaign. The media may have felt that it was not in their best interest to publicize the fact that they had been so easily fooled by the Canadian intelligence agency. However, the real victims in this whole affair are not to be found in the media, but rather in the Muslim community. The excessive attention the media devoted to the CSIS hoax could only contribute to the rise of Islamophobia within the Quebec population. The media passed up on the opportunity to set things right; a failure that is all the more galling given how much remains unknown in the Breault affair.

We still know very little, for example, about Breault's activities outside Canada on behalf of CSIS. Yet when journalist André Noël met with the former informant in 2001, Breault said he had visited a variety of countries at the taxpayers' expense:

> He listed at least 21 countries that he had visited, sometimes repeatedly, between 1985 and 1999. He claims to have been to Libya, Palestine, Afghanistan, and even to have met Osama bin Laden in Sudan, where the latter took refuge between 1992 and 1996.
>
> He also claimed that CSIS had paid him $7,000 per month (in salary, expenses and airfare).[84]

Normand Lester explains how CSIS botched an "opportunity to infiltrate Al Qaeda" with Breault:

> In December 1993, Breault-Mouammar was invited to attend a conference in Khartoum, Sudan, which brought together fundamentalist organizations from around the world. This was a unique opportunity for CSIS to gather intelligence that it could share and thereby increase its prestige with the British and American services, which gave it much more information than they received from it.
>
> In Khartoum, Breault-Mouammar befriended the conference organizer, Hassan al-Tourabi, a Sorbonne graduate who spoke impeccable French. At Tourabi's house, the Quebecker met a Saudi exile who

had taken refuge in Sudan, a certain Osama bin Laden. Mouammar even visited one of the camps that bin Laden had established in Sudan to train jihadists. By using Mouammar, CSIS missed the opportunity to introduce one of its agents.[85]

Al-Qaeda was just one of several jihadist organizations active at the time; it was not widely known and had yet to declare war on the West. But the fact remains that the only tangible result of Joseph Gilles Breault's work was his amplification of national insecurity. CSIS certainly seems less concerned with keeping people safe than it is with ensuring its control, even if this means fostering groundless fears. For reasons known only to him, the former informant chose to keep his true allegiance a mystery, suggesting to André Noël: "Was Youssef working for CSIS or was he using CSIS money to finance Al-Qaeda [...] and the Islamic World Front?"[86] A question that has remained unanswered and that seems to be of no interest to anyone in the media, SIRC, the opposition parties, or the government.

In fact, documents that could provide answers may simply not exist anymore, following a major fire at the CSIS regional office in Montreal at 715 Peel Street, on December 21, 2001.[87] There had never been a fire like this before at a CSIS office, and this one occurred just one week after *La Presse* had devoted a full-page article to exposing CSIS's involvement with Breault. Were there people at CSIS worried the *La Presse* story would breathe new life into the RCMP's investigation of Breault? Remember that the RCMP had gone so far as to prepare a search warrant to go through the intelligence agency's files ...

With its usual lack of transparency, CSIS refused to say whether any documents had been destroyed or even damaged in the blaze. However, journalist Raymond Gervais reported that "the water and smoke damage is considerable, especially on the upper floors" where the intelligence agency's offices are located.[88] The report produced by the Service de Sécurité Incendie de Montréal (SSIM), which the author obtained through an access to information request, describes the nature of the fire as "accidental" and attributes it to "an installation too close to a combustible material."[89] So the mystery remains.

CSIS has admitted to destroying evidence in the past in order to assist their informants. For example, in January 2000, a CSIS officer admitted to two *Globe and Mail* reporters that he had destroyed audio recordings of interviews with two of the intelligence agency's moles. This was particularly

9. TERROR THREATS, COURTESY OF CSIS

serious because it was done despite orders to hand the tapes over to RCMP officers investigating the June 23, 1985, bombing of Air India Flight 182, which killed 329 people.[90] The unnamed CSIS officer explained that he used an incinerator on the roof of the intelligence agency's Vancouver office. Sources in the intelligence community told the Toronto newspaper that the incinerator had been used on many occasions to dispose of compromising documents ...

Conclusion

J. Michael Cole, who worked at CSIS from 2003 to 2005, wrote in 2008 that "the Service may on occasion feel compelled to bend the rules by which it usually operates, or even break Canadian laws" in order to make itself look good to the intelligence services of major foreign powers.[1] According to Cole, the "Global War on Terror" created a permissive atmosphere that opened the door to illegal acts by CSIS.[2]

In its 2014–15 annual report, SIRC revealed that "some CSIS activities [are] in contravention of Canadian regulations related to United Nations Security Council (UNSC) resolutions," specifically the *United Nations Al Qaeda Taliban Regulations* (UNAQTR).[3] These regulations prohibit, among other things, the provision of funds to any person linked to the Taliban or al-Qaeda. However, SIRC

> found that CSIS lacked a procedure to systematically verify whether the human source operations it conducts against Al Qaeda and Taliban threats are in contravention of the UNAQTR. Second, SIRC found that CSIS cannot systematically attest as to whether or not its past human source operations have already violated the UNAQTR.[4]

One might wonder how all this sits with the relatives and family members of the 158 members of the Canadian Armed Forces who lost their lives in Afghanistan between 2002 and 2011 during deployments to fight the Taliban and al-Qaeda.[5] But these people are probably not aware of these allegations against CSIS anyway, since the Canadian print media has never written a single line about them.

CSIS has participated in this "global war on terror" by using informants who are themselves involved in terrorist activities. Such is the case of Mohammed Al-Rashed, a Syrian refugee who approached the Canadian Embassy in Jordan for asylum but was instead recruited by CSIS to provide intelligence on Daesh (aka ISIS). Canada didn't look too good when Al-Rashed was arrested by police in Turkey on February 28, 2015, for helping three British teenage girls, aged 15 and 16, join Daesh in Syria. This is just the tip of the iceberg, as al-Rashed has admitted to serving as a human smuggler for twelve other individuals seeking to join the jihadist group, all at the request of CSIS, which had promised him eventual Canadian citizenship in exchange for his cooperation.[6] First revealed in 2015, the scandal came back in Canadian and international mainstream media after new details were disclosed in a book published in 2022. Written by British award-winning investigative journalist Richard Kerbaj, *The Secret History of the Five Eyes* is unfortunately not available on the Canadian market.[7]

"The source was bringing in foreign fighters, that in itself is an illegal activity, because you are facilitating terrorism," former CSIS agent Huda Mukbil said. Human trafficking is also an offence, both regarding criminal law and an international protocol on the practice to which Ottawa is a signatory. "So everything he was doing, you needed ministerial approval to do," adds Mukbil. But Steven Blaney, the Conservative public safety minister responsible for CSIS at the time, was kept in the dark. "I can hardly see how we could have let this happen or authorized it," he says. CSIS also violated its own rules for operations that were in place in February 2015, which state: "human sources will carry out their tasks on behalf of [CSIS] without engaging in illegal activities." The Ministerial Directions for Operations also requires that CSIS must consider the impact on "Canadian foreign-policy interests and objectives" while conducting covert operations. And the al-Rashed affair did damage Canada's relation with Turkey, which retaliated by limiting the number of CSIS agents operating at the Canadian embassy in Ankara. Al-Rashed spent more than seven years in a Turkish prison for terrorism and smuggling charges before regaining his freedom on August 5, 2022.[8]

Two of the three British teenage girls are now believed to have died in Syria. The third, Shamima Begum, is leading a miserable life as a prisoner of war in a Kurdish prison camp, where she gave birth to three children, all of whom died in harsh conditions.[9] She told the BBC that al-Rashed "organized the entire trip from Turkey to Syria .... I don't think anyone would have been able to make it to Syria without the help of smugglers."[10] Still, Canada's prime minister, Justin Trudeau, publicly defended CSIS's actions. "The fight against terrorism requires our intelligence services to continue to be flexible and to be creative in their approaches," he said following the release of Kerbaj's book.[11] Up until then, Canada had declined to confirm CSIS's role in this affair.

In this global—and apparently never-ending—war on terror, the ends seem to justify the means. This is also true of the RCMP, which never stopped being a major player in counter-terrorism. "After the McDonald Commission, the RCMP continued to assume responsibility for conducting national security investigations from a law enforcement perspective," noted Justice Denis O'Connor in his report on the Maher Arar Inquiry.[12] O'Connor added that the number and intensity of RCMP security-related investigations only increased after the September 11th attacks in the United States.[13] The increased importance in the role of the RCMP is largely a result of Parliament's passing Bill C-36, the *Anti-terrorism Act*. Creating a range of new criminal offences related to terrorist activity, this bill was largely viewed as a response to the September 11th attacks.

But the RCMP's involvement in the "war on terror" has also involved serious excesses, as evidenced by the revelations surrounding the trial of the couple John Nuttall and Amanda Korody. Living on welfare in Surrey, BC, Nuttall and Korody are two former drug addicts who converted to Islam and became radicalized by the Internet. On July 1, 2013, the couple was arrested on charges of planting three bombs on the grounds of the provincial legislature, for which they could have faced life in prison.[14] After a series of lengthy court proceedings, Nuttall and Korody were finally acquitted on July 29, 2016, after BC Supreme Court Justice Catherine Bruce found that the RCMP itself had "carefully orchestrated" the terrorist plot by abusing the immunity enjoyed by police officers to commit criminal acts.[15]

According to Justice Bruce, "[RCMP officers] violated the Criminal Code in order to accomplish their objectives and almost all of their actions were unapproved and beyond the scope of the RCMP's authorization to commit certain criminal offences."[16] The federal police had only obtained one authorization, for the possession of C4 explosives, and that was for only two RCMP agents. However, the trial revealed that the police investigation, dubbed Project Remembrance, involved no less than 240 RCMP officers.[17] The court found that the RCMP officers had committed several other criminal offences, including facilitating terrorist activity, providing goods or services for terrorist purposes, making or possessing an explosive substance with intent to endanger life or cause serious damage to property or to enable another person to do so, placing explosives in or against a public place or government facility with intent to cause death or serious bodily harm, and conspiracy to commit a criminal act.

CONCLUSION

It is unfortunate, to say the least, that the media passed up on the opportunity this verdict offered to engage in a much-needed public debate on the legal immunity police enjoy, without which the RCMP would probably not have been able to go to such lengths to entrap the couple. That said, the judgment, which was upheld on appeal, was historic in that it marked the first time that police provocation has been successfully used as a defence in a Canadian terrorism trial.[18] The RCMP's conduct was all the more egregious, as the court noted, given Nuttall's vulnerability, specifically "his inability to think logically, his childish behaviour and his inability to remain focused on a task."[19] Justice Bruce did not mince her words in expressing disapproval of the RCMP: "There are enough terrorists in the world already. We don't need the police to create more of them with marginalized people who don't have the ability or motivation to become them themselves."[20]

It is also unfortunate that the court was not able to shed light on the role played by CSIS in this case. Not the least of which being that it was CSIS itself that first set the RCMP on Nuttall's trail in February 2013.[21] The defence has even alleged that the couple may have been "radicalized" by someone acting as an agent provocateur for CSIS, before the RCMP even began its investigation.[22] Attempting to get to the bottom of this, on June 25, 2015, the court ordered the Crown to instruct CSIS to turn over all information provided to the RCMP about Nuttall between December 2012 and July 1, 2013.[23] CSIS was unwilling to cooperate, however, to the point that Justice Bruce even threatened to charge the organization with contempt of court.[24] In the end, however, the agency's stonewalling proved greater than the accused's will to get to the bottom of the matter, with the result that in April 2016 the defence withdrew its applications to the court regarding the disclosure of CSIS information.[25] Keep in mind that time was not on Nuttall and Korody's side, as the two had been in custody since the time of their arrest.

Like their activities, the identities of CSIS moles are a closely guarded secret. Case law effectively obliges the Canadian state to protect the identity of CSIS informants.[26] Also, as previously mentioned, the CSIS Act makes it an offence to disclose information that might identify a Canadian intelligence "human source," with a maximum sentence of five years in prison.[27] As if that were not enough, the anti-terrorist Bill C-36 has added to this penalty: since 2002, persons "Permanently Bound to Secrecy," which includes current and former CSIS employees, can face up to fourteen years in prison if found guilty of communicating or confirming "Special Operational Information."[28]

In writing this book, I myself got a taste of the intelligence service's lack of transparency when I submitted an access to information request to CSIS for all of the agency's current and previous directives or guidelines on the use of "human sources," dating back to its inception.[29] CSIS responded belatedly, sending 111 pages of documents that were so highly redacted that they reveal next to nothing of value.[30] In its report, the McDonald Commission argued that the guidelines outlining the "principles which govern the use of human sources and members undercover by the security agency [...] should be open to public scrutiny."[31]

Today, as in the past, whenever there is a question of "national security," the public is treated as an inconvenient witness, one who should be removed from the scene as quickly as possible. As if it were none of our business. As if the search for truth and the right to information were a threat to their skittish "national security." For it is not our security, either as individuals or collectively, that is at stake, but rather the security of the state and its established order: when CSIS and the RCMP exaggerate or fabricate threats, going so far as to invent them out of thin air, it is clear that this is first and foremost to protect the security of the state, not our own. There are no limits in the pursuit of this "national security." Hence the state says as little as possible and hides as much as possible, for what lies behind the thick curtain of "national security" is often not very pretty. Indeed, if "national security" were a closet, it would be overflowing with skeletons.

Former CSIS employee J. Michael Cole has seen the intelligence agency from the inside; his book, *Smokescreen: Canadian Security Intelligence after September 11, 2001*, is far from flattering. He paints a picture of an agency rife with ignorance and intellectual laziness, one that engages in racial and religious profiling and monitors "targets" for tenuous reasons at best.[32] These "targets" are themselves dehumanized and openly treated with the utmost contempt by surveillance officials, who refer to them with offensive epithets such as "scumbags," "idiots," and "pieces of shit."[33] The idea, Cole writes, is to create "emotional distance" from the "targets" so that CSIS agents can do their jobs without too much cognitive dissonance.[34] He might have added that it is easier to abuse a person's rights when you feel nothing but contempt for them. In the end, CSIS investigations are evaluated in purely quantitative terms: "Inaction—even when the opponent is himself inactive—is unacceptable," writes Cole. "Absence of activity is construed as a sign that the opponent excels at what it is doing."[35]

CONCLUSION

The strange and paranoid world of intelligence work can knock one off balance, mentally and psychologically. The Canadian Civil Liberties Association once reported that informants are often unstable people, citing the case of Sara Jane Moore, an FBI informant who attempted to assassinate US President Gerald Ford in San Francisco on September 22, 1975.[36] There can be no doubt that undercover work is not without its risks to mental health. Leading a double life often involves spending one's every waking minute lying and living in constant fear of being found out, which can have consequences that are all too real, even if they may not be immediately apparent. Dr. Ed Kramer of the RCMP's Psychological Services has observed that

> In undercover part of your role is to appear as someone you are not, and in doing that you are involved in a group that may, for some people, become for more interesting or more attractive than the group to which you belong [...] They may not be personally vulnerable, but they are vulnerable if they go through that kind of experiencing too long.[37]

The longer the undercover assignment, the more disciplinary and substance abuse problems occur, according to psychologist Michel Girodo, who has conducted research on forty-eight agents from different US federal agencies. His work shows that 66% of the subjects studied employed their false identity outside of the operational context. Other studies have found that up to one-quarter of those involved in undercover operations have psychological problems.[38] The RCMP and CSIS are not exempt from these problems. We have seen, for example, how RCMP undercover officer John Leopold became an alcoholic and how CSIS informant Marc-André Boivin engaged in high-risk sexual behaviour. Were Breault's delusional communiqués related to some psychological issue stemming from his double life, rather than from his superiors' directives? We may never know.

It is important to note that the psychological consequences for the victims of secret service abuse are much less well documented. We have seen how the campaign of psychological harassment conducted by CSIS informant Grant Bristow damaged the lives of several anti-racist activists. More generally, people who discover that they have trusted an informant cannot help but be more suspicious of others. First Nations activists understandably felt betrayed when they learned that Rosie Douglas had introduced them to the RCMP agent provocateur Warren Hart.[39] Similarly, according to journalist Fabrice de Pierrebourg, the Breault affair is still having repercussions for some converts to Islam today:

> In Montreal mosques, where many still remember the manipulations of Joseph Gilles Breault, alias Youssef Mouammar—the CSIS mole in the 1990s—they avoided these new Muslims like the plague, suspecting them of being police infiltrators.[40]

But such fallout is unlikely to bother those who experience undercover missions as "extremely exhilarating," to borrow the words of former SQ police officer Louis Sansfaçon.[41] Sansfaçon infiltrated the criminal underworld for nine long years before being sentenced to seven years in prison for drug trafficking in January 1992. In his words, "the best way to stay a cop in your head is to wear a uniform."[42] But "staying a cop in your head" is not an issue for informants, who were never members of any police force in the first place. There is no code of ethics or police academy for moles, which perhaps makes this category of individuals particularly prone to all sorts of wrongdoing.

More than a lacking code of ethics, however, is the basic nature of undercover work itself. As Federal Court Justice Henry S. Brown writes,

> Human sources live what some would consider unsavoury lives. [...]

> I take it as a given that violent extremists are comfortable associating with those who to a greater or lesser degree, live as they do, that is, those who may and often do live outside the norms of both Canadian morality and law. [...] Their very unsavouriness may indeed best enable them to obtain access and valuable intelligence information from and concerning even more unsavoury people [...]

> I take it as a given that good information may also be provided by human sources who themselves are of unsavoury or bad character.[43]

At the same time, like Sansfaçon, snitches are often looking for an adrenaline rush. Like Carole de Vault, who said she "enjoyed the game" when explaining why she continued her undercover work after the October Crisis.[44] As for Grant Bristow, according to his former co-worker Bill Cooke at the CISB Group security company,

> If he could have been a James Bond he'd have jumped at the opportunity ... He loved to see himself as a superman in civilian clothing

without going into the phone booth routine. He'd play a role and play it to the hilt.[45]

In an interview with *Le Soleil*, Sansfaçon suggested that undercover missions should not exceed three years.[46] That's a lot of time, especially keeping in mind that Keable had recommended that no person or group should be undercover for more than a year at a time. But it is still less time than John Leopold, Carole de Vault, Warren Hart, Marc-André Boivin, Grant Bristow, and Joseph Gilles Breault spent undercover. As to the latter three cases, it should be noted that these CSIS informants radicalized—to borrow a buzzword—their actions over time. Boivin went from incitement to direct participation in bombings. Bristow set up his harassment campaign against antiracists after spending a few years in the white supremacist movement. Nor did Breault become a prolific author of threats overnight.

The extended infiltration of groups is particularly noxious for the victims of state agents, since those targeted are often highly vulnerable to manipulation, given the resources that moles can offer them, especially on a long-term basis. As the American sociologist Gary T. Marx pointed out in a text published in 1973,

> The agent's entry and rise to a position of leadership in an organization may be facilitated by the structure of that organization; those groups that are dedicated to unpopular or visionary causes are often small, experience high rates of turnover, and lack resources and people willing unselfishly to undertake the routine and time-consuming tasks required of activists, as well as the dangerous and daring tasks that may be called for. The agent often brings badly needed special skills and resources.[47]

Agents provocateurs can also be very useful to the state in justifying the surveillance of different groups, as Keable noted in his report:

> A group, whose activities are unrelated to violent action, but which includes among its members, even if unknowingly, one or more persons suspected of engaging in terrorism or sympathizing with violent action, becomes itself suspected of being manipulated by these persons. It thus becomes the object of surveillance. It will remain so, even if the persons suspected of manipulating it for their own ends have left it.[48]

This could be an apt description of the undercover operations to which Marc-André Boivin devoted some fifteen years of his life.

CSIS appears to have a strong preference for proactive infiltration. Boivin and Bristow held leadership positions in their respective groups, while Breault seems to have been the sole figure behind a series of paper organizations; under the direction of the intelligence agency, the latter two were even actively involved in the creation of organizations considered by CSIS to pose a threat to "national security." While Boivin was in a different situation—infiltrating an already established labour organization—his actions were no less insidious. These three agents provocateurs added to the threat by building it up, promoting it, legitimizing it, acting as its mouthpiece. They became part of the threat, the very threat that CSIS claimed to be fighting, thereby rendering the line between threat and state imperceptible. Through its secret services, the state can be a bomber, a seditious subversive, a terrorist conspirator, or a neo-Nazi extremist. And by creating its own threats, the state simultaneously invents the need for security, i.e. its own actions serve to justify its intervention. In short, the state produces its own raison d'être.

Apologists for provocation will argue that to do their job, a mole must convince the enemy that they are one of them. And to do this, they must behave in a manner that is as similar as possible to that of their adversary. In short, a good infiltrator must be a chameleon. But who benefits from the fact that informants are so good at imitating their targets that we can no longer distinguish between the crook and the cop, the spy and the subversive, the informant and the terrorist? In other words, who gets the final word when the state becomes what it claims to fight?

Of course, infiltration is not necessarily synonymous with provocation. An informant who, for example, adopts a low profile and simply reports information to his handler does not meet the definition of an agent provocateur. But like a worm in an apple, the informant's mere presence has the effect of contaminating its target. As Gary T. Marx notes,

> Even when social control by the informant does not go beyond passive observation and participation, the informant helps perpetuate a contentious group by offering resources and moral support from another so-called sympathizer, thus helping those who take unpopular positions and engage in illegal actions to remain committed. The nature of the group cannot be unaffected by the presence of such outsiders, even in the absence of illegal actions.[49]

CONCLUSION

In the world of intelligence, intelligence is often an end in itself that takes precedence over everything else, including moral considerations and even the arrest of criminal offenders. CSIS has proven that it will stop at nothing to advance its own agenda, even if this means destroying evidence, intimidating bothersome media outlets, or going against directives from Parliament or the responsible minister. Certainly, the best way to carry out the kind of activities you don't want to have to admit to is in secret. "The natural cure to the tyranny of secrecy is the public nature of government information and police files," wrote Jean-Claude Leclerc, an editor at *Le Devoir*, in a collection of essays on the secret police in Quebec. According to former CSIS employee J. Michael Cole,

> The only real system of accountability that remains today is the media. It is newspapers that, when at their best and facing the threat of legal action, nevertheless choose to go ahead and publish a story that the government would rather keep secret.[50]

The former CSIS employee was probably disappointed that his book went completely unnoticed in the Canadian print media. The silence is difficult to explain, as it is obvious that his account was of public interest, as not many former CSIS employees have written about their experiences and observations. This media apathy will certainly not encourage others to speak out. Cole, however, was under no illusions about the Fourth Estate. The media, he wrote, "assists CSIS in its exploitation of fear."[51] Perhaps one of the only ways out of this media psychosis is to turn fear on its head—by going after the powers that be and not the public.

To be fair, not everything is rotten in the media realm. After all, much of the information in this book comes from journalistic sources, as the footnotes attest. But the media is failing at its job when it does not report information that is clearly and indisputably in the public interest, such as that contained in Cole's book or even in SIRC's 2014–15 annual report. The media can—and should—do a much better job of shining a light on Canada's secret services and subjecting the issue of provocation to public debate.

The investigative role of the media is all the more essential in the face of the Canadian government's skeletal oversight of CSIS activities. Stephen Harper's Conservative government even found a way to further weaken these anemic accountability mechanisms by quietly abolishing the office of the CSIS Inspector General in 2012, a decision that was not even officially announced: in fact, the measure was buried in the 452-page omnibus federal budget implementation bill, C-38.[52] Not many people spoke up to denounce the abolition of this agency, which according to François Lavigne, who works as an analyst in the Solicitor General's office after a career at CSIS, "had already been whittled down to nothing a long time ago anyway."[53]

Bill C-38 also called for SIRC to provide more information on CSIS activities, without specifying what information and without providing any additional resources.[54] This was at a time when SIRC's already threadbare credibility had been further damaged by the controversial resignations of two of its chairs, both of whom were appointed by the Harper government. Arthur Porter resigned on November 10, 2011, after the *National Post* reported that he had entered into a $200,000 financial transaction with Ari Ben-Menashe, a wealthy arms dealer who once worked for Israeli military intelligence and now lives in Montreal.[55] Then, on January 24, 2014, it was the turn of former Conservative Minister Chuck Strahl to resign as SIRC Chair, following allegations of conflict of interest.[56] Strahl was acting as a lobbyist for Enbridge's Northern Gateway pipeline, a project that had met with considerable opposition from environmentalists, at the same time as he was the chair of SIRC, which had recommended that CSIS monitor "environmental terrorism" in one of its annual reports.[57]

The *Anti-terrorism Act* of 2015 (or Bill C-51) provides that SIRC must review each year "at least one aspect" of the "measures" taken by CSIS "to reduce threats to the security of Canada."[58] A minimum threshold which is far from a complete review. In its three annual reports published after the adoption of C-51, SIRC provides the results of its various reviews. However, the data offered to the public remains very vague. Thus, at the end of its first review, SIRC reports that CSIS has "approved or considered to date, approximately two dozen" of those "measures" without specifying their number or how many of them have been implemented.[59] Furthermore, the report does not contain any information on the nature of the "measures," nor on the context that led CSIS to wish to use its new powers of disruption. SIRC is also evasive in its 2016–17 report, limiting itself to reporting that "CSIS had approved fewer than a dozen threat reduction measures, which were executed in full or in part by CSIS."[60] In the following annual report, SIRC simply refers to "around a half-dozen cases of threat reduction measures approved and executed between January 1, 2017 and October 31, 2017."[61]

C-51 also provided that SIRC's annual reports must specify whether

CONCLUSION

CSIS has sought and obtained a Federal Court warrant to exercise its disruption powers.[62] As mentioned earlier, obtaining judicial authorization is mandatory when the CSIS "measure" violates the law or the Canadian Charter of Rights and Freedoms. However, the 2016–17 SIRC report is silent on this. As for the reports of the previous year[63] and the following year,[64] they indicate that CSIS did not apply for a warrant to this effect. Furthermore, the three SIRC reports conclude that all of the "actions" taken by the intelligence agency "complied with the CSIS Act, Ministerial Direction, and [CSIS] operational policy."[65] No surprise here from a watchdog historically reluctant to bark. SIRC contented itself with formulating timid criticisms, such as blaming CSIS for not having a "process for tracking best practices on threat reduction measures"[66] or that "CSIS's process for developing and reporting on the impacts of the measures lacked some of the thoroughness found in the approval and consultation process."[67]

Under Justin Trudeau's Liberals, Parliament created new oversight mechanisms for Canada's secret services. First there was the creation of a "National Security and Intelligence Committee of Parliamentarians" (NSICOP), in 2017.[68] In itself, the idea was not new: the McDonald Commission in its time had also recommended the creation of a "Joint Parliamentary Committee on Security and Intelligence."[69] And later, in November 2005, Paul Martin's Liberal minority government introduced Bill C-81 to create a "National Security Committee of Parliamentarians."[70] But Bill C-81 died when the various opposition parties joined forces to defeat the Martin government. Over the years, the situation had become increasingly embarrassing for Canada, which was the only Five Eyes country whose intelligence agency was operating without parliamentary oversight.[71] Bill C-22, tabled in June 2016 by the Trudeau government, corrected this shortcoming.[72]

To the NSICOP were added the Office of the Intelligence Commissioner (IC) and the National Security Intelligence Review Agency (NSIRA)—which was the official successor to SIRC—two bodies created by the National Security Act of 2017 (or Bill C-59).[73] However, unlike SIRC, the NSIRA is not only to be the watchdog of CSIS, but also of the Communications Security Establishment (CSE)—the Canadian equivalent of the US National Security Agency (NSA)—in addition to reviewing the "national security" and intelligence-related activities of any federal department. It must also investigate complaints against the RCMP when they relate to "national security," as well as those filed by persons who have been refused a security clearance.[74] For its part, the IC has jurisdiction over both CSIS and CSE.[75] NSICOP's mandate is also rather broad since it must review "the legislative, regulatory, policy, administrative and financial framework for national security and intelligence" and also "any activity carried out by a department that relates to national security or intelligence."[76] However, both the IC[77] and the members of the NSIRA[78] exercise their functions only on a part-time basis. Ditto for the NSICOP since its members are MPs or senators.[79]

While the NSIRA must ensure that CSIS and the CSE comply with the law and ministerial directives, it does not have any power to sanction.[80] When completing a complaint investigation, the NSIRA can only offer findings and recommendations, period.[81] The NSICOP is equally toothless, its mandate being further limited by the fact that it cannot look into "ongoing operations" when the responsible minister determines that "the review would be injurious to national security."[82] The NSIRA is required to suspend any of its inquiries when continuation "would compromise or seriously hinder an ongoing criminal investigation or proceeding."[83]

As for the IC, it can only approve or not approve the authorizations granted to CSIS or the CSE and adjudicate on the "reasonable" nature of the "determinations" made in relation to these two organizations.[84] This includes approving or not approving the offences that the Minister of Public Security authorizes CSIS to commit.[85] The IC can therefore exercise a kind of veto power since "the Minister's determination comes into effect only on the IC's approval."[86] In the absence of such approval, the law provides that the "designated employee" of CSIS is not justified in committing the offence.[87]

Furthermore, neither the IC,[88] the NSIRA[89] nor the NSICOP[90] have any right of access to the "confidence" of the King's Privy Council for Canada—which includes the Federal cabinet. Moreover, all the activities of these surveillance bodies are governed by the law of silence. Indeed, both the IC and the members—former or current—of the NSIRA and the NSICOP are "permanently bound to secrecy."[91] In other words, they are restricted as much in what they can say as in what they can see. The creation of these three watchdogs therefore doesn't do much to resolve the problem of the intelligence services' lack of transparency and the appalling inefficacy of the various surveillance mechanisms in place.

At the time of publication, the NSICOP has published four annual reports, all of which have been redacted. None of the public versions of these reports contain information about the use of CSIS's new disruption pow-

CONCLUSION

ers or its criminal immunity regime. In fact, the themes addressed by the NSICOP in its annual reports vary from year to year. The number of pages too: its first report in 2018 had 206 pages, while the following year's had only 129, and those for 2020 and 2021 contained only fifty and twenty-two pages, respectively.

With respect to the IC, the law provides that its annual reports must, among other things, include statistics relating to the "determinations" of classes of offences made by the Minister of Public Safety in connection with the activities of CSIS.[92] In its 2019 report, the IC commented on three such determinations. The IC writes that "the Minister's first determination for classes of otherwise unlawful acts or omissions did not include any ministerial conclusions." He therefore "was not satisfied that the conclusions were reasonable and he did not approve the determination." The second determination "identified seven classes" of offences all of which received the IC's approval, except one. "The IC found the ministerial conclusions that were the basis of the seventh class were not reasonable, and did not approve that class," says the report. In the last case, the "IC found the Minister's conclusions were reasonable, and consequently approved the determination of all seven classes."[93] The report does not provide any additional information to understand the reasons for the findings of the IC, nor does it identify the classes of offence in question. The same goes for the two subsequent annual reports, which say only that all of the Minister's "determinations" relating to CSIS were endorsed.[94]

As for the NSIRA, the law obliges it to produce annual reports relating in particular to "the compliance of [CSIS] with the law and any applicable ministerial directions" as well as "the reasonableness and necessity of [CSIS's] exercise of its powers."[95] The most recent annual report also contains data on the "non-compliance incidents processed by CSIS, 2019–2021," which totaled 237 for the given period. These "incidents" are classified into four categories: "Administrative," "Operational," "Canadian laws" and "Canadian Charter of Rights and Freedoms." The total number of cases of "non-compliance" with "Canadian laws" is 60. The report, however, does not specify the laws in question and does not offer any details on the "incidents" thus listed. The data also seem to be incomplete regarding "Administrative," "Operational," and "Canadian Charter" incidents.[96]

This same report also contains data on offences committed with the authorization of CSIS, again during the years 2019–21. The total number of these offences is 408. The data table indicates that the total number of "directives to commit" offences is 232. The total number of offences committed by CSIS is 107. The NSIRA also reports the absence of emergency designations allowing the authorization process to be bypassed. It should be noted that the report does not provide any information on the nature of the offences authorized and/or committed. However, the table shows that the number of authorizations, directives, and offences committed is increasing from one year to the next.[97]

The law also requires that the NSIRA "review, each calendar year, at least one aspect of the taking" of "threat reduction measures" (TRM) by CSIS.[98] Thus, a minimum threshold identical to that of its predecessor, SIRC. The NSIRA delivered the results of its first review of TRMs in 2021. "The sample reviewed by NSIRA consisted of TRMs that were employed to disrupt threats to Canadian democratic institutions in relation to the 2019 federal election," says the report.[99] The report does not specify the nature of CSIS's intervention in the election. It should also be noted that two of the nine "findings" formulated by the NSIRA at the end of its examination were completely redacted in the public version of its annual report.[100]

"For a certain type of TRM, the NSIRA considers that the requirements set out in the Ministerial Direction have been met," the report says.[101] "For most of the measures taken by CSIS, NSIRA noted that the measures satisfied the requirements of the [CSIS] Act."[102] However, these conclusions must be qualified in light of the fact that "the NSIRA also found gaps and inconsistencies in CSIS's documentation, which had the effect of hindering NSIRA's compliance review."[103] The NSIRA also complained that "in a limited number of cases, CSIS selected individuals for inclusion in the TRM without a rational link between the selection of the individual and the threat. As a result, these measures were not 'reasonable and proportional' as required under the CSIS Act."[104]

"NSIRA finds that CSIS did not adequately consider whether a *Charter* right would be limited by the reviewed TRM," the report also says.[105] However, "NSIRA was struck by the potential for a class of TRMs to affect rights and freedoms protected under the *Charter*."[106] This is all the more problematic since CSIS is required to obtain a warrant from the Federal Court when a TRM contravenes the Charter. However, as the 2021 annual report reveals, CSIS has never made a single application of this type since Parliament granted it disruptive powers with the passage of the *Anti-terrorism Act of 2015*. The

CONCLUSION

report also indicates that in a matter of seven years, CSIS has approved a total of 114 TRMs—an average of 16.2 per year—of which ninety-two have been implemented.[107] In other words, 80% of approved TRMs have been executed, amounting to 13.1 each year.

The report does not contain any information on the nature of the TRMs in question. However, the report of NSIRA's first examination, also heavily redacted, establishes that "there are three broad categories of TRMs implemented by CSIS: messaging, leveraging, and interference."[108] The NSIRA acknowledges that it "did not complete an in-depth examination of all three types of TRMs." According to the watchdog, "the leveraging category has seen the greatest growth in the number of proposals put forward" over the years. But, according to the NSIRA, "these appear to carry the highest risk of limiting Charter-protected rights and freedoms."[109]

In its second review, the NSIRA looked at "a larger number of TRMs, wherein CSIS disclosed information to external parties, and in doing so, provided the external party the opportunity to take action, at their discretion and pursuant to their authorities, to reduce identified threats." The annual report thus reveals that "several different kinds of external parties were involved in the TRMs."[110] Which is to say that CSIS practices a form of subcontracting in this matter. "According to CSIS, leveraging involves providing threat information to private companies for them to take action, at their discretion and pursuant to their authorities, to impede a person's ability to obtain services," says the second review report.[111] NSIRA stresses that these TRMs "can have significant and lasting impacts on the subjects and their families."[112]

However, "NSIRA also found that CSIS did not always document the outcomes of a specific TRM, or the actions taken by external parties to reduce a threat,"[113] leading the watchdog to recommend "that CSIS comply with its record-keeping policies."[114] NSIRA also recommended "that CSIS seeks a warrant when a proposed TRM could infringe on an individual's *Charter* rights, or where it would otherwise be contrary to Canadian law, regardless of whether the activity would be conducted by CSIS directly, or via an external party to whom CSIS discloses information."[115] The watchdog also says that it "fundamentally disagrees with CSIS's understanding of and approach to the legal analysis of determining whether a warrant is required for proposed TRMs."[116] They are not the only ones. The International Civil Liberties Monitoring Group has denounced the fact that "CSIS is farming out threat reduction measures to third parties," saying that the agency is "using that as a reason to avoid considering whether they need a warrant in the first place."[117]

Thus, the absence of a warrant application from CSIS does not mean that the agency did not act outside the law or in contravention of constitutional rights in exercising its new powers of disruption. In fact, the history of CSIS reveals that the intelligence agency shows little respect either for the law or for the Federal Court. Moreover, just recently, CSIS was rebuffed by the three different Federal justices in 2020 and 2021 for not complying with its duty of candour to the court (although their decisions were redacted to varying degrees). As Justice Brown points out, the importance of the duty of candour imposed on CSIS stems from the fact that the hearings to apply for such warrants are "conducted in secret," and so "the Court does not generally hear from anyone except [CSIS]."[118] In other words, "decisions are made based on information provided by [CSIS]."[119]

The facts that gave rise to these new controversies were recounted in detail in a Federal Court of Appeal decision, also partially redacted. CSIS originally approached the Federal Court for warrants in the context of an investigation about Canadian citizens wishing to join jihadist groups fighting overseas. While Judge Simon Noël was hearing one of these warrant applications, in April 2018, the CSIS representative revealed that the intelligence agency "had provided payments over a few years to an individual or individuals known to be facilitating or carrying out terrorism," the court wrote. However, "there was nothing in counsel's submissions to Justice Noël, or in the affiant's affidavit or her initial testimony, to suggest that there was anything potentially illegal about the payments." When the court raised questions about the legality of these payments, counsel for the Department of Justice's National Security Litigation and Advisory Group (NSLAG) "explained that he had not brought the potential illegality of the payments to the attention of the Court as he was not aware of the terrorist financing provisions of the *Criminal Code*."[120] The warrants requested by CSIS were nevertheless issued.

"In addition to the potential illegality arising from the payments [...] six additional instances of potential illegality were reported to the Court as this matter proceeded. The identified illegality involved [CSIS] or human sources acting on [CSIS]'s behalf making payments or providing goods," wrote Federal Court Judge Patrick K. Gleeson.[121] In one case, "CSIS provided [...] payments over a few years, totaling less than $25,000, to an individual known to be facilitating or carrying out terrorism." In another, "CSIS directed [...] to provide a target with goods valued at less than $2,000." Another case also mentions a payment "at the direction of" CSIS, this one with a value of "less than $1000 to a target."¹²²

At a case management conference held in May 2018, the new lawyer for the NSLAG recognized the importance of the issues raised by Justice Noël and proposed to start the process from scratch by submitting a new warrant application in order to respond to the court's concerns. The new application was heard by Judge Gleeson in September 2018. During the hearing, the court expressed concern about information provided by CSIS in support of the warrant application. The Court wondered "whether information obtained [by CSIS] had been legally obtained, or potentially involved the commission of criminal offences."¹²³ The warrants issued by his colleague Noël, however, remained in force "so as to avoid any gaps in [CSIS]'s operational capabilities."¹²⁴ In the meantime, CSIS has made "additional payments"¹²⁵ even though, by the admission of an agency official, such payments "could be construed as financing a terrorist." As the court pressed for answers, the CSIS lawyer "intervened to advise the Court that the Department of Justice had been consulted with respect to the legality of payments being made by the Service to those engaged in terrorist activities, and that its analysis was subject to solicitor-client privilege."¹²⁶

Then, in January 2019, the NSLAG's senior general counsel wrote to the Federal Court advising that CSIS "had become aware that information that it had relied upon in two other warrant applications," one granted by the judge Catherine M. Kane and the other by Justice Brown, "may engage provisions of the *Criminal Code*."¹²⁷ CSIS then said it "would no longer approve operations that were likely illegal."¹²⁸ The agency's lawyer acknowledged that the existence of the illegal activities "ought to have been disclosed to the issuing judge." Feeling the heat, CSIS Director David Vigneault waived the solicitor-client privilege protecting the NSLAG's legal opinions.¹²⁹ Notices dealing with the payments made revealed that CSIS had been advised by the NSLAG that "[t]here is little doubt here that most of the elements of the financing terrorism offen[c]e would be met." However, Michel Coulombe, director of CSIS at the time of the payments, nevertheless approved these activities on the grounds that their "value outweighs the [legal] risks."¹³⁰ In the end, Judge Gleeson issued the warrants requested by CSIS.¹³¹

In February 2019, Judge Brown was made aware of "four types of potential criminality related to the human source information in this file."¹³² "The first type of potential criminality dealt with relatively small payments" that the court finds to be "trivial matters, albeit technically perhaps criminal in nature."¹³³ As for the "second type of potential criminality," it involved the "assistance provided to the targets by human sources." Again, the judge didn't appear to care much. "While perhaps technically contraventions [...] this category also involves trivial matters with very little if any benefit," he wrote. The paragraph dealing with the "third type of potential criminality involved human sources" is so redacted that it is difficult to extract any information. "It seems to me that while the targets benefited, so too did [CSIS]," the court noted. "While this might technically constitute an offence, again it is trivial and a truly *de minimis* [*non curat lex*] one-off activity in respect of which there was also an entitlement"¹³⁴ The Latin is an "expression to the effect that the law does not care for small or trifling matters."¹³⁵ The judge went on to write that "the same may be said of the fourth activity, namely assisting on occasion [...] a target."¹³⁶

The court therefore leniently concluded that "the seriousness of these activities is minor and the illegality does not constitute a broader pattern of conduct; [...] I am also of the view, especially given the minor nature of the activities, that they do not undermine the credibility or reliability of the human source information provided."¹³⁷ And anyway, Justice Brown believed that he was "not required to assess whether or not crimes were actually committed by anyone providing human source information; this is not a criminal court."¹³⁸ Accordingly, "no information obtained from potential illegal activities of human sources should be excised from the record."¹³⁹ Then, in September 2019, the judge was informed of the existence of "further potentially unlawful conduct" on the part of CSIS, but these were "essentially of the same nature the Service disclosed in January and February 2019."¹⁴⁰

The judgment also mentioned that "evidence of activities before the issuance of the 2018 Warrants, does raise the issue of the validity of those warrants."¹⁴¹ Again, the paragraphs devoted to this additional information are heavily redacted; there is a mention of "unsubstantiated allegations made by others of more serious activity" but the redactions leave no clue as to their nature. Another paragraph mentions that CSIS "directed potentially unlawful activities," but no more is revealed. "Nor am I able to find these transactions to be serious crimes," wrote Judge Brown.¹⁴² That said, the court found that the "the newly disclosed information should have been disclosed in October 2018."¹⁴³

Finally, Judge Brown noted that Director Vigneault approved an operation involving a human source that "posed a high legal risk" in March 2018. But "the Minister was not advised for some four months." The previous year, however, Vigneault had written to the minister that he "will immediately notify you of high risk operations I approve, should any be identified."[144] The court was particularly alarmed "that human source activity was assessed as 'high legal risk' was not discussed at the Warrant Review Committee."[145] "This omission is important," the judge wrote, adding that CSIS "should have informed the Court when it applied for the 2018 Warrants that [there] was a report from the Director of CSIS to the Minister on July 3, 2018 based on operational high legal risk."[146] Despite these circumstances, the court chose to conclude that "there was no intent to conceal."[147]

As for Justice Kane, her decision reveals the existence of a CSIS memo revealing that "35% of the Service's human source activity was high risk (i.e., having likely engaged in one or more of the terrorism offences)." Given the agency's lack of candour, it's reasonable to think the true percentage is likely higher. Moreover, as the court points out, the note dated January 2017 "was not communicated until September 2020."[148]

In a ruling released May 15, 2020, Justice Gleeson writes that "the evidence discloses a number of institutional failures that contributed to the candour breach" by CSIS.[149] The court laments that "many individuals involved in the review and approval process were at least aware of the issue of illegality,"[150] adding: "It appears only the Court was left in the dark.[151] [...] The circumstances disclosed here suggest a degree of institutional disregard for—or, at the very least, a cavalier institutional approach to—the duty of candour and regrettably the rule of law."[152] Despite all these admonishments, when asked whether the Federal Court can "consider and rely on information probably gathered illegally," Judge Gleeson gave a positive answer. "I am of the view that this Court should consider three factors when determining whether information connected to illegal conduct should be admitted in support of a warrant application: (1) seriousness of the illegal activity; (2) fairness; and (3) societal interest," he wrote.[153]

Judge Brown's decision was handed down the following December 31. "There is no doubt, he writes, that [CSIS] failed in its duty of candour"[154] by "not disclosing that human source information relied upon might have been derived from activities that potentially contravened the *Criminal Code*," and by "failing to disclose information that had the potential to reflect adversely on the reliability and credibility of Service human sources relied upon." For the judge, "both breaches occurred through a combination of institutional and systemic negligence," adding that he is "unable to find any intention to mislead or deceive the Court."¹⁵⁵ Deploring the "regrettable frequency with which [CSIS] has breached its duty of candour," the tribunal notes that "despite previous and frequent judicial admonitions and commissioned expert reports, [CSIS] has failed to respect, and failed to instill respect for, the duty of candour within it."¹⁵⁶ Despite all this, "the 2018 Warrants are not set aside" since "they could have [been] issued even if this information had been disclosed."¹⁵⁷

As for Judge Kane's decision, it was rendered on June 7, 2021. "There was sufficient information to support the issuance of the warrants without reliance on the information gathered from illegal activities,"¹⁵⁸ the court found, adding that "the information gathered as a result of the execution of the 2017 and 2018 warrants need not be destroyed or isolated."¹⁵⁹

The case does not end there, however. "The circumstances and events that resulted in the Service engaging in illegal conduct contrary to legal advice warrants a comprehensive and detailed review," recommended Justice Glesson, "a review that is mandated to consider broad issues of institutional structure, governance and culture within both [CSIS] and relevant elements of the Department of Justice."¹⁶⁰

The review was entrusted to the NSIRA, which published the results in its 2021 annual report.¹⁶¹ The watchdog "conclude[d] that repeated failures" of the duty of candour were caused by "deep-seated cultural and governance patterns."¹⁶² Thus, CSIS and its counsels "struggle to organize themselves in a manner that enables them to meet their legal obligations, including to the Federal Court."¹⁶³ Their relations themselves appear problematic since "some at CSIS perceive the Department of Justice as presenting a roadblock."¹⁶⁴ Specifically, "NSIRA finds that the Justice Legal Risk Management Framework is misunderstood at the working level at CSIS and further that it does not provide an appropriate framework for the unequivocal communication of unlawful conduct to CSIS."¹⁶⁵ The watchdog also concluded that "CSIS has not always shared all relevant information with NSLAG, prompting a degree of mistrust and limiting Justice's ability to provide responsive legal advice."¹⁶⁶

In 2019, in an attempt to improve the agency's tarnished reputation with the Federal Court, "CSIS sought to professionalize affiant work by creating an Affiant Unit."¹⁶⁷ However, "CSIS has not supported the unit with resources commensurate with the importance of this unit in fulfilling CSIS's mission."

CONCLUSION

As a result, the Affiant Unit "is currently at risk of collapse."[168]

Although the NSIRA has made no less than twenty recommendations, the watchdog itself does not seem to be overflowing with optimism for the future. "No one reform is likely to succeed unless each is pursued as part of a coherent package," writes NSIRA.[169] Especially since "CSIS does not track or measure the outcome of past reforms adequately and has no performance metrics for assessing success."[170] In fact, past reforms themselves seem to be more part of the problem than part of the solution, because "many reforms appear to have contributed to the bureaucratic complexity of the warrant process, without addressing candour issues."[171] Moreover, "CSIS acknowledges that it is currently not a learning organization and does not have a learning culture."[172] The damning findings, however, raise questions that are missing from the NSIRA report: Isn't an organization that refuses to learn doomed to reproduce the same behaviours? How can an organization that prefers opacity to frankness be worthy of any trust?

Instead of drawing the necessary conclusions, the legislature chose to once again rubber-stamp the veil of secrecy behind which CSIS hides in order to commit various illegal acts and provocations. But the political class faces a conundrum when dealing with an agency like CSIS. On the one hand, it is in their own interests, given likely future political developments, to have an effective surveillance apparatus on hand, even if this clashes with the legal protections and rights that they also must pay lip service to in an attempt to retain public support (or apathy). To do its surveillance job, an agency like CSIS must be able to operate without being held back by the concerns or qualms of whomever happens to have won the last election. On the other hand, however, there are certain risks involved in an "out of control" surveillance body. An out of control CSIS may pose a threat not only to dissent but to everyone, including individual members of Parliament. There is nothing to prevent an agent provocateur from using the immunity that Parliament has so kindly granted them to make public death threats to members of the governing party, as RNWMP informant Robert Gosden did back in the day.

Similarly, there are those who will argue that Canada's allies would lose confidence in the Canadian secret service if it were to develop a reputation for being an intelligence "sieve," by virtue of being under an obligation to disclose any of its secrets to the public. Yet some of the cases of agents provocateurs examined in this book suggest that CSIS's failings may do even greater damage to Canada's image in "friendly" countries. How did it make Canada look when France's Judge Bruguière was informed that the man who had made repeated death threats against him with impunity was actually working for the Canadian secret service? And what did German authorities think when they learned that Ottawa had not informed them that it had authorized CSIS to send one of its informants to Germany to attend a neo-Nazi rally held in contravention of the laws of that country?

From the perspective of the state's victims, one small measure that might be hoped for is that the institutionalized impunity enjoyed by the Canadian secret services be balanced by an obligation of transparency, which criminal law concedes with regard to certain covert operations carried out in the course of police investigations.[173] This right to disclosure covers, among other things, activities carried out by undercover civilian agents in order to gather evidence that could incriminate the person charged. The accused can then learn the extent of the surveillance before their trial begins.

Only those formally charged in criminal court have the right to disclosure, however. Since from the outset CSIS investigations are not designed to gather evidence to lay charges, individuals who have been the direct or indirect target of undercover and covert surveillance may never be informed that they have been spied upon by the state, or that someone they thought was a trusted comrade was not who they claimed to be. Unless, of course, the informant's double-dealing comes to light. But for every Marc-André Boivin, Grant Bristow, or Joseph Gilles Breault whose clandestine activities are splashed across the pages of major newspapers, how many others remain safely tucked away in their protective shroud of secrecy, never to be discovered? We find ourselves in a situation that is paradoxical, to say the least, where a person involved in a criminal organization has a greater chance of being informed of the degree of state intrusion in his or her private life than a person working in a completely legal political organization where he or she is in contact with individuals who, rightly or wrongly, have been targeted by the secret services.

Likewise, the Criminal Code provides that any person who has been the subject of wiretaps must be notified in writing by the authorities, within a period of time ranging from 90 days to 3 years, depending on whether the investigation is extended and the nature of the offence under investigation.[174] But there is no similar provision that people must be notified that they have been the target of an undercover operation, an investigative method that is

CONCLUSION

often much more intrusive than electronic surveillance.

Supreme Court of Canada jurisprudence also recognizes the public's right to know about controversial police operations. In a unanimous decision in 2001, the country's highest court allowed the contents of so-called "Mr. Big" undercover police operations be revealed for the first time.[175]

> A fundamental belief pervades our political and legal system that the police should remain under civilian control and supervision by our democratically elected officials; our country is not a police state. The tactics used by police, along with other aspects of their operations, is a matter that is presumptively of public concern. Restricting the freedom of the press to report on the details of undercover operations that utilize deception, and that encourage the suspect to confess to specific crimes with the prospect of financial and other rewards, prevents the public from being informed critics of what may be controversial police actions.[176]

In another unanimous decision, this one rendered in 2010, the Supreme Court also ruled in favour of a lawyers' association seeking to obtain documents relating to a police investigation that resulted in several abuses:

> Without the desired access, meaningful public discussion and criticism on matters of public interest would be substantially impeded. As Louis D. Brandeis famously wrote in his 1913 article in *Harper's Weekly* entitled "What Publicity Can Do": "Sunlight is said to be the best of disinfectants...." Open government requires that the citizenry be granted access to government records when it is necessary to meaningful public debate on the conduct of government institutions.[177]

Secret services abhor this type of disinfectant; like moles that must flee the sun and scurry about in the dark, they are unable to stand the light of day. As such, one measure that might provide some relief to the state's victims would be a permanent commission of inquiry, which would do more good than the fortune in public funds spent to pay lawyers to obstruct access to information and to fund oversight mechanisms whose effectiveness is questionable at best. Unfortunately, the Canadian state, regardless of which party is in power, seems to have chosen opacity in matters of "national security" in order to protect CSIS's secrets big and small, even if this ensures provocation and abuse of all kinds will continue.

If the state refuses us the right to know what abuses are being committed in the name of "national security," then we should return the favour by refusing to provide the "security intelligence" that it apparently holds so dear. Without the public's cooperation, CSIS would have a hard time conducting its investigations. If you're tired of being taken for a ride by the Canadian secret service, there's nothing in the law that says you have to answer when CSIS comes knocking on your door.

There is no simple solution to the problem of police provocation and manipulation; in fact, they are likely to continue as long as the police and secret services exist. This is not an excuse to do nothing or wallow in defeatism. Many movements start with the denunciation of an injustice, and this book wishes to be a modest step in that direction. I hope that the history recounted here will outrage you as much as I have been outraged while writing about the despicable conduct of secret agents in the service of the Canadian state.

Endnotes

Introduction: In the Name of the Law

1. Montréal-Nord Républik is a collective that was formed following the August 10, 2008, riot in Montréal-Nord, to demand the resignation of the borough's mayor and an end to racial profiling. Its members founded the annual Hoodstock event and the Montreal North Social Forum.

2. I contacted Martineau myself, to explain the role I had played in calming things down. He didn't want to hear it, remaining adamant as to his characterization. I complained to the Quebec Press Council, which censured Martineau for "opening the door to an abusive generalization" by failing to report on the otherwise successful efforts of the demonstration organizers to stop things from getting out of hand. (*Popovic v. Martineau*, Quebec Press Council, 2010, 2009-08-014).

3. *Popovic v. Noël et al.*, Police Ethics Commissioner, 2013, 10-0429.

4. Louise Letarte, counsel for the Commissioner, communicated to me in a letter dated August 6, 2013, that they had decided to "discontinue the process."

5. Originating in West Germany in the 1980s, the "black bloc" refers to a tactic used by anarchist-affiliated groups during demonstrations in which participants conceal their identities and dress all in black to disrupt police efforts to distinguish one from another.

6. "Sommet de Montebello—La SQ passe aux aveux," *Radio-Canada*, Montreal, August 23, 2007, http://ici.radio-canada.ca/nouvelle/364528/sq-reax-youtube.

7. A Latin phrase used in law meaning "caught in the act."

8. *Coles v. Police Ethics Commissioner*, Police Ethics Committee, 2009, R-2009-1418.

9. The citation accused them of disrespecting and being rude to a person (count 1), using abusive language and obscene language (count 2), refusing to identify themselves when asked to do so (count 3), abusing their authority by using force (count 4), and inciting people to violence (count 5). However, Inspector Savard was cleared due to "insufficient evidence."

10. It should be noted that Sergeant Boucher had argued that his behaviour had been entirely consistent with the training provided in preparation for the Summit of the Americas, held in Quebec City in April 2001. At the time, the training provided required that plainclothes police teams take on the appearance of protesters "by using the equipment necessary for their dress and by adopting their behaviour and language." Judging by his conduct at Montebello, Sergeant Boucher seemed to have concluded that protesters are assholes and bullies. (*Police Ethics Commissioner v. Boucher*, Police Ethics Committee, 2011, C-2009-3584-1.)

11. *Boucher v. Simard*, Court of Quebec, 2012, 500-80-019385-112, p. 17, para. 56.

12. *Ibid, para. 57.*

13. Commission of Inquiry into Certain Activities of the RCMP (McDonald Commission), *Second Report—Freedom and Security under the law*, Ottawa, Canadian Government Publishing Centre, 1981, p. 55.

14. Steven R. Hewitt, "Old Myths Die Hard: The Transformation of the Mounted Police in Alberta and Saskatchewan 1914–1939," PhD thesis in history, University of Saskatchewan, 1997, pp. 272–273.

15. McDonald Commission, *Third Report—Certain R.C.M.P. Activities and the Question of Governmental Knowledge*, p. 133.

16. The SS was responsible for the RCMP's national security activities. This department went by different names at different points in time. It began as the Intelligence Section in 1936 and became the Special Branch ten years later. In 1956, it was renamed the Security and Intelligence Service (also known as I Branch). It finally became the SS in 1970.

17. McDonald Commission, *Second Report*, op. cit., p. 399.

18. *Ibid.*, p. 400.

19. *Ibid.*

20. McDonald Commission, *Third Report, op. cit.*, p. 35.

21. *Ibid.*, p. 44.

22. *Ibid.*, p. 70.

23. *Ibid.*, p. 64.

24. *R. v. Bond*, Alberta Court of Appeal, 1993, 135 A.R. 333 (C.A.).

25. *R. v. Mack*, Supreme Court of Canada 1988, 2 SCR 903-094.

26. *Regina v. Campbell et al.*, Ontario Court of Appeal, 1997, 32 O.R. (3d) 181 (Ont. C.A.).

27. Chad Skelton, "Police pose as drug dealers in $1.2-million cocaine sting to nab 3 biker gang suspects," *The Vancouver Sun*, September 26, 1998, p. A1. Chad Skelton, "Reverse sting law slipped in to aid police," *The Vancouver Sun*, October 6, 1998, p. A1.

28. *R. v. Campbell*, Supreme Court of Canada, 1999, 1 SCR 593–594.

29. Department of Justice, *Law Enforcement and Criminal Liability—White Paper 2000*, Ottawa, Justice Canada, 2000.

30. Cristin Schmitz, "Ottawa looks to give some immunity to police," *National Post*, May 29, 1999, p. A1.

31. Nahlah Ayed, "Justice Minister tables draft legislation on police conduct," Canadian Press, June 22, 2000.

32. Andrew Duffy, "Cops would be allowed to break law," *Montreal Gazette*, June 23, 2000, A9.

33. Gilles Toupin, "Une immunité limitée pour les policiers," *La Presse*, August 24, 2000, p. B1.

34. Sections 25.1 to 25.4 of the *Criminal Code* provide the legal framework under which members of police forces may commit criminal offences.

35. Jim McNulty "Sound the alarm—Anti-gang bill lets cops break law," *The Province*, June 1, 2001, p. A15.

36. Ligue des droits et libertés, "La proposition du ministère fédéral de la Justice d'amender l'article 25 du Code criminel est inacceptable dans une société libre et démocratique fondée sur la primauté du droit et l'égalité devant la loi," Canada NewsWire, October 11, 2000.

37. Jim Bronskill, "Even police wary of new powers," *Ottawa Citizen*, April 11, 2001, p. A1.

38. Vincent Westwick, "Police not wary of increased powers," *Ottawa Citizen*, April 16, 2001, p. A11.

39. Yves Prud'Homme, "Antigang: va-t-on trop loin? Non," *La Presse*, May 30, 2001, p. A15.

40. Anne-Marie Boisvert, "La protection des collaborateurs de la justice : éléments de mise à jour de la politique québécoise—Rapport final présenté au ministre de la Sécurité publique," Quebec City, Ministère de la Sécurité publique, 2005, p. 4.

41. Yet another category consists of those who agree to testify against their accomplices "in exchange for certain benefits." While such turncoats are generally viewed with disgust, they are referred to by the Quebec government with the sanitized term "repentant witness." Boisvert, *op. cit.*, p. 5.

42. Review Committee on the CSIS Act and the Security Offences Act, "Proceedings," Ottawa, House of Commons, May 15, 1990, p. 31:5.

43. *R. v. B., G., et al.*, Ontario Court of Appeal, 2000, 146 CCC (3d) 465 (Ont. C.A.).

44. Catharine Tunney, "RCMP officers given permission to break the law a record 73 times in 2017, report shows," *CBC*, November 25, 2018; Éric Thibault & Félix Séguin, "Un policier a forgé un document de cour," *Journal de Montréal*, May 7, 2022.

45. Section 25.1(9)(b) of the *Criminal Code* provides for the possibility of bypassing the need for authorization where "it is not feasible in the circumstances to obtain the authorization and that the act or omission is necessary to (i) preserve the life or safety of any person, (ii) prevent the compromise of the identity of a public officer acting in an undercover capacity, of a confidential informant or of a person acting covertly under the direction and

control of a public officer, or (iii) prevent the imminent loss or destruction of evidence of an indictable offence"

46. The report said there were four, but actually named five offences.

47. Unfortunately, the data contained in the RCMP annual reports is far from consistent. Some do not mention the number of authorizations followed by deed, while others do not specify the number of offences concerned by the authorizations.

48. *Canadian Security Intelligence Services Act (Re)*, 2020 FC 616, [2021] 1 FCR 417, canlii.ca/t/j8mjx, para. 42.

49. The official name of bill C-51 is *An Act to amend the Criminal Code, the Official Secrets Act, the Canada Evidence Act, the Proceeds of Crime (Money Laundering) Act and other Acts, and to enact measures respecting the registration of charities, in order to combat terrorism.*

50. 2020 FC 616, *op. cit.*, para. 42–43.

51. *Ibid.*, para. 67.

52. *Ibid.*, para. 128–29.

53. *Ibid.*, para. 44–46.

54. *Canadian Broadcasting Corp. v. Attorney General (Ontario)*, 1959 CanLII 2 (SCC), [1959] S.C.R. 188, (1959).

55. 2020 FC 616, *op. cit.*, para. 44–46.

56. *Ibid.*, para. 47.

57. *Ibid.*

58. *Ibid.*, para. 48.

59. C-51, *op. cit.*, s. 42.

60. David Vienneau, "Canada's spymaster fired," *Toronto Star*, September 12, 1987, p. A1.

61. *X (Re)*, Federal Court, 2013 CSIS-30-08, canlii.ca/t/g2rl7.

62. Jim Bronskill, "CSIS illegally retained personal data, federal court says," *Canadian Press*, November 3, 2016.

63. "Les espions canadiens contrariés par les tribunaux," Montreal, *Radio-Canada*, November 30, 2010, http://ici.radio-canada.ca/nouvelle/495420/wikileaks-judd-scrs.

64. Colin Freeze, "Divisive terror law losing traction in Ottawa," *Globe and Mail*, September 21, 2009, p. A1.

65. Colin Freeze, "CSIS spy-warrant requests meet with little opposition, documents reveal," *Globe and Mail*, November 15, 2004, p. A6.

66. 2020 FC 616, *op. cit.*, para. 54–55.

67. *Ibid.*, para. 57.

68. *Ibid.*, para. 150.

69. *Ibid.*, para. 58.

70. *Ibid.*, para. 64.

71. *Ibid.*, para. 103.

72. *Ibid.*, para. 108.

73. *Ibid.*, para. 144.

74. Government of Canada, "Our Security, Our Rights—National Security Green Paper," 2016, p. 3.

75. Public Safety Canada, "National Security Consultations—What We Learned Report," 2017, p. 4.

76. House of Commons, "Protecting Canadians and their Rights: A New Road Map for Canada's National Security," Report of the Standing Committee on Public Safety and National Security, May 2017, p. 39.

77. C-59, s. 99.

78. *Ibid.*, s. 98(3.2).

79. *Ibid.*, s. 107.

80. *Ibid.*, s. 103(1.1).

81. *Ibid.*, s. 101(2–3) and (18).

82. *Ibid.*, s. 101(6–8) and (12).

83. *Ibid.*, s. 101(5–6).

84. Thomas Walkom, "Trudeau's security bill is a lot like Harper's," *Toronto Star*, June 23, 2017, p. A13.

85. 2020 FC 616, *op. cit.*, para. 114.

Chapter 1. Confederation and Provocation

1. Allan Greer, "The Birth of the Police in Canada," in Allan Greer and Ian Radforth [eds], *Colonial Leviathan: State Formation in Mid-Nineteenth-Century Canada*, Toronto, University of Toronto Press, 1992, p. 32.

2. Greer, *op. cit.*, pp. 33–38.

3. *Ibid.*, p. 40.

4. Greer, p. 49.

5. Peter Edwards, *Delusion: The True Story of Victorian Superspy Henri Le Caron*, Toronto, Key Porter Books, 2008, pp. 30–34.

6. Gregory S. Kealey, "The Empire Strikes Back: The Nineteenth-Century Origins of the Canadian Secret Service," *Journal of the Canadian Historical Association*, vol. 10, no. 1, 1999, p. 11.

7. The Dominion Police consisted of a dozen officers. In addition to espionage, their mandate was to protect government buildings and investigate violations of federal laws.

8. David Ricardo Williams, *Call in Pinkerton's: American Detectives at Work for Canada*, Toronto, Dundurn Press, 1998, p. 22.

9. Donald Creighton, *John A. Macdonald : le 1er ministre du Canada*, trans. I. Steenhout, Montreal, Éditions de l'Homme, 1981, p. 379.

10. Richard Gwyn, *John A.: The Man Who Made Us. The Life and Times of John A. Macdonald*, Toronto, Random House Canada, 2009, p. 356.

11. Kealey, *op. cit.*, pp. 11–14.

12. Edwards, *op. cit.*, pp. 30–34.

13. *Ibid.*, p. 46.

14. Edwards, *op. cit.*, pp. 64–65.

15. *Ibid.*, p. 86.

16. *Ibid.*, p. 67.

17. Henry Le Caron, *Twenty-five years in the secret service: the recollections of a spy*, London, William Heinemann, 1892, pp. 53–54.

18. Edwards, *op. cit.*, p. 86.

19. Le Caron, *op. cit.*, p. 55.

20. Edwards, *op. cit.*, p. 75.

21. *Ibid.*, p. 66.

22. Edwards, *op. cit.* Added to this were the many factional struggles that fuelled internal dissent, and the fact that, by the end of 1869, O'Neill had begun dipping into the organization's coffers to support himself. Finances were so bad that the Fenians could no longer pay Le Caron (Le Caron, *op. cit.*, pp. 73–74).

23. Edwards, *op. cit.*, p. 87.

24. Le Caron, *op. cit.*, p. 82.

25. Receiving a hero's welcome in Ottawa, Le Caron was awarded a $2,000 bonus from the Canadian government (Edwards, *op. cit.*, p. 93).

26. *Ibid.*, pp. 100–102.

27. Le Caron, *op. cit.*, p. 98.

28. *Ibid.*

29. Edwards, *op. cit.*, p. 101.

30. Not to be confused with the Northwest Territories, a present-day federal territory in Canada's north bordered by the Yukon to the west, Nunavut to the east, and British Columbia, Alberta, and Saskatchewan to the south.

31. Alexandre-Antonin Taché, *Louis Riel et les troubles du Nord-Ouest: de la Rivière-Rouge à Batoche*, Montreal, Éditions du Méridien, 2000, p. 203.

32. The modest commando never entered Canada, as it was quickly intercepted by American soldiers.

33. Edwards, *op. cit.*, pp. 104–106.

34. Le Caron, *op. cit.*, p. 276.

35. Edwards, *op. cit.*, p. 293.

36. Donald G. McLean, *1885 Métis Rebellion or Government Conspiracy?* Winnipeg, Pemmican Publications, 1985, pp. 27–28.

37. George Woodcock, *Gabriel Dumont: The Metis Chief and His Lost World*, Peterborough, Broadview Press, 2003, p. 121.

38. McLean, *op. cit.*, p. 38.

39. Responsible for the management of Ottawa lands, Indian affairs, and the development of natural resources before it was abolished in 1936.

40. Woodcock, *op. cit.*, pp. 148–149.

41. Lorne Brown & Caroline Brown, *An Unauthorized History of the RCMP*, Toronto, James Lewis & Samuel, 1973, p. 12.

42. Hewitt, *Old Myths Die Hard, op. cit.*, p. 32.

43. Woodcock, *op. cit.*, p. 123.

44. *Ibid.*, p. 124.

45. *Ibid.*, p. 155.

46. McLean, *op. cit.*, p. 40.

47. *Ibid.*, p. 49.

48. Woodcock, *op. cit.*, p. 155.

49. McLean, *op. cit.*, p. 35.

50. Lawrence Clarke played a major role in the negotiation of Treaty 6 with the Cree and Assiniboine, among others (*Ibid.*, p. 41).

51. *Ibid.*, p. 47; Bob Beal and Rod MacLeod, *Prairie Fire: The 1885 North-West Rebellion*, Toronto, McClelland & Stewart, 1994, p. 101.

52. McLean, *op. cit.*, pp. 49–50.

53. *Ibid.*, p. 90.

54. Beal and Macleod, *op. cit.*, pp. 109–115.

55. Taché, *op. cit.*, pp. 159–160.

56. McLean, *op. cit.*, pp. 90–91.

57. *Ibid.*, p. 91.

58. *Ibid.*, p. 93.

59. *Ibid.*, pp. 92–94.

60. Joseph Boyden, *Louis Riel et Gabriel Dumont*, Montreal, Boréal, 2011, pp. 60–61.

61. McLean, *op. cit.*, p. 96.

62. Beal and Macleod, *op. cit.*, pp. 134–136.

63. Taché, *op. cit.*, pp. 160–161.

64. *Ibid.*, p. 137.

65. Joseph Kinsey Howard, *Strange Empire: A Narrative of the Northwest*, St. Paul, Minnesota Historical Society Press, 1994, p. 380.

66. McLean, *op. cit.*, p. 97.

67. Taché, *op. cit.*, p. 162.

68. McLean, *op. cit.*, p. 98.

69. Woodcock, *op. cit.*, p. 172.

70. Howard, *op. cit.*, p. 228.

71. Murray Dobbin, "Thomas Flanagan's Riel: An Unfortunate Obsession—A Review," *Alberta History*, Spring 1984, vol. 32, no. 2, p. 25.

72. McLean, *op. cit.*, p. 103.

73. *Ibid.*, p. 108.

74. Beal and Macleod, *op. cit.*, p. 155.

75. McLean, *op. cit.*, p. 113.

76. Taché, *op. cit.*, p. 173.

77. McLean, *op. cit.*, p. 119.

78. J. M. Bumsted, *Louis Riel v. Canada: The Rebel Years*, Winnipeg, Plains, 2005, p. 337.

79. Beal and Macleod, *op. cit.*, p. 337–338. The other Cree were A-pis-chas-koos (Little Bear), Manchoose (The Bad Arrow), Nahpase (Iron Body), Kit-ahwah-ke-ni (Wretched Man), and Pahpah-me-kee-sick (Walking the Sky). The Assiniboine were Waywahnitch (Man without Blood) and Itka (Crooked Leg).

80. McLean, *op. cit.*, p. 122.

81. The National Policy had three related pillars: the introduction of tariffs of 30–35% on manufactured goods to encourage the industrialization of Canada, the extension of the railroad to secondary cities and the West to facilitate trade, and bringing in settlers to "develop" the West and encourage the growth of the Canadian economy.

82. Gwyn, *op. cit.*, p. 337.

83. David Cruise and Alison Griffiths, *Lords of The Line. The Men Who Built the CPR*, New York City, Viking, 1988.

84. Gwyn, *op. cit.*, p. 366.

85. Cruise and Griffiths, *op. cit.*, pp. 154–155.

86. Quoted in McLean, *op. cit.*, p. 121.

87. *Ibid.*, p. 122.

Chapter 2. Seeing Red

1. Brown and Brown, *op. cit.*, p. 51.

2. The title "Royal" was added to the name of the North West Mounted Police in 1904, after members of the force took part in the Second Boer War (1899–1902) alongside British troops.

3. Brown and Brown, *op. cit.*, p. 46.

4. Hewitt, *Old Myths Die Hard, op. cit.*, p. 163.

5. Steve Hewitt, *Spying 101: The RCMP's Secret Activities at Canadian Universities, 1917–1997*, Toronto, University of Toronto Press, 2002.

6. Hewitt, *Old Myths Die Hard, op. cit.*, p. 163.

7. In the world of intelligence, processing officers, also known as "controllers," recruit and manage informants.

8. Hewitt, *Old Myths Die Hard, op. cit.*, p. 173.

9. *Ibid.*, p 184.

10. Michael Butt, "Surveillance of Canadian Communists: A case study of Toronto RCMP intelligence networks, 1920–1939," PhD thesis in history, Memorial University of Newfoundland, 2003, p. 172.

11. *Ibid.*, pp. 107–110.

12. Williams, *op. cit.*, p. 152.

13. *Ibid.*

14. *Ibid.*, p.154.

15. *Ibid.*

16. Founded in the United States in 1905, the IWW is an international syndicalist movement advocating self-management, the abolition of wage-labour, and the inclusion of all members of the working class in a single union. Mark Leier, "Portrait of a Labour Spy: The Case of Robert Raglan Gosden, 1882–1961," *Labour/Le Travail*, vol. 42, Fall 1998, pp. 56–63.

17. *Ibid.*, pp. 56 and 64.

18. *Ibid.*, p. 63.

19. *Ibid.*, pp. 64–65.

20. *Ibid.*, p. 69.

21. *Ibid.*, pp. 66–70.

22. James Dubro and Robin Rowland, *Undercover: Cases of the RCMP's Most Secret Operative*, London, Octopus Publishing, 1991, p. 13.

23. *Ibid.*, p. 25.

24. As the First World War raged for nearly four years, at Britain's request Ottawa amended the Military Service Act to send more men to the front. The measure proved highly unpopular in French-speaking Quebec, which did not identify with the British Empire.

25. Dubro and Rowland, *op. cit.*, p. 29.

26. *Ibid.*, pp. 29–35.

27. Scott C. Eaton, "Capitalism on Trial: Section 98, the Communist Party of Canada, and the Battle for Legality in the Interwar Period," PhD thesis in history, Memorial University of Newfoundland, 2012, p. 16.
PC 2384 expired on April 1, 1919, and was not renewed.

28. Brown and Brown, *op. cit.*, p. 37.

29. G.W.L. Nicholson and Mark O. Humphries, *Canadian Expeditionary Force, 1914–1919: Official History of the Canadian Army in the First World War*, Montreal, McGill-Queen's University Press, 2015, p. 519.

30. Alan Philips, *The Living Legend: The Story of the Royal Canadian Mounted Police*, New York, Little, Brown and Company, 1957, p. 88.

31. Hewitt, *Old Myths Die Hard*, *op. cit.*, p. 156.

32. Philips, *op. cit.*, p. 88.

33. Andrew Parnaby and Gregory S. Kealey, "How the 'Reds' Got Their Man: The Communist Party Unmasks an RCMP Spy," *Journal of Labor Studies*, vol. 40, Fall 1997, p. 255.

34. Philips, *op. cit.*, p. 88.

35. *Ibid.*, p. 87.

36. Leier, *op. cit.*, p. 71.

37. *Ibid.*, pp. 72–73.

38. *Ibid.*, pp. 73–74.

39. *Ibid.*

40. In addition to his ineptitude at avoiding detection, the RNWMP was not particularly pleased that Gosden submitted a report that was virtually identical to the one he had written on the Calgary Convention. His "reports were considered unreliable and, in some cases, false. He was considered untrustworthy," noted one of his case officers. One of his colleagues, while acknowledging that Gosden "provided the most useful information," lamented the fact that he was "too restless and unstable to hold a regular job" (*Ibid.*, p. 75).

41. Dubro and Rowland, *op. cit.*, pp. 38–41.

42. *Ibid.*, pp. 48–50.

43. *Ibid.*, p. 51.

44. *Ibid.*, pp. 69–70.

45. According to Section 123(5) of the Criminal Code at the time, "a seditious conspiracy is an agreement or understanding between two or more persons to carry out a seditious intention."

46. Brown and Brown, *op. cit.*, pp. 42–43.

47. Dubro and Rowland, *op. cit.*, pp. 73–75.

48. Brown & Brown, *op. cit.*, p. 51.

49. Quoted in Dubro and Rowland, *op. cit.*, pp. 77–78.

50. *Ibid.*, p. 79.

51. Hewitt, *Spying 101, op. cit.*, pp. 22–23.

52. Brown and Brown, *op. cit.*, p. 36.

53. Dubro and Rowland, *op. cit.*, pp. 86–87.

54. *Ibid.*, p. 98.

55. William Rodney, *Soldiers of the International: A History of the Communist Party of Canada, 1919–1929*, Toronto, University of Toronto Press, 1968, p. 47.

56. Quoted in Philips, *op. cit.*, p. 88.

57. *Ibid.*, p. 89.

58. The Worker's Party of Canada changed its name to the Communist Party of Canada in April 1924, after Ottawa decided not to renew the *War Measures Act*.

59. Hewitt, *Old Myths Die Hard, op. cit.*, p. 157.

60. *Ibid.*

61. Parnaby and Kealey, *op. cit.*, p. 255.

62. Hewitt, *Old Myths Die Hard, op. cit.*, p. 158.

63. Philips, *op. cit.*, pp. 89–90.

64. Butt, *op. cit.*, pp. 155–156.

65. Parnaby and Kealey, *op. cit.*, p. 260.

66. *Ibid.*, pp. 121–123.

67. *Ibid.*, p. 138.

68. Butt, *op. cit.*, p. 146.

69. *Ibid.*, pp. 147–148.

70. Hewitt, *Old Myths Die Hard, op. cit.*, p. 159.

71. Butt, *op. cit.*, pp. 160–161.

72. Nicola Sacco and Bartolomeo Vanzetti were two American anarchists of Italian origin. They were convicted of murder on questionable evidence, sentenced to death, and executed in the electric chair on August 27, 1927.

73. Butt, *op. cit.*, pp. 164–166.

74. Philips, *op. cit.*, p. 90.

75. Parnaby and Kealey, *op. cit.*, p. 256.

76. *Ibid.*, pp. 263–265.

77. Butt, *op. cit.*, p. 169.

78. It should be noted that the charge of seditious conspiracy was dropped on appeal. The indictment, based on Section 98(3) of the Criminal Code at the time, was amended by the court so that the accused were charged with being both members and officials of an illegal organization. Section 98 was repealed in 1935.

79. Barbara Roberts, *Whence They Came: Deportation from Canada, 1900–1935*, Ottawa, University of Ottawa Press, 1988, p. 128.

80. Penner, *op. cit.*, p. 119.

81. Butt, *op. cit.*, pp. 251–252.

82. Hewitt, *Old Myths Die Hard*, *op. cit.*, p. 198.

83. Roberts, *op. cit.*, pp. 129–130.

84. Hewitt, *Old Myths Die Hard*, *op. cit.*, p. 160.

85. Butt, *op. cit.*, p. 173.

86. Bill Waiser, *All Hell Can't Stop Us: The On-to-Ottawa Trek and Regina Riots*, Markham, Fifth House, 2003, p. 37.

87. Hewitt, *Old Myths Die Hard*, *op. cit.*, p. 162.

88. Quoted in Hewitt, *Old Myths Die Hard*, *op. cit.*, p. 156.

89. Brown & Brown, *op. cit.*, pp. 54–55.

90. Leier, *op. cit.*, pp. 77–78.

91. *Ibid.*

92. Hewitt, *Old Myths Die Hard*, *op. cit.*, pp. 174–175.

93. Brown and Brown, *op. cit.*, p. 80.

94. Hewitt, *Old Myths Die Hard*, *op. cit.*, p. 188.

95. *Ibid.*, pp. 200–203.

96. Brown and Brown, *op. cit.*, p. 82.

97. Hewitt, *Old Myths Die Hard, op. cit.*, p. 177.

Chapterv 3. On the Trail of the FLQ

1. Quoted in Louis Fournier, *F.L.Q. Histoire d'un mouvement clandestin*, Montreal, Éditions Québec/Amérique, 1982, p. 44.

2. *Ibid.*, pp. 47–48.

3. In French, it is common to make an adjective out of pronouncing an initialism as if it were a word. The resulting word also refers to members or supporters of the group. Felquiste is pronounced "fell-KEEST."

4. Gérard Pelletier, *La crise d'octobre*, Montreal, Éditions du jour, 1971, pp. 225–253.

5. Also called "Direction I."

6. Fournier, *op. cit.*, p. 42.

7. McDonald Commission, *Second Report, op. cit.*, p. 451.

8. Founded in 1960, the RIN became a political party three years later. It was disbanded in 1968, its members merging into the fledgling Parti Québécois.

9. Like many post-war national liberation struggles, the FLQ always featured a tension between those who prioritized nation/nationalism and those who prioritized class/socialism.

10. Serge Savard, a young unemployed man, was arrested at the same time. Savard would be sentenced to six months in jail.

11. Fournier, *op. cit.*, pp. 149–150. After entering provincial politics in 1994, Serge Ménard served as Minister of Public Safety for seven of the subsequent nine years of PQ governments, under Jacques Parizeau, Lucien Bouchard, and Bernard Landry. He also sat as a Bloc Québécois MP from 2004 to 2011, and would chair the Special Commission to Review the Events of Spring 2012.

12. Fournier, *op. cit.*, p. 175.

13. *Ibid.*, pp. 223–224.

14. These other demands were: 1) no police search for the hostage; 2) the release of the FLQ manifesto to the media; 3) the release of twenty-three political prisoners; 4) the rehiring of the "Lapalme boys" (alluding to the 450 truckers of the private company Lapalme who had been fired following the loss of a postal contract with the federal government); 5) safe passage to Cuba or Algeria; and 6) the imposition of a "voluntary tax" of $500,000 to be placed on board the plane.

15. During the Prévost raid, police seized three sawed-off rifles, revolvers and ammunition, hoods and handcuffs, detonators and timers, and $28,260 (half of the proceeds of a robbery at the Université de Montréal). Another search, this time of an apartment on Henri-Bourassa Boulevard in Montreal, resulted in the seizure of materials with which the FLQ had printed its communiqués and Manifesto.

16. Centre d'analyse et de documentation, *Front de libération du Québec 1963–1975*, Quebec City: Ministère du Conseil exécutif, September 15, 1975, p. 10. Dubbed Bourassa's "political police," the CAD kept files on 6,000 groups and 30,000 individuals in the 1970s. The organization was dismantled in 1987, but some of its records were transferred to the Ministry of Public Security.

17. Fournier, *op. cit.*, pp. 267–268.

18. CAD, *op. cit.*, p. 1.

19. Jean-François Duchaîne, *Rapport sur les événements d'octobre 1970*, Quebec City, Ministère de la Justice, 1980, p. 92.

20. Germain Dion, *Une tornade de 60 jours*, Hull, Éditions Asticou, 1985, p. 73.

21. Dion, *op. cit.*, pp. 99–100.

22. Fournier, *op. cit.*, p. 300.

23. This refers to an assembly in support of the FLQ held at the Centre Paul-Sauvé on October 15. After Pierres Vallières (recently released from prison for FLQ activity) said "The FLQ is each and every one of you" in his speech, the large crowd chanted "FLQ! FLQ! FLQ!"

24. Duchaîne, *op. cit.*, p. 556.

25. Fournier, *op. cit.*, pp. 310–311.

26. CAD, *op. cit.*, p. 10.

27. Duchaîne, *op. cit.*, p. 211.

28. *Ibid.*, pp. 254–255.

29. Nicknamed "Monsieur," Jacques Parizeau (1930–2015) was Minister of Finance in René Lévesque's government from 1976 to 1984, before being elected Premier of Quebec in 1994, a position he left immediately following the defeat of the pro-independence camp in the 1995 referendum.

30. Carole de Vault and William Johnson, *The Informer: Confessions of an Ex-terrorist*, Toronto, Fleet Books, 1982, p. 110.

31. "Information" refers to the cell's focus on releasing communiqués.

32. Duchaîne, *op. cit.*, p. 162.

33. De Vault, *op. cit.*, pp. 131–134.

34. *Ibid.*, pp. 139–143.

35. *Ibid.*, p. 157.

36. Duchaîne, *op. cit.*, p. 163.

37. De Vault, *op. cit.*, p. 189.

38. *Ibid.*, p. 160.

39. *Ibid.*, p. 165.

40. *Ibid.*, p. 170.

41. *Ibid.*, pp. 182–185.

42. McDonald Commission, *Third Report*, *op. cit.*, pp. 194–195.

43. Fournier, *op. cit.*, pp. 323–325.

44. Duchaîne, *op. cit.*, p.231.

45. Jean-Paul Brodeur, "La Crise d'octobre et les commissions d'enquête," *Criminologie*, vol. 13, no. 2, 1980, p. 94.

46. In all likelihood, this was François "Fritz" Séguin, discussed below. *Ibid.*, pp. 231–232.

47. The other members of the Libération Cell also received prison sentences after their return from exile. Jacques Lanctôt received the most severe sentence for refusing to express regret in court, namely three years in prison. Yves Langlois and Jacques and Louise Cossette-Trudel received two years less a day in prison, while Marc Carbonneau received twenty months.

48. McDonald Commission, *Third Report*, op. cit., p. 30.

49. Quoted in *Ibid.*, p. 27.

50. Quoted in *Ibid.*, p. 32.

51. At the end of the year, only four people—considered movement leaders—remained incarcerated from the War Measures Act arrests: Michel Chartrand, Robert Lemieux, Pierre Vallières, and Charles Gagnon. Paul Rose and Francis Simard were finally released on parole in 1982, while Jacques Rose and Bernard Lortie were released in 1978.

52. Commission of Inquiry into Police Operations on Quebec Territory (Keable Commission), *Rapport de la commission d'enquête sur des opérations policières en territoire québécois*, Quebec City, Direction générale des publications gouvernementales, 1981, p. 228.

53. *Ibid.*, pp. 219–221.

54. *Ibid.*, pp. 229–230.

55. The police had been warned by de Vault in late December 1970 that Comeau was planning to steal explosives from a quarry in St. Paul-d'Abbotsford. Comeau and Séguin were under surveillance when they went to the site to check it out. On January 3, 1971, the *felquistes* went into action and got their hands on 137 sticks of dynamite and 397 electric detonators. Two days later, Sergeant Bernard Fréchette of the SAT communicated the names of Comeau and Séguin to the person in charge of the investigation, SQ Officer Guy Laplante. Strangely enough, however, Detective Lieutenant Giguère would soon afterwards state that "they were not the right suspects" and the investigation was not pursued (*ibid.*, pp. 171 and 175).

56. *Ibid.*, pp. 201 and 205.

57. *Ibid.*, p. 218.

58. De Vault, *op. cit.*, p. 247.

59. McDonald Commission, *Third Report*, *op. cit.*, p. 197.

60. Carole de Vault, *Toute ma vérité : les confessions de l'agent S.A.T. 945-171*, Montréal, Stanké, 1981, p. 246. This passage, which appears in the original French version of de Vault's book, does not appear in the English version.

61. De Vault and Johnson, *op. cit.*, pp. 246–247.

62. Brink's had alienated many independence supporters after nine of its armoured vans were used to transport equipment from the Montreal offices of Royal Trust Financial Institution to Toronto on April 26, 1970—just two days before the Quebec general election (the first in which the Parti Québecois had run candidates). The spectacle, dubbed "the Brink's coup," made headlines and was used to scaremonger about the possibility of capital flight in the event of a PQ victory.

63. Keable Commission, *op. cit.*, pp. 131–133.

64. De Vault and Johnson, *op. cit.*, p. 240; Keable Commission, *op. cit.*, p. 143.

65. *Ibid.*, p. 145,

66. *Ibid.*, pp. 151–153. Cf. Chapter 5. Moles come out of their holes.

67. Keable Commission, *op. cit.*, p. 153.

68. De Vault and Johnson, *op. cit.*, p. 256.

69. Keable Commission, *op. cit.*, p. 154.

70. Michèle Gauthier was a twenty-eight-year-old pregnant woman who died as a result of an asthma attack caused by the riot police attacking a demonstration in support of striking workers at the *La Presse* newspaper, on October 29, 1971.

71. Keable Commission, *op. cit.*, pp. 147–148.

72. De Vault and Johnson, *op. cit.*, p. 260.

73. Keable Commission, *op. cit.*, pp. 147–148.

74. *Ibid.*, pp. 149–151.

75. Fournier, *op. cit.*, p. 346.

76. De Vault and Johnson, *op. cit.*, pp. 249–250.

77. *Ibid.*

78. *Ibid.*

79. "According to available police records, Séguin was recruited as an informant in May 1972 by the SAT. His source number is 945-226." Fournier, *op. cit.*, p. 332.

80. Keable Commission, *op. cit.*, p. 160.

81. *Ibid.*, pp. 89–90.

82. The exception being Communiqué #1 of the Joseph Duquet Cell. *Ibid.*, p. 83.

83. The ten communiqués were issued in the name of the André Ouimet, Jalbert, Narcisse Cardinal, Viger, Michèle Gauthier, Joseph Duquet, and Wolfred Nelson Cells (*ibid.*).

84. The "joint communiqué" dated October 23, 1971, was signed by the Amable Daunais, André Ouimet, Narcisse Cardinal, Viger, Wolfred Nelson, Joseph Duquet, Pierre-Louis Bourret, and De Lorimier Cells (*ibid.*).

85. The two she claims not to have mentioned to police are the Frères Chasseurs Communiqué #1, issued on October 17, 1971, and the Narcisse Cardinal Communiqué, issued on November 25, 1971.

86. De Vault and Johnson, *op. cit.*, p. 306.

87. Keable Commission, *op. cit.*, pp. 103–104.

88. *Ibid.*, pp. 89–90.

89. Sergeant Langevin came by this information second hand, however. *Ibid.*, pp. 114–115. The McDonald Commission also addressed this question; its report briefly mentions the hypothesis that paper for writing communiqués that was found during the search on Des Récollets Street was

subsequently given to "Poupette" by the Montreal police. "We note that the copy of the Montreal Police reports of the search, as found in an RCMP file, are incomplete, in that some pages are missing," noted the Commission, whose investigation "proved inconclusive" on this point. McDonald Commission, *Third Report, op. cit.*, p. 196.

90. Keable Commission, *op. cit.*, p. 51.

91. *Ibid.*, pp. 59–60.

92. *Ibid.*

93. *Ibid.*, p. 199.

94. Fournier, *op. cit.*, p. 370.

95. Keable Commission, *op. cit.*, pp. 60–62.

96. *Ibid.*, pp. 68–70.

97. In its report, the Keable Commission was unable to confirm that this document was in fact produced by the RCMP. The McDonald Commission, however, confirmed this on page 219 of its *Third Report*.

98. Keable Commission, *op. cit.*, pp. 62–63.

99. *Ibid.*, p. 210.

100. *Ibid.*, pp. 65–66.

101. McDonald Commission, *Third Report, op. cit.*, p. 219.

102. *Ibid.*, p. 200.

103. Established in 1970 and disbanded three years later, Section G's mandate in Quebec was to deal with the "terrorist" and "subversive" activities of the Quebec independence movement, those of foreign powers that might influence Quebec's place within Confederation, and "subversive" events occurring among the French-speaking population of other Canadian provinces. "C" Division refers to the RCMP in Quebec.

104. McDonald Commission, *Third Report, op. cit.*, p. 196.

105. *Ibid.*, p. 219.

106. Fournier, *op. cit.*, p. 360.

107. McDonald Commission, *Third Report, op. cit.*, p. 219.

108. The communiqué was issued in the name of the Frères Chasseurs Cell: "We spend sleepless nights thinking about the fact that Quebec is dying a bit each day because of you. We often think of you and we will soon come to visit you." The second, dated the same day, was issued in the name of the Pierre Louis Bourret Cell, which claimed to know the whereabouts of "the guilty," who should be "afraid of receiving a 'visit.'" The third, dated October 23, 1971, and issued in the name of the same cell, stated that "Several judges have already signed their own death warrants" for having conducted political trials. Quoted in McDonald Commission, *Third Report, op. cit.*, pp. 197–199.

109. McDonald Commission, *Third Report, op. cit.*, p. 199.

110. Quoted in Fournier, *op. cit.*, p. 381.

111. Laurent Poulin, an RCMP illustrator, was asked to draw an Old Patriot similar to the one found in the background of FLQ communiqués; Section G's Corporal Bernard Dubuc was asked to assemble the materials needed to make the communiqué: paper and plastic gloves to avoid leaving fingerprints behind.

112. Keable Commission, *op. cit.*, p. 92.

113. François Barbeau, "La GRC n'avait pas infiltré la 'Minerve,'" *Le Devoir*, February 21, 1979, p. 7.

114. "La cellule 'Minerve' rejette l'électoralisme," *Montréal-Matin*, December 20, 1971, p. 2.

115. François Barbeau, "Des 50 cellules du FLQ—Aucune n'avait été infiltrée par un agent de la police," *Le Devoir*, February 14, 1979, p. 1.

116. *Montréal-Matin, op. cit.*

117. Keable Commission, *op. cit.*, p. 93.

118. Mary Trueman, "Fake FLQ message is final impropriety of RCMP, Fox says," *Globe and Mail*, January 10, 1978, p. 1.

119. Keable Commission, *op. cit.*, pp. 91–92.

120. Barbeau, "Des 50 cellules du FLQ," *op. cit.*

121. François Barbeau, "Au moins 3 communiqués attribués au FLQ ont été écrits de la même main," *Le Devoir*, February 15, 1979, p. 3.

122. Patricia Poirier, "Dynamite: McCleery voulait 'neutraliser' un présumé terroriste," *Le Devoir*, September 20, 1978, p. 3.

123. Fournier, *op. cit.*, p. 392.

124. *Ibid.*, pp. 393–394. A suspended sentence specifies a period of time during which certain conditions must be met; if the conditions are not met, the convicted person may be called back to court and have the sentence that the court suspended imposed.

125. For over a century, the Solicitor General of Canada was the federal minister responsible for police and prisons. Since 2005, this office has been known as the Minister of Public Safety and Emergency Preparedness.

126. Fournier, *op. cit.*, pp. 402–403.

127. *Ibid.*

128. Robert Dion, *Les crimes de la police montée*, Montreal, Éditions coopératives Albert Saint-Martin, 1979.

129. Daniel Rioux, "Avec l'arrestation de Raynald Lévesque—La police annihile un plan felquiste de piraterie," *Le Journal de Montréal*, November 14, 1972, p. 3.

130. Alain Duhamel, "Fox nie toute participation de la GRC au projet de détournement," *Le Devoir*, November 19, 1977, p. 1.

131. Roger Drouin, "Trudeau forcé de démissionner?" *Le Devoir*, November 19, 1977, p. 2.

132. Fournier, *op. cit.*, p. 411.

133. *Ibid.*, p. 406.

134. Close to the labour and poor people's movements, the APLQ was founded in 1968. It published the weekly *Bulletin d'information* from 1971

to 1973, which gave way to the bi-monthly *Bulletin populaire* from 1973 to 1976, when the APLQ ceased its activities. Regarding this break-in, see R. Dion, *op. cit.*, pp. 15–18.

135. *Ibid.*, pp. 97–107.

136. Fournier, *op. cit.*, pp. 375–376 and 397–398.

137. De Vault and Johnson, *op. cit.*, p. 285.

138. *Ibid.*, p. 294.

Chapter 4. An Agent Provocateur "Made in the USA"

1. McDonald Commission, *Second Report, op. cit.*, pp. 501–502.

2. David Austin, *Fear of a Black nation : race, sex and security in sixties Montreal*, Toronto, Between the Lines, 2013, p. 164.

3. *Ibid.*, p. 157.

4. *Ibid.*, p. 164.

5. Keable Commission, *op. cit.*, p. 327.

6. Hewitt, *Spying 101, op. cit.*, p. 154.

7. Dennis Forsythe (ed.), *Let the Niggers Burn! The Sir George Williams University Affair and its Caribbean Aftermath*, Montreal, Our Generation Press, 1971, p. 7.

8. Hewitt, *Spying 101, op. cit.*, p. 151.

9. Austin, *op. cit.*, p. 145. Ward Churchill, *Agents of Repression: the FBI's Secret Wars Against the Black Panther Party and the American Indian Movement*, New York, South End Press, 2002, p. 53.

10. *Ibid.*, p. 48.

11. Austin, *op. cit.*, p. 26.

12. LeRoi Butcher, "The Anderson Affair," in Forsythe, *Let the Niggers Burn, op. cit.*, p. 97.

NOTES TO PAGES 72–74

13. "Sir George Williams—Ottawa étudie le dossier des étrangers arrêtés," *Le Devoir*, February 14, 1969, p. 1.

14. Austin, *op. cit.*, p. 137.

15. "Le sac de SWG—$1 million de dégâts et 79 arrestations," *Le Devoir*, February 12, 1969, p.1. House of Commons, Journal of Debates, 28th Parliament, 1st session, vol. 5, January 21–February 18, 1969, p. 5426.

16. Édouard Anglade would become the first Black officer on the Montreal police force in 1974.

17. Cathy Lord, "Black cultural awards advance beyond province to national stage,"*Edmonton Journal*, October 3, 2003, p. B1.

18. Charles Earl Jones, *The Black Panther Party (reconsidered)*, Baltimore, Black Classic Press, 1998, p. 131.

19. Marshall Eddie Conway, *Marshall Law: The Life & Times of a Baltimore Black Panther*, Oakland, AK Press, 2011, p. 48.

20. Jeff Sallot, "Mounties bugged solicitor-general, Commons is told," *Globe and Mail*, February 23, 1978, p. 1.

21. John Burns, "Lawyer says Sir George suspect 'known' by Diefenbaker," *The Globe and Mail*, February 27, 1969, p. 2.

22. Ronald Lebel, "38 remain in Montreal jail as legal arguments continue," *Globe and Mail*, February 21, 1969, p. 2.

23. "3 found guilty of obstructing use of university's computer," *Globe and Mail*, April 23, 1971, p. 8.

24. "Two sent to jail for leadership in Sir George riot," *Globe and Mail*, May 1, 1971, p. 1; Don Butler, "Waiting for Rosie, Part One,"*Ottawa Citizen*, July 16, 2000, p. C7.

25. Jon Ferry, "Suspected Hart was agent, Douglas says," *Globe and Mail*, February 23, 1978, p. 8.

26. "Spurned arms offers, natives say," *Globe and Mail*, May 26, 1980, p. 9. McDonald Commission, *Third Report, op. cit., p.* 484.

27. Sallot, *op. cit.*

28. Richard Fidler, *RCMP: The Real Subversives*, New York, Vanguard Publications 1978, p. 76.

29. Linda McQuaig, "The Man with the Guns," *Today Magazine (The Gazette)*, June 13, 1981, p. 9.

30. Robert Sheppard, "Hart: the unsecret secret agent," *Globe and Mail*, January 14, 1980, p. 10.

31. Jon Ferry, "'We used to laugh in his face'—Avowed RCMP agent 'a joker,' blacks say," *Globe and Mail*, February 24, 1978, p. 10.

32. McDonald Commission, *Third Report, op. cit.*, p. 489.

33. McQuaig, *op. cit.*, p. 10.

34. *Ibid.*, p. 8.

35. *Ibid.*, pp. 9–10.

36. Rob Tripp, "Last chance for bank robber," *National Post*, April 9, 2011, p. A18.

37. *Ibid.*

38. George Russell, "Lawyer fights bid to man waiting for appeal," *Globe and Mail*, December 13, 1971, p. 5.

39. McDonald Commission, *Third Report, op. cit.*, p. 493.

40. "Scheme to disrupt trials Concordia rector warned of plot to kill him," *Globe and Mail*, March 6, 1978, p. 5.

41. Eric Siblin, "Rosie the Red stops smashing the state," *Saturday Night*, May 27, 2000, p. 27.

42. McQuaig, *op. cit.*, p. 10.

43. These were actually offences that Hart had committed at events to maintain his cover as an undercover FBI agent.

44. McDonald Commission, *Third Report, op. cit.*, p. 485.

45. "Ottawa defers bid to deport West Indian," *Globe and Mail*, December 17, 1971, p. 5.

46. "Deportation of Roosevelt is ordered," *Globe and Mail*, October 17, 1972, p. 35.

47. "En récompense, un informateur de la GRC s'est fait expulser," *La Presse*, January 9, 1980, p. A3.

48. Austin, *op. cit.*, p. 156.

49. Robert Sheppard, "Probe to study allegation RCMP protecting murderer," *Globe and Mail*, January 10, 1980, p. 8.

50. "Mounties went with him, CTV told," *Globe and Mail*, February 27, 1978, p. 5.

51. McDonald Commission, *Third Report, op. cit.*, p. 484.

52. *Ibid.*, p. 493.

53. *Ibid.*, p. 492.

54. *Ibid.*, p. 494.

55. Robert Sheppard, "Informer ordered to hide guns on farm, Mountie probe told," *Globe and Mail*, April 23, 1980, p. 20.

56. Sheppard, "Informer ordered to hide guns," *op. cit.*

57. "Roosevelt Douglas a risk to security, ministers tell board," *Globe and Mail*, June 2, 1973, p. 5.

58. Butler, "Waiting for Rosie," *op. cit.*

59. Isabel Vincent, "Premier's politics forged in Montreal riot," *National Post*, February 23, 2000, p. A3.

60. Siblin, "Rosie the Red stops smashing the state," *op. cit.*

61. "Rosie Douglas to be released," *Globe and Mail*, November 5, 1974, p. 2.

62. McDonald Commission, *Third Report, op. cit.*, p. 246.

63. *Ibid.*, pp. 243–244.

64. *Ibid.*, p. 244.

65. Sallot, *op. cit.*

66. Siblin, *op. cit.*

67. McDonald Commission, *Third Report, op. cit.*, p. 257. Allmand was not the only Member of Parliament to be recorded by Hart. The informant also recorded a conversation between Douglas and John Rodriguez, NDP MP for Nickel Belt, Ontario, in 1975. Hart and Rodriguez had crossed paths at an anti-racist town hall meeting held in the basement of a Toronto church. When the event ended, Hart offered to drive the federal MP, who was supporting Douglas in his fight against deportation. The "General's" bugged car captured their entire conversation (Mary Trueman, "Rodriguez recalls possible bugging incident," *Globe and Mail*, February 23, 1978, p. 8).

68. The McDonald Commission wrote that "Mr. Hart accompanied Mr. Douglas to Kenora, Ontario in 1974 when Anicinabe Park at Kenora was occupied by some Indians." This is likely an error since Rosie Douglas was still in prison at the time of the occupation. McDonald Commission, *Third Report, op cit.*, p. 488.

69. Fidler, *op. cit.*, p. 76.

70. Scott Rutherford, *Canada's Other Red Scare: Rights, Decolonization, and Indigenous Political Protest in the Global Sixties*, Master's thesis in History, Queen's University, 2011, pp. 120–121.

71. Quoted in McDonald Commission, *Second Report, op. cit.*, p. 504.

72. From February 27 to May 8, 1973, Wounded Knee was put under siege by the FBI, the US Marshal Service, Bureau of Indian Affairs police, and a paramilitary organization known as the GOONs, who were provided with assault rifles, limitless ammunition and state-of-the-art radio equipment by the FBI. During the course of the siege, at least two Indigenous people were killed by pro-government forces and several others "disappeared." The GOONs reign of terror only intensified after the siege had ended: over the following three years over sixty American Indian Movement members and supporters were killed on Pine Ridge Reservation, and over 340 others suffered violent physical assaults.

73. "Wounded Knee talks will resume," *Globe and Mail*, March 16, 1973, p. 10.

74. "No role for U.S. Indian militants north of the border: Canadian leader," *Globe and Mail*, September 21, 1973, p. 3.

75. McQuaig, *op. cit.*, pp. 10–11.

76. *Ibid.*

77. McDonald Commission, *Third Report, op. cit., p.* 489.

78. McQuaig, *op. cit.*, p. 11.

79. *Globe and Mail*, "Spurned arms offers, natives say," *op. cit.*

80. McQuaig, *op. cit.*, p. 11.

81. "Citizens speak out on McDonald probe," *Globe and Mail*, June 22, 1979, p. 8.

82. McDonald Commission, *Third Report, op. cit.*, p. 497.

83. Robert Sheppard, "RCMP did not trust paid U.S. informer, officer tells inquiry," *Globe and Mail*, April 30, 1980, p. 9.

84. Robert Sheppard, "Rosie Douglas loses appeal," *Globe and Mail*, May 9, 1975, p. 1.

85. Sheppard, "Probe to study allegation," *op. cit.*

86. "Deportation to Dominica avoided—Douglas emigrating to Jamaica," *Globe and Mail*, April 30, 1976, p. 9.

87. Eric Siblin, "Douglas drops in for visit—Dominica PM led '69 computer riot," *Montreal Gazette*, May 26, 2000, p. A4.

Chapter 5. Moles Come Out of Their Holes

1. Richard Cléroux, *Pleins feux sur les… services secrets canadiens : révélations sur l'espionnage au pays*, Montreal, Éditions de l'Homme, 1993, pp. 63–65.

2. *Ibid.*, p. 68.

3. Quoted in *ibid.*, pp. 70–73.

4. R. Dion, *op. cit.*, p. 81.

5. Bernard Morrier, "Le cambriolage de l'APLQ—Les 3 policiers sont libérés sans condition," June 17, 1977, p. 1.

6. "Québec veut plus de lumière sur l'affaire," *Le Devoir*, June 17, 1977, p. 1.

7. Alain Duhamel, "La commission Keable entend faire la lumière sur d'autres opérations," *Le Devoir*, November 10, 1977, p. 8.

8. Lise Bissonnette, "Ottawa institue une enquête sur les pratiques illégales de la GRC," *Le Devoir*, July 7, 1977, p. 1.

9. Cléroux, *op. cit.*, p. 78.

10. Federal prosecutors filed three motions for stays in 1977 (all of which were rejected) and two motions for evocation (one rejected by the Superior Court, the other granted by the Court of Appeal). Dominique Bernard, *La Commission d'enquête sur des opérations policières en territoire québécois: portée réelle et limites du rapport Keable*, Master's thesis in political science, UQAM, 2008, Annexe I, p. 159.

11. *Ibid.*, pp. 125–127.

12. Conrad Bernier, "L'avenir de la commission Keable pourrait se jouer devant la Cour supérieure," *La Presse*, November 29, 1979, p. A1.

13. Bernard, *op. cit.*, p. 101.

14. *Ibid.*, p. 93.

15. *Ibid.*, p. 155.

16. Jean Keable, "Un abcès qu'il fallait crever," *Le Devoir*, November 29, 1979, p. 4.

17. Conrad Bernier, "Keable identifie François Séguin comme un informateur de police," *La Presse*, November 28, 1979, p. A1.

18. "Francois Seguin, or the tactics of an informer," *In Struggle!*, no. 252, May 26, 1981 https//www.marxists.org/history/erol/ca.secondwave/is-seguin.htm.

19. Martha Gagnon, "En devenant indicatrice de police—Elle ne voulait qu'une chose : décapiter le FLQ," *La Presse*, March 1, 1980, p. A8.

20. *Ibid.*

21. *Ibid.*

22. Marc Laurendeau, "Des révélations qui heurtent des sensibilités," *La Presse*, November 24, 1979, p. A5.

23. Jean-Guy Martin, "En 1971, la police de la CUM laissait émettre de fausses communiqués du FLQ," *Le Journal de Montréal*, November 22, 1979, p. 6.

24. De Vault and Johnson, *op. cit.*, p. 339.

25. Keable Commission, *op. cit.*, p. 236.

26. *Ibid.*

27. Robert Sheppard, "Six operations cited in Quebec probe—Police should be charged, Keable says," *Globe and Mail*, March 7, 1981, p. 1.

28. Ferry, *op. cit.*

29. McDonald Commission, *Third Report, op. cit.*, p. 500.

30. Rutherford, *op. cit.*, p. 224.

31. Quoted in McQuaig, *op. cit.*, p. 12.

32. *Ibid.*, p.13.

33. *Ibid.*

34. McDonald Commission, *Third Report, op. cit.*, p. 489.

35. *Ibid.*

36. See Section 22 of the *Criminal Code*, which was in force at the time.

37. McDonald Commission, *Third Report, op. cit.*, p. 500.

38. "Informer's treatment criticized," *The Vancouver Sun*, June 5, 1987, p. A12.

39. Lawrence Martin, "Blais admits he was wrong to say RCMP 'surreptitious entries' legal," *Globe and Mail*, May 3, 1978, p. 1.

40. John Gray, "Hundreds escape justice," *Globe and Mail*, August 1, 1983, p. 1.

41. McDonald Commission, *Second Report, op. cit.*, p. 518. Robert Sheppard, "RCMP files on citizens 'will be cut back,'" *Globe and Mail*, August 27, 1981, p. 1.

42. Cléroux, *op. cit.*, at 104.

43. "'Astonished' at turndown, Quebec says," *Globe and Mail*, November 19, 1977, p. 13.

44. During the hearings, federal counsel categorized under the broad heading of "government documents" all files relating to the deliberations of Cabinet and its committees, documents relating to any other form of consultation between Ministers, between public servants, or between Ministers and public servants, as well as documents originating from Ministers or public servants relating to the decision-making or policy development process, agendas and minutes of Cabinet meetings, and even documents containing quotations from the above documents.

45. McDonald Commission, *Second Report, op. cit.*, p. 1177.

46. *Ibid.*, p. 1180.

47. *Ibid.*, p. 1191.

48. *Ibid.*, p. 1179.

49. Jeff Sallot, "Ottawa vs. RCMP," *Globe and Mail*, October 27, 1978, p. 1.

50. Jeff Sallot and Mary Trueman, "Three solicitors-general informed of illegal acts, ex-RCMP chief testifies, but Allmand denies it," *Globe and Mail*, October 25, 1978, p. 1.

51. Huguette Laprise, "Keable exonère les politiciens," *La Presse*, March 7, 1981, p. F13.

52. Keable Commission, *op. cit.*, p. 403.

53. *Ibid.*, pp. 424–425.

54. Cléroux, *op. cit.*, p. 120.

55. Victor Malarek, "RCMP officers face charges in Quebec," *Globe and Mail*, June 13, 1981, p. 1.

56. Those charged with breaking into the Parti Québécois's offices and stealing its membership list were former Assistant Commissioner Howard Draper; Inspectors Claude Vermette, Kenneth Hollas, and Alcide Yeller; Superintendent Alcide Nowlan; Staff Sergeants Gilbert Albert and Robert Potvin; Sergeants Dale Boire, Gérard Boucher, and Maurice Goguen; and former Constable and computer expert Ken Burnett.

Those charged with setting fire to the barn at Sainte-Anne-de-la-Rochelle were former Staff Sergeant Donald McCleery, Sergeants Claude Brodeur and Bernard Dubuc, Inspector Bernard Blier and Constable Richard Daigle.

Those charged with the theft of dynamite in Saint-Grégoire were Daigle, Dubuc, and McCleery—also charged with the barn fire—and Corporal Normand Chamberland.

57. Those charged with these kidnappings were Bernard Blier, Richard Daigle, and Bernard Dubuc—who were already charged in other cases—and Constable Laurent Hugo. "4 Mounties charged with kidnapping pair of Montreal men," *The Globe and Mail*, August 18, 1981, p. 8.

58. Cléroux, *op. cit.*, p. 100.

59. Rodolphe Morissette, "La Commission McDonald propose de créer un service civil de sécurité," *Le Devoir*, 26 August 1981, p. 1. McDonald Commission, *Second Report*, *op. cit.*, p. 24.

60. *Ibid.*, pp. 405 and 101, respectively.

61. McDonald Commission, *Third Report*, *op. cit.*, p. 68.

62. McDonald Commission, *Second Report*, *op. cit*, p. 538.

63. *Ibid.*, p. 539.

64. *Ibid*, pp. 525–526.

65. *Ibid.*, p. 536.

66. *Ibid.*, p. 550.

67. *Ibid.*, pp. 541–542.

68. *Ibid.*, pp. 543–544.

69. *Ibid.*, p. 543.

70. *Ibid.*, pp. 550–551.

71. *Ibid.*, p. 533.

72. *Ibid.*, pp. 533–534.

73. *Ibid.*, p. 527.

74. *Ibid.*

75. *Ibid.*, p. 1032.

76. *Ibid.*

77. *Ibid.*

78. Rodolphe Morissette, "Kaplan rejette la critique généralisée de la GRC," *Le Devoir*, August 26, 1981, p. 1.

79. Jean-Claude Leclerc, "La fin d'une puissance," *Le Devoir*, August 27, 1981, p. 6.

80. John Gray, "Some violations called necessary RCMP will continue breaking law: Kaplan," *Globe and Mail*, August 27, 1981, p. 1.

81. *Ibid.*

82. Barry Nelson, "Illegal act permissible, Kaplan says," *Globe and Mail*, August 28, 1981, p. 10.

83. Nelson, *op. cit.*

84. "4 provinces study cases on RCMP," *Globe and Mail*, August 28, 1981, p. 1.

85. "Trials delaying release of report," *Globe and Mail*, October 31, 1983, p. 9.

86. John Gray, "Hundreds escape justice—Prosecution of Mounties too much work: Ottawa," *Globe and Mail*, August 23, 1983, p. 1.

NOTES TO PAGES 90–91

87. Victor Malarek, "They did it, but where? Mounties absolved in dynamite theft," *Globe and Mail*, September 23, 1982, p. 1. Inspector Bernard Blier was acquitted of setting fire to the Petit Québec Libre barn after admitting his participation in the February 1983 kidnapping of the attorney André Chamard, a crime for which he received an absolute discharge ("RCMP inspector cleared in Quebec barn burning," *Globe and Mail*, February 10, 1983, p. 8; "Guilty in FLQ case, Mountie is absolved in dynamite theft," *Globe and Mail*, September 23, 1982, p. 1; "Guilty in FLQ case, Mountie is freed," *Globe and Mail*, November 20, 1982, p. 2). Constable Richard Daigle was also acquitted in both cases (Victor Malarek, "Acquittal by Quebec jury leaves Mountie in tears," *Globe and Mail*, December 8, 1982, p. 8; "Mountie acquitted on kidnap charge," *Globe and Mail*, February 11, 1983, p. 3). It should be noted that Ottawa did agree to pay Chamard $23,000 in compensation ("Ottawa pays $23,000 for detaining lawyer," *Globe and Mail*, May 4, 1984, p. 2). Inspector Laurent Hugo was acquitted of the kidnapping and confinement of André Laforest in February 1983 (*Globe and Mail*, "Mountie acquitted," *op. cit.*), a verdict that led in short order to the withdrawal of charges against Sergeant Bernard Dubuc in the same case ("RCMP officer receives acquittal," *Globe and Mail*, February 26, 1983, p. 13).

88. Victor Malarek, "Mountie given suspended sentence for stealing PQ tapes," *Globe and Mail*, May 18, 1983, p. 10.

89. René Laurent, "Too late to try Mounties charged in 1973 theft, Appeals Court rules," *Montreal Gazette*, May 8, 1991, p. A4. The eleventh accused, Superintendent Alcide Nowlan, had died in the interim.

90. "Les agents de la GRC accusés d'un incendie relié au FLQ sont libérés," *La Presse*, September 6, 1991, p. C11.

91. Robert Sheppard, "Ottawa yields on civilian agency, other moves to wait," *Globe and Mail*, August 26, 1981, p. 13.

92. "Ex-Mountie derides reform, terms charges 'a travesty,'" *Globe and Mail*, August 28, 1981, p. 10.

93. *Canadian Security Intelligence Service Act*, Section 2.

94. *Ibid.*, Section 13.

Chapter 6. The Birth of a Monster

1. Cléroux, *op. cit.*, pp. 61–62.

2. *Report of the Royal Commission on Security*, Ottawa, Privy Council Office June 1969, p. 21.

3. *Ibid.*

4. Quoted in McDonald Commission, *Third Report, op. cit.*, p. 73.

5. Robert Sheppard, "Civilian agency would have more trouble, Fox says," *Globe and Mail*, March 5, 1980, p. 8.

6. McDonald Commission, *Second Report, op. cit.*, p. 773.

7. Bill C-157's official name was *An Act to establish the Canadian Security Intelligence Service, to enact legislation respecting the prosecution of certain security and related offences and to make consequential amendments to other Acts.*

8. Jeff Sallot, "New security agency can break law: bill," *Globe and Mail*, May 19, 1983, p. 1.

9. *Ibid.*

10. Quoted in Cléroux, *op. cit.*, pp. 113–114.

11. *Ibid.*

12. John Cruickshank, "Provinces call security force a huge threat," *Globe and Mail*, May 28, 1983, p. 1.

13. *Ibid.*

14. Sylvia Stead, "McMurtry turns to constitutional experts," *Globe and Mail*, June 2, 1983, p. 3.

15. Jeff Sallot, "Allmand says powers should be narrower," *Globe and Mail*, June 24, 1983, p. 8.

16. Jeff Sallot, "Public in dark on security threats: MP," *Globe and Mail*, September 16, 1983, p. 8.

17. Jeff Sallot, "Security bill powers 'a problem,'" *Globe and Mail*, September 14, 1983, p. 5.

18. Barreau du Québec, *Mémoire présenté par le Comité du Barreau du Québec sur le Bill C-157, Service canadien du renseignement de sécurité* (Québec: Service de recherche du Barreau du Québec, 1983), p. 11.

19. Robert Stephens, "Lifetime wiretaps in use now: Kaplan," *Globe and Mail*, June 17, 1983, p. 1.

20. Jeff Sallot, "Spy agency to see secret census data," *Globe and Mail*, June 3, 1983, p. 1.

21. Philip Rosen, *The Canadian Security Intelligence Service*, Library of Parliament, Ottawa, 24 January 2000, p. 6. https://publications.gc.ca/collections/Collection-R/LoPBdP/CIR-e/8427-e.pdf

22. It should be noted that Pitfield was present at the notorious Cabinet Committee on Priorities and Planning meeting of December 1, 1970, at which the Director General of the Security Service, John Starnes, had claimed that the RCMP had been "doing illegal security and intelligence work for twenty years and not getting caught." Yet Pitfield, then Deputy Secretary to the Cabinet, testified before the McDonald Commission that he did not remember what had transpired at the meeting (McDonald Commission, *Third Report, op. cit.*, p. 45).

23. *Report of the special committee of the senate on the Canadian security intelligence service: delicate balance : a Security Intelligence Service in a democratic society*, Senate Journals, November 3, 1983, p. 3333.

24. *Ibid.*, pp. 3332–3333.

25. *Ibid.*, p. 3334.

26. *Ibid.*

27. Its official name was *An Act to establish the Canadian Security Intelligence Service, to enact An Act respecting enforcement in relation to certain security and related offences and to amend certain Acts in consequence thereof or in relation thereto.*

28. Rosen, *op. cit.* Section 25 of the Criminal Code provides that "every one who is […] authorized by law to do anything in the administration or enforcement of the law […] (b) as a peace officer or public officer […] is, if he acts on reasonable grounds, justified in doing what he is required or authorized to do and in using as much force as is necessary for that purpose."

29. Rosen, *op. cit.*, p. 10.

30. *Ibid.*

31. *Bill C-9: An Act to establish the Canadian Security Intelligence Service*, first reading, January 18, 1984, 32nd Parliament, 2nd session. It should be noted, however, that section 18 of the CSIS Act, which establishes this offence, also sets out, in paragraph 2, the circumstances in which such information may be lawfully disclosed. In particular, disclosure may be "for the purposes of the performance of duties and functions under this Act or any other Act of Parliament or the administration or enforcement of this Act or as required by any other law."

32. Pitfield Committee, *op. cit.*, p. 3318.

33. *Ibid.*, p. 3334.

34. *Ibid.*, pp. 3337 and 3339.

35. Cléroux, *op. cit.*, p. 114.

36. *Ibid.*, p. 11.

37. "MPs applaud Kaplan as security bill passes," *Globe and Mail*, June 22, 1984, p. 5.

38. Rosen, *op. cit.*, p. 9.

39. André Cédilot, "Des espions au-dessus des lois," *La Presse*, October 20, 2002, p. F3.

40. Cléroux, *op. cit.*, p. 120.

41. *Ibid.*, pp. 115–116. Cléroux even reports that CSIS was using "RCMP forms, manuals and equipment for several more months, if not years. It was not until 1989 and 1990 that CSIS had its own training and operations manuals" (*ibid.*, p. 133).

42. John Picton, "Security service favors Mounties," *Toronto Star*, April 6, 1986, p. A12.

43. Quoted in Andrew Mitrovica, *Entrée clandestine: Crimes et mensonges dans les services secrets canadiens*, Montreal, Trait d'Union, 2002, p. 16.

44. SIRC, *Annual Report 1990–1991*, Ottawa, Public Services and Supply Canada, 1991, p. 57.

45. "Hausse importante de l'effectif et du budget des services secrets fédéraux," *La Presse*, November 19, 1991, p. A10.

46. Pitfield Committee, *op. cit.*, p. 3339.

47. Quoted in Mitrovica, *op. cit.*, p. 19.

48. Cléroux, *op. cit.*, p. 129.

49. Mitrovica, *op cit.* p. 19.

Chapter 7. Paid for by the CSN ... and CSIS

1. Normand Lester, *Enquêtes sur les services secrets*, Montreal, Éditions de l'Homme, 2002, p. 78.

2. Monique Giguère, "La CSN a braqué les projecteurs sur moi," *Le Soleil*, January 5, 1989, p. A1.

3. *Ibid.*

4. Security Intelligence Review Committee, *Section 54 Report to the Solicitor General of Canada on CSIS' use of its investigative powers with respect to the Labor Movement*, Public Services and Procurement Canada, Ottawa, March 25, 1988, p. 5, https://www.securitepublique.gc.ca/lbrr/archives/jl%2086.s4%20s43s%201988-eng.pdf.

5. Giguère, *op. cit.*, p. A1.

6. Monique Giguère, "Boivin prêt à perdre sa chemise contre la CSN," *Le Soleil*, January 6, 1989, p. A1.

7. "Le conseiller délateur de la CSN était un véritable agent secret," *La Presse*, June 13, 1987, p. A2.

8. Monique Giguère, " Marc Boivin voulait éviter le bain de sang," *Le Soleil*, January 3, 1989, p. A1.

9. SIRC, *Section 54 Report, op. cit.*, p. 5.

10. *Ibid.*

11. Quoted in Lester, *op. cit.*, pp. 83–84.

12. SIRC, *Section 54 Report*, op. cit., pp. 5–6.

13. As historian David Milot notes: "The Quebec [Marxist-Leninist] experiment lasted ten years, from the creation of the group EN LUTTE! by Charles Gagnon and the newspaper's team in 1973 to the fall of EN LUTTE! and the Communist Workers' Party (CWP) in 1982 and 1983, respectively" (David Milot, "Histoire du mouvement marxiste-léniniste au Québec 1973–1983—Un premier bilan," *Bulletin d'histoire politique*, Montreal, AQHP/Lux Éditeur, vol. 13, no. 1, Fall 2004, p. 12).

14. SIRC, *Section 54 Report*, op. cit., p. 14.

15. Quoted in Lester, op. cit., pp. 84–85.

16. Simon Durivage, "L'affaire Boivin," *Téléjournal—Le Point*, Montreal, Radio-Canada, January 6, 1989.

17. "Boivin aurait aussi infiltré le Parti communiste du Québec," *Le Devoir*, October 9, 1987, p. A3.

18. "Boivin a déjà été membre du Parti communiste pendant quelques mois," *Le Soleil*, October 9, 1987, p. A4.

19. It should be noted that the promise to appear initially signed by Boivin indicates that he was actually supposed to be charged under Section 157 of the *Criminal Code*. This provision provides for a maximum sentence of five years imprisonment while Section 169 provides for a maximum sentence of six months imprisonment; so it would seem that the informant received a "discounted" charge.

20. "Boivin a été condamné pour des actes indécents," *Le Devoir*, July 18, 1987, p. A3.

21. National security has long been used as a pretext to investigate the sexual habits of Canadians, especially those outside the heteronormative framework, as Gary Kinsman and Patrizia Gentile recount in *The Canadian Wars on Queers: National Security as Sexual Regulation*, published by UBC Press (Vancouver) in 2010. In the era of the RCMP-SS, "sexual proclivity" was considered a "character trait" that could leave one vulnerable to blackmail (p. 340). CSIS subsequently persisted in this war on "sexual deviance" (p. 428).

22. "Le 'Tough de La Malbaie' broie du noir," *La Presse*, November 10, 1993, p. D8

23. Quoted in Lester, *op. cit.*, pp. 84–85.

24. Louise Lemieux, "Pour les frères Boivin, la vie est devenue difficile," *Le Soleil*, September 12, 1987, p. A3.

25. Sarah Scott, "Choke hold led to Harvey's death: MD," *The Montreal Gazette*, December 12, 1986, p. A1.

26. The blast was so powerful that it woke up the forty or so people staying in the motel next door, as well as people living in a trailer park 500 meters away.

27. Isabelle Jinchereau, "Contre une propriété de Raymond Malenfant— Attentat à la bombe," *Le Soleil*, May 24, 1987, p. A1. This amount was later increased to $100,000, to take into account the loss of revenue from room rentals after the incident (Louise Lemieux, "La CSN furieuse du récit du procureur de la Couronne," *Le Soleil*, September 12, 1987, p. A3).

28. Giguère, "Marc Boivin voulait éviter le bain de sang," *op. cit.*, p. A1.

29. *Ibid.*

30. SIRC, *Section 54 Report, op. cit.*, p. 8.

31. *Canadian Security Intelligence Service Act*, para. 19(2)a.

32. SIRC, *Section 54 Report, op. cit.*, pp. 8 and 13.

33. Manon Cornellier, "Boivin n'a pas 'infiltré' la CSN, soutient le SCRS," *Le Devoir*, March 30, 1988, p. A1.

34. Lemieux, "Pour les frères Boivin," *op. cit.*

35. Monique Giguère, "Les policiers ne me croyaient pas," *Le Soleil*, January 4, 1989, p. A1.

36. Gilles Paquin, "Le SCRS aurait infiltré quatre autres syndicats," *La Presse*, September 24, 1987, p. A1.

37. "Le gouvernement nie l'ingérence de l'agence de sécurité," *Le Soleil*, September 25, 1987, p. A3.

38. SIRC, *Section 54 Report, op. cit.*, p. 13.

39. Régys Caron, "Trois conseillers de la CSN accusés," *Le Soleil*, June 6, 1987, p. A1.

40. Michel Truchon, "L'enquête de la SQ aurait été mise en branle par Marc Boivin," *Le Soleil*, June 6, 1987, p. A4.

41. Guy Dubé, "Boivin protected by the SQ," *Le Soleil*, June 9, 1987, p. A1.

42. Michel David, "Le présumé délateur 'n'est pas en état d'arrestation', reconnait Latulippe," *Le Soleil*, June 16, 1987, p. A3.

43. Giguère, "Les policiers ne me croyaient pas," *op. cit.*

44. *Ibid.*

45. Louise Lemieux, "Déplacements et appels téléphoniques surveillés," *Le Soleil*, May 5, 1988, p. A4.

46. *Ibid.*

47. Louise Lemieux, "Après ses révélations, Boivin a signé une entente avec la SQ," *Le Soleil*, May 5, 1988, p. A1.

48. Giguère, "Les policiers ne me croyaient pas," *op. cit.*

49. Michel Auger, "La Sûreté du Québec cherchait des documents compromettants dans les locaux de la CSN," *Le Journal de Montréal*, June 10, 1987, pp. 2–3.

50. *Ibid.*

51. Michel Auger, "Boivin, un informateur du Service canadien de renseignement de sécurité," *Le Journal de Montréal*, June 10, 1987, p. 3.

52. "Boivin : un agent de la GRC," *Le Soleil*, June 10, 1987, p. A1.

53. Normand Girard, "Larose convaincu que Boivin est un délateur," *Le Journal de Montréal*, June 10, 1987, p. 2.

54. William Marsden, "CNTU head suggests police frameup," *The Montreal Gazette*, June 11, 1987. p. A4.

55. *La Presse*, "Le conseiller délateur de la CSN," *op. cit.*, However, a Crown prosecutor indicated that the exact remuneration the informant received could not be disclosed to the court because of CSIS's objections ("Kelleher confirme que Boivin était un informateur," *La Presse*, September 16, 1987).

56. "Marc Boivin informerait la GRC depuis 1971," *Le Soleil*, June 13, 1987, p. A2.

57. Louise Lemieux, "Paule Gauthier a peine à croire que Boivin œuvre pour la CIA canadienne," *Le Soleil*, June 16, 1987, p. A3.

58. Pierre-Paul Noreau, "Kaplan demande si le comité de surveillance a bien fait son travail," *Le Soleil*, June 25, 1987, p. A10.

59. Comité spécial d'examen de la Loi constituant le Service canadien du renseignement de sécurité et de la Loi sur les infractions en matière de sécurité, *Procès-verbaux et témoignages* (No. 17), Ottawa, Solicitor General Canada, February 22, 1990, p. 17:21.

60. *Ibid.*, p. 17:26.

61. Pitfield Committee, *op. cit.*, p. 3337.

62. Louise Lemieux, "Ce n'est pas du SCRS qu'on saura si Marc Boivin est l'un de ses agents," *Le Soleil*, June 18, 1987, p. A3.

63. Giguère, "La CSN a braqué," *op. cit.*, p. A1.

64. Louise Lemieux, "De nouvelles accusations contre deux conseillers de la CSN," *Le Soleil*, June 12, 1987, p. A1.

65. "La famille Boivin se dit traumatisée et grandement humiliée," *Le Soleil*, June 13, 1987, p. A3.

66. Louise Lemieux, "La Couronne exige la prison pour les Boivin," *Le Soleil*, September 12, 1987, p. A1.

67. Lemieux, "La CSN furieuse," *op. cit.*

68. Nancy Wood, "Fourth CNTU man held in bomb plot plans to ask court for bail tomorrow," *The Montreal Gazette*, June 18, 1987, p. A7.

69. Louise Lemieux, "Le syndicaliste Rénald Tardif remis en liberté en attendant son enquête préliminaire," *Le Soleil*, June 20, 1987, p. A3.

70. "1. conspiracy to cause an explosion in connection with the bombing, on May 23, 1987 of the kitchen of the hotel in Chicoutimi owned by Raymond Malenfant; 2. being party to the bombing in Chicoutimi on May 23, 1987 referred to in 1; 3. conspiracy to cause an explosion in relation to a car bombing in Ste-Foy on October 7, 1986 which occurred in the parking lot of a hotel owned by Raymond Malenfant; 4. for causing the explosion in relation to the car bombing referred to in 3; 5. for conspiracy between the dates of May 27 and June 5, 1987, in relation to a planned bombing of a hotel in Drummondville owned by Raymond Malenfant; and 6. for conspiracy between the dates of May 27 and June 5, 1987 in relation to a planned bombing of a hotel in Montreal owned by Raymond Malenfant." (Security Intelligence Review Committee, *op. cit.*, pp. 8–9.)

71. Louise Lemieux, "Les frères Boivin plaident coupable," *Le Soleil*, June 30, 1987, p. A3.

72. *Ibid*. The Peace and Sessions Court dated from the colonial era and was abolished in 1988, its jurisdiction being subsequently entrusted to the Criminal and Penal Division of the Court of Quebec.

73. It was revealed that Marc-André Boivin's property on Île d'Orléans was worth $160,000, while his apartment building was worth $90,000. The mortgages on these two properties totalled $80,000. Richard Boivin still owed $40,000 on a house worth $124,000.

74. I sent an access to information request to CSIS (No. 117-2016-198) asking for the total amount of money paid to Boivin, including the total amount of money paid as reimbursement for expenses, as well as the total amount of any other money paid to him after he stopped providing his services. CSIS refused to provide me with any information, citing Sections 15(1), 16(1)(a), 16(1)(c), 19(1) of the *Access to Information Act*, and Section 24(1) of the *CSIS Act*.

75. Lemieux, "Les frères Boivin plaident coupable," *op. cit.*

76. "Québec ne poursuivra pas le Service de renseignement," *Le Devoir*, July 9, 1987, p. A3.

77. SIRC, *Section 54 Report, op. cit.*, at 2.

78. *Ibid.*, p. 14.

79. Special Committee on the Review of the Act..., *op. cit.*, p. 17:16. Pierre-Paul Noreau, "Enquête sur une possible infiltration à la CSN," *Le Soleil*, June 30, 1987, p. A3.

80. Suzanne Dansereau, "Boivin entre en cour par la porte réservée aux policiers," *Le Devoir*, July 10, 1987, p. A1.

81. "Boivin est encore à la barre des témoins," *Le Devoir*, July 14, 1987, p. A3.

82. Louise Lemieux, "Des objections au témoignage de Boivin," *Le Soleil*, July 11, 1987, p. A1.

83. Louise Lemieux, "Un 4e permanent de la CSN cité à son procès," *Le Soleil*, September 19, 1987, p. A3.

84. "Boivin gets 15 months in motel bombings," *The Montreal Gazette*, October 3, 1987, p. A5.

85. "Le syndicaliste Boivin: 15 mois de prison," *Le Journal de Montréal*, October 3, 1987, p. 4.

86. Louise Lemieux, "Quinze mois de prison pour l'ex-syndicaliste Marc-André Boivin, dix pour son frère," *Le Soleil*, October 3, 1987, p. A3.

87. "Mise au point de la CSN—Une question d'équité," *Le Devoir*, January 10, 1989, p. 2.

88. "Acquittement du permanent syndical Rénald Tardif," *La Presse*, December 2, 1988, p. C14.

89. "Quebec unionist was spy-agency informer minister confirms," *The Montreal Gazette*, September 16, 1987, p. A1.

90. *Ibid.*

91. Paquin, "Le SCRS aurait infiltré quatre autres syndicats," *op. cit.*

92. Georges Lamon, "Larose accuse Boivin d'avoir fomenté des projets criminels, mais ne donne pas de preuves," *La Presse*, January 22, 1988, p. A4.

93. Louise Lemieux, "La CSN accuse Boivin d'être un provocateur," *Le Soleil*, January 22, 1988, p. A1.

94. Noreau, "Enquête sur une possible infiltration à la CSN," *op. cit.*

95. Quoted in Lester, *op. cit.*, pp. 84–85.

96. SIRC said it tried to reach Larose by phone twice to apologize for the delay in responding to his letter, to explain how the *CSIS Act* works for filing complaints, and to answer his questions, but that he never returned their calls. "This is a flat-out fabrication," Larose stated, "We have never had any contact with the Supervisory Committee apart from this letter of January 13. Never, neither verbally nor in writing, were we asked to come and testify." Louise Lemieux, "Le SCRS réplique que Larose n'a pas donné suite à ses appels," *Le Soleil*, January 22, 1988, p. A3.

97. Pierre April, "Le SCRS n'a jamais demandé à Boivin d'inciter des syndiqués à commettre des actes criminels," *La Presse*, January 23, 1988, p. B1.

98. *Ibid.*

99. Marc Laurendeau, "Le SCRS: bourdes et 'provocation,'" *La Presse*, January 25, 1988, p. B3.

100. "Boivin l'informateur est en liberté conditionnelle," *La Presse*, March 5, 1988, p. A4.

101. SIRC, *Section 54 Report...*, *op. cit.*, p. 1.

102. *Ibid.*, pp. 3–4.

103. "We tried to arrange a meeting with Mr. Boivin after the courts had ruled on his case. Mr. Boivin expressed his desire to cooperate fully with the investigation, but he was not yet ready to meet with SIRC. However, he did have several lengthy telephone conversations with the Executive Secretary of the Committee," reads the fourth page of the report.

104. *Security Intelligence Review Committee*, *op. cit.*, pp. 13 and 17.

105. Jim Brown, "Spy agency's anti-subversive branch to be disbanded in wake of criticism," *Toronto Star*, November 29, 1987, p. A4.

106. SIRC, *Section 54 Report*, *op. cit.*, p. 18.

107. *Ibid.*, p. 10.

108. *Ibid.*, p. 14. See also *Ibid.*, p. 11

109. *Ibid.*

110. *Ibid.*, p. 1.

111. Gilles Paquin, "Le SCRS blâmé pour ses liens avec Marc Boivin," *La Presse*, March 30, 1988, p. A1.

112. Clayton Ruby, "Still reason to fear security intelligence service," *Toronto Star*, July 18, 1988, p. A15.

113. "CSIS cleared of inciting Quebec union violence," *The Montreal Gazette*, March 30, 1988, p. B1.

114. Raymond Giroux, "Un mouton noir parmi les espions," *Le Soleil*, March 31, 1988, p. B3.

115. Paquin, "CSIS Blamed," *op. cit.*

116. Louise Lemieux, "Marc-André Boivin contestera la décision du Tribunal du travail," *Le Soleil*, September 1, 1988, p. A10. During a radio interview, Gérald Larose replied sarcastically to Marc-André Boivin's complaint: "We should open a position for a double agent, an agent provocateur, a liar … but we don't have such a position yet" (Andrée Roy, "La CSN n'a pas de poste d'agent double pour Marc Boivin—Gérald Larose," *Le Soleil*, January 7, 1989, p. A1).

117. Lemieux, "Après ses révélations," *op. cit.*, p. A1.

118. André Bellemare, "Boivin perd contre la CSN," *Le Soleil*, June 29, 1988, p. A1.

119. In these interviews, Boivin never disclosed how much he earned from his "job" at CSIS, saying only that he was "probably making less" than he had made at the CSN. "I had a base salary, more dependent on events that might take place," he added. The former mole was also vague when Radio-Canada TV host Simon Durivage asked him about how often he met with his CSIS handler. "We had meetings as needed," he said. "It's like in any kind of work, when they needed information on certain targets, or certain problems that were emerging, we met." Durivage, "L'affaire Boivin," *op. cit.*

120. *Ibid.*

121. "CSIS agent in union sues Ottawa," *The Montreal Gazette*, March 24, 1989, p. A3.

122. Page 8 of "Détails fournis en réponse à des demandes de particularités," document dated August 24, 1992, filed in Federal Court by Boivin's counsel.

123. *Ibid.*

124. "Marc-André Boivin poursuit le SCRS," *Le Devoir*, March 25, 1989, p. A6.

125. "The Defence for Her Majesty The Queen and the Attorney General of Canada," document dated June 28, 1993, filed in the Federal Court of Canada, p. 9.

126. This is according to a letter dated March 2, 1999, and signed by Mr. Pierre Giroux, one of the federal lawyers. The Federal Court record does not mention whether Boivin received any damages.

127. Marco Fortier, "M.-A. Boivin se met au service du patronat et passe pour un 'dur,'" *Le Soleil*, October 10, 1993, p. A3. In April 2007, it was learned that the Verreault shipyard in Les Méchins had retained Boivin's services in a labour dispute with workers unionized with the CSN. According to a shipyard spokesperson, Boivin was hired "to give training to management employees on how to act in situations like ours" (Carl Thériault, "Un bateau entre au chantier Verreault en fin de semaine," *Le Soleil*, April 28, 2007, p. 52).

128. Élisabeth Fleury, "Marc-André Boivin coupable de recel," *Le Soleil*, January 17, 2007, p. 13.

129. *Criminal Code*, s. 464.

Chapter 8. A Big Thank You from the Neo-Nazis

1. Stewart Bell, *Bayou of Pigs*, Mississauga, John Wiley and Sons, 2008, p. 17.

2. "Matrai is found guilty of assault on Kosygin, free on bail until sentencing in the new year," *Globe and Mail*, December 24, 1971, p. 1.

3. Michael Smith, "$50,000 offered for Kosygin assassination, inquiry told," *Globe and Mail*, January 26, 1972, p. 5.

4. "Attacked Kosygin, man jailed 3 months by judge in Ottawa," *Globe and Mail*, January 8, 1972, p. 4.

5. "Burker society leader denies Kosygin assassination planned," *Globe and Mail*, March 3, 1972, p. 5.

6. "Burkers using rifles for 'country's defense,'" *Globe and Mail*, March 25, 1972, p. 12.

7. Bell, *op. cit.*, pp. 17–18.

8. McDonald Commission, *Second Report, op. cit.*, at 500.

9. "Don't confuse us with John Birch Society, Edmund Burke group ask," *Globe and Mail*, August 7, 1968, p.5.

10. Gunther Latsch and Klaus Wiegrefe, "Munich Olympics Massacre—Files Reveal Neo-Nazis Helped Palestinian Terrorists," *Spiegel Online*, June 18, 2012.

11. Benjamin Weinthal, "'Leftists, not neo-Nazis, helped in Munich massacre," *The Jerusalem Post*, June 24, 2012.

12. Bell, *op. cit.*, p. 18.

13. Michael Keating, "Driver for Western Guard 'hit and run' raids," *Globe and Mail*, November 24, 1977, p. 5. Michael Keating, "Man paid by RCMP broke windows for Western Guard," *Globe and Mail*, November 23, 1977, p. 1.

14. Michael Keating, "Bomb-making manual found in garage, Western Guard trial is told," *Globe and Mail*, November 26, 1977, p. 5.

15. "2 ex-Guard members guilty of plotting arson, mischief," *Globe and Mail*, February 2, 1978, p. 12.

16. *Globe and Mail*, "2 ex-Guard members," *op. cit.*

17. "Anti-Semitic material is called rotten," *Globe and Mail*, December 22, 1977, p. 5. "Racial slur in magazine caption—Called blacks garbage, Western Guard head testifies," *Globe and Mail*, December 21, 1977, p. 3.

18. "Letter for Jew amusing, Guard member tells trial," *Globe and Mail*, January 20, 1978, p. 38.

19. Michael Keating, "2 in Western Guard jailed in racist plot," *Globe and Mail*, February 18, 1978, p. 19.

20. Tu Thanh Ha, "CSIS probed Liberals, Conservatives in 1980s," *Globe and Mail*, December 17, 1994, A1.

21. Security Intelligence Review Committee, *The Heritage Front Affair: Report to the Solicitor General of Canada* (File No. 2800-54), Ottawa, Public Services and Supply Canada, December 9, 1994, ch. III, p. 2.

22. *Ibid.*

23. *Ibid.*, ch. III, p. 3.

24. Drew Fagan, "Toronto pair guilty of promoting hatred against Jews, blacks," *Globe and Mail*, December 10, 1985, p. A19.

25. SIRC, *The Heritage Front Affair, op. cit.*, ch. III, p. 3.

26. *Ibid.*

27. Andrew Mitrovica, "Front Man," *The Walrus*, September 2004, http://thewalrus.ca/front-man/.

28. SIRC, *The Heritage Front Affair, op. cit.*, ch, III, p. 4.

29. See *Bayou of Pigs*, a book by journalist Stewart Bell published in 2008 (and quoted above), entirely devoted to Operation Red Dog.

30. Bell, *op. cit.*, pp. 249–250.

31. "Affidavit of Wolfgang Droege," Federal Court of Canada, court file no. T-567-96.

32. SIRC, *The Heritage Front Affair, op. Cit.*, ch. III, p. 14. Norm Ovenden, "Offer of free security opened Reform to racists," *Edmonton Journal*, December 24, 1994, p. A3.

33. "Affidavit of Wolfgang Droege," *op. cit.*

34. SIRC, *The Heritage Front Affair, op. cit.*, ch. III, p. 6.

35. David Pugliese, "CSIS unveiled: How Bristow got inside ultra-right," *Ottawa Citizen*, December 30, 1994, p. A1.

36. SIRC, *The Heritage Front Affair, op. cit.*, ch. III, p. 10.

37. "Affidavit of Wolfgang Droege," *op. cit.*

38. SIRC, *The Heritage Front Affair, op. cit.*, ch. III, p. 11.

39. "Affidavit of Wolfgang Droege," *op. cit.* According to American researcher Leonard Zeskind, the "white nationalism" or "white separatism" that groups like the Heritage Front claim to adhere to is in fact simply an attempt to make white supremacism more palatable (Leonard Zeskind, *Blood and Politics: The History of the White Nationalist Movement from the Margins to the Mainstream*, New York, Farrar Straus Giroux, 2009, pp. 489 and 538).

40. SIRC, *The Heritage Front Affair, op. cit.*, ch. III, p. 11.

41. "Affidavit of Wolfgang Droege," *op. cit.*

42. SIRC, *The Heritage Front Affair, op. cit.*, ch. III, p. 14.

43. *Ibid.*, ch. XIII, p. 2.

44. "Affidavit of Wolfgang Droege," *op. cit.*

45. SIRC, *The Heritage Front Affair, op. cit.*, ch. III, p. 14, and ch. XIII, p. 2. The Airborne Regiment was a Canadian army unit that was disbanded after some of its members were involved in the torture and murder of Shidane Arone, a 16-year-old Somali, during the "Operation Restore Hope" in Somalia in 1992–93.

46. "Affidavit of Wolfgang Droege," *op. cit.*

47. SIRC, *The Heritage Front Affair, op. cit.*, ch. III, p. 12; SIRC, *Annual Report 2000–2001*, Ottawa, Public Services and Supply Canada, 2001, p. 17.

48. Andrew Mitrovica, *Covert Entry: Spies, Lies and Crimes Inside Canada's Secret Service*. Toronto: Random House Canada, 2002, p. 135.

49. *Ibid.*, p. 147.

50. SIRC, *The Heritage Front Affair*, op. cit., ch. III, p. 15.

51. *Ibid.*

52. *Ibid.*, p. 14.

53. *Ibid.*, ch. IV, p. 5.

54. "CSIS sent informer to spy in Germany," *Toronto Star*, October 18, 1994, p. A13.

55. R. v. Zundel, Supreme Court of Canada, 1992, 2 SCR 731; SIRC, *The Heritage Front Affair*, op. cit., ch. IV, p. 2.

56. D. Brazao, P. Cheney, J. Lakey, C. Millar, and G. Swainson, "Portrait of the vanishing spy," *Toronto Star*, September 10, 1994, p. A1.

57. *Ibid.*

58. SIRC, *The Heritage Front Affair*, op. cit., ch. IX, p. 1.

59. "Affidavit of Wolfgang Droege," op. cit.

60. SIRC, *The Heritage Front Affair*, op. cit., ch. IX, pp. 1–2.

61. "Affidavit of Wolfgang Droege," op. cit.

62. SIRC, *The Heritage Front Affair*, op. cit., ch. IX, p. 3.

63. *Ibid.*, ch. IV, p. 4.

64. House of Commons—Subcommittee on National Security, Testimonies, 35th Parliament 1st Session, June 13, 1995.

65. See for example, https://www.youtube.com/watch?v=oceN4FJK8bE. After Bristow was exposed as an agent, the Heritage Front even produced a ninety-five-minute video, entitled *The Best of Bristow*, in which one could view various verbal interventions by the CSIS informant at meetings of the far-right group.

66. SIRC, *The Heritage Front Affair*, op. cit., ch. XIII, p. 2.

67. *Ibid.*

68. "Affidavit of Wolfgang Droege," op. cit.

69. "Affidavit of Gerry Lincoln."

70. SIRC, *The Heritage Front Affair*, op. cit., ch. V, pp. 35–36.

71. *Ibid.*, ch. V, p. 37.

72. *Ibid.*, ch. V, p. 1.

73. Nicolaas van Rijn, "Video shows Bristow's role in racist Front," *Toronto Star*, February 20, 1995, p. A14.

74. House of Commons—Subcommittee on National Security, Evidence, *op. cit.*

75. Founded in 1987 in Western Canada, the Reform Party became the Canadian Alliance in 2000, which subsequently merged with the Progressive Conservative Party in 2003 to create the Conservative Party of Canada. The Conservative Party was in government from 2006 to 2015 under Prime Minister Stephen Harper.

76. Daphne Bramham, "Manning lays down the Reform Party line," *The Vancouver Sun*, February 12, 1991, p. A12.

77. SIRC, *The Heritage Front Affair*, op. cit., ch. VII, p. 13.

78. *Ibid.*, ch. VII, p. 4.

79. *Ibid.*, ch. IV, pp. 3–4.

80. *Ibid.*, ch. VII, p. 10.

81. *Ibid.*, ch. VII, p. 17.

82. *Ibid.*, ch. VII, p. 19.

83. *Ibid.*, ch. VII, p. 27.

84. *Ibid.*, ch. VII, pp. 21–22.

85. *Ibid.*, ch. VII, p. 24.

86. *Ibid.*, ch. VII, p. 25.

87. *Ibid.*, ch. XIII, p. 7.

88. *Ibid.*, ch. VII, p. 31.

89. *Ibid.*, ch. VII, p. 25.

90. *Ibid.*, ch. VII, p. 26.

91. *Ibid.*, ch. VII, p. 29.

92. Peter Krivel, "Reform party probes racist connections," *Toronto Star*, February 28, 1992, p. A9.

93. "Reform party panel to try to weed out racists," *Toronto Star*, March 11, 1992, p. A10.

94. As a result of these lawsuits, the line was shut down and then set up again seven times (SIRC, *The Heritage Front Affair, op. cit.*, ch. V, p. 3).

95. *Ibid.*

96. David Hilderley, "Supremacist group uses rock to spread message," *Globe and Mail*, June 7, 1993, p. A11.

97. Ian Timberlake, "Skin Head," *The Windsor Star*, February 20, 1993, p. E1.

98. D. Brazao et al., "Portrait of the vanishing spy," *op. cit.*, p. A1.

99. SIRC, *The Heritage Front Affair, op. cit.*, ch. IV, p. 7.

100. Elisa Hategan, *Race Traitor: The True Story of Canadian Intelligence's Greatest Cover-up*, Incognito Press, 2014, https://incognitopress.files.wordpress.com/2015/10/race-traitor-excerpt-by-elisa-hategan.pdf

101. *Ibid.*

102. *Ibid.*

103. SIRC, *The Heritage Front Affair, op. cit.*, ch. V, p. 1.

104. *Ibid.*

105. *Ibid.*, ch. V, p. 8.

106. *Ibid.*, ch. V, p. 11.

107. *Ibid.*, ch. V, p. 12.

108. *Ibid.*, ch. V, pp. 14–15.

109. Dale Brazao, "Agency fostered racism, activist says Heritage Front member paid by security service," *Toronto Star*, August 17, 1994, p. A19.

110. House of Commons—Subcommittee on National Security, Evidence, *op. cit.*

111. *Ibid.*

112. SIRC, *The Heritage Front Affair, op. cit*, ch. V, p. 11.

113. *Ibid.*, ch. XIII, p. 4.

114. Hategan, *op. cit.*

115. *Ibid.*

116. *Ibid.*

117. SIRC, *The Heritage Front Affair, op. cit.*, ch. XIII, p. 2.

118. According to SIRC, "the Source invented the 'IT' scenario in an attempt to avoid criminal threatening charges." *Ibid.*, ch. V, p. 9.

119. *Ibid.*, ch. V, p. 9.

120. *Ibid.*, ch. V, p.15.

121. House of Commons—Subcommittee on National Security, "Evidence," *op. cit.*

122. SIRC, *The Heritage Front Affair, op. cit.*, ch. V, p. 13.

123. SIRC, *The Heritage Front Affair, op. cit.*, ch. XIII, p. 4. "In any event, CSIS senior management at Headquarters in Ottawa apparently knew little or nothing, at the time, of the harassment program that occurred in late 1992 and early 1993." *Ibid.*, ch. XIII, p. 5.

124. *Ibid.*, ch. V, p. 15.

125. *Ibid.*, ch. IV, p. 10.

126. House of Commons—Subcommittee on National Security, Evidence, *op. cit.*

127. Mitrovica, "Front Man," *op. cit.*

128. SIRC, *The Heritage Front Affair, op. cit.*, ch. V, p. 4.

129. Michael Tenszen and Moira Welsh, "3 protesters, one officer hurt in anti-racist clash," *Toronto Star*, January 25, 1993, p. A1.

130. Mike Shahin and Peter Hum, "600 anti-racist protesters battle police," *Ottawa Citizen*, May 30, 1993, p. A1.

131. SIRC, *The Heritage Front Affair, op. cit.*, ch. V, p. 24.

132. Jennifer Lewington, "Anti-racists vent anger on white supremacist," *Globe and Mail*, June 12, 1993, p. A1.

133. House of Commons—Subcommittee on National Security, Evidence, *op. cit.*

134. Founded in Florida in 1973, the Church of the Creator was a white supremacist religious organization; its Canadian section was affiliated with the Heritage Front.

135. Geoffrey York, "Military's hands tied, House Leader declares," *Globe and Mail*, May 8, 1993, p. A10; "Military watching white racist activity in its ranks," *Ottawa Citizen*, May 7, 1993, p. A4.

136. In his testimony years later, Droege would note that "Bristow was not at the concert which was extremely unusual as he always attended all HF events in the city of Toronto as security chief. This was the first event he had missed." ("Affidavit of Wolfgang Droege," *op. cit.*).

137. "Affidavit of Tyrone Mason."

138. The White Berets were the Church of the Creator's paramilitary group.

139. "Affidavit of Tyrone Mason," *op. cit.*

140. "Man denied bail in Tamil's beating," *Toronto Star*, June 10, 1993, p. A18.

141. Jack Lakey, "Man pleads guilty in racial attack," *Toronto Star*, March 8, 1994, p. A2.

142. Dottie O'Neill and Peter Small, "Worker partly paralyzed after vicious beating," *Toronto Star*, June 7, 1993, p. A22.

143. Donn Downey, "Former skinhead pleads guilty in vicious assault," *Globe and Mail*, March 8, 1994, p. A14.

144. Peter Small, "Beaten Tamil slowly rebuilds his life," *Toronto Star*, September 4, 1993, p. A4.

145. *Toronto Star*, "Man denied bail in Tamil's beating," *op. cit.*

146. Jack Lakey, "Sobbing skinhead jailed 4 years for beating," *Toronto Star*, March 9, 1994, p. A9.

147. Peter Small, "Mayor condemns racial violence," *Toronto Star*, June 11, 1993, p. A8; Peter Small, "Refugee slashed by 2 men in third attack on Tamils," *Toronto Star*, June 22, 1993, p. A6.

148. Donn Downey, "Racial attacks decried as dangerous trend," *Globe and Mail*, June 23, 1993, p. A14.

149. Hategan, *op. cit.*

150. Rachel Mendleson, "Former neo-Nazi's journey from HATE to healing," *Toronto Star*, May 5, 2015, p. A3.

151. Hategan, *op. cit.*

152. Mendleson, "Former neo-Nazi's," *op. cit.*

153. "Affidavit of Wolfgang Droege," *op. cit.*

154. *Ibid.*

155. Hategan, *op. cit.*

156. Chambre des Communes—Sous-comité sur la sécurité nationale, Témoignages, *op. cit.*

157. Hategan, *op. cit.*

158. SIRC, *The Heritage Front Affair*, *op. cit.*, ch. V, p. 20.

159. *Ibid.*

160. House of Commons—Subcommittee on National Security, Evidence, *op. cit.*

161. "Neo-Nazis to stand trial over brawl," *Toronto Star*, December 8, 1993, p. A9.

162. Mitrovica, "Front man," *op. cit.*

163. SIRC, *The Heritage Front Affair*, op. cit., ch. IV, p. 12.

164. SIRC, *The Heritage Front Affair*, op. cit., ch. IV, p. 10.

165. Mitrovica, "Front man," *op. cit.*

166. House of Commons—Subcommittee on National Security, Evidence, *op. cit.*

167. Mitrovica, "Front man," *op. cit.*

168. Kirk Makin, "Is Canada's spy agency out of control?," *Globe and Mail*, September 10, 1994. p. A1.

169. D. Brazao et al., "Portrait of the vanishing spy," *op. cit.*, p. A1.

170. "Le Service du renseignement à l'aide des néonazis," *Le Devoir*, August 15, 1994, p. A3.

171. Kirk Martin, "Front enjoying media attention," *Globe and Mail*, August 27, 1994, A1.

172. *Ibid.*

173. Makin, "Is Canada's spy agency out of control?," *op. cit.*

174. Martin, "Front enjoying media attention," *op. cit.*

175. William Boei, "Blood on Jew's steps coincided with informant's visit," *The Vancouver Sun*, December 16, 1994, p. A4. However, the SIRC report states that Bristow knew absolutely nothing about Elterman (SIRC, *The Heritage Front Affair*, op. cit., ch. V, p. 33).

176. Kirk Martin, "Lawyers assail Bristow tactics, Role in trials questioned," *Globe and Mail*, December 8, 1994, p. A1.

177. Jim Sheppard, "Meet mysterious CSIS spy," *The Montreal Gazette*, September 11, 1994, p. A5.

178. Amber Nasrulla, "Ottawa probes claims about CSIS informant," *Globe and Mail*, August 16, 1994, p. A5.

179. Brazao, "Agency fostered racism," *op. cit.*

180. Larry Welsh, "Reform Party wants parliamentary probe of CSIS spy," *The Montreal Gazette*, August 24, 1994, p. A10.

181. Elizabeth Payne, "Spy agency placed Jewish 'lives in danger,'" *Ottawa Citizen*, September 10, 1994, p. A3.

182. Mitrovica, "Front man," *op. cit.*

183. Jim Sheppard, "CSIS watchdog to review claims that spy directed neo-Nazi front," *Ottawa Citizen*, August 16, 1994, p. A1.

184. Nicolaas van Rijn, "Spy agency probed over hate group link," *Toronto Star*, August 16, 1994, p. A4.

185. "Fox loses 4th bid to stop inquiry into RCMP affairs," *Globe and Mail*, December 17, 1977, p. 12; Sallot, "Ottawa vs. RCMP," *op. cit.*

186. Doug Ward, "MP demands inquiry into spy body's link with neo-Nazi," *The Vancouver Sun*, August 16, 1994, p. B4.

187. Sheppard, "CSIS watchdog," *op. cit.*

188. Kirk Makin, "Front member Manning's 'shadow,'" *Globe and Mail*, August 23, 1994, A.1.

189. *Ibid.*

190. The Reform Party won fifty-two seats, compared to fifty-four for the Bloc Québécois, an ironic outcome for the sovereigntist political party.

191. Norm Ovenden, "Tories used CSIS files—Reformer,'" *Edmonton Journal*, September 14, 1994, p. A3.

192. *Ibid.* In support of their allegations, Reformers pointed to the fact that the minister responsible for CSIS during Operation Governor, then–Solicitor General Doug Lewis, was also co-chair of the Progressive Conservative campaign in Ontario ("Le scandale de l'"informateur' Bristow éclairci aujourd'hui," *Le Soleil*, October 18, 1994, p. A8). Meredith also pointed out that her party only managed to win one seat in the prov-

ince. (Kenny Eoin, "Ex-Tory aide arrested for CSIS leak," *Ottawa Citizen*, August 26, 1994, p. A1).

193. "L'affaire Bristow: Doug Lewis ne collabore pas," *Le Devoir*, October 19, 1994, p. A2.

194. "Le Parti réformiste et le Bloc québécois surveillés?," *Le Devoir*, October 20, 1994, p. A4.

195. SIRC, *The Heritage Front Affair*, op. cit., ch. XIII, p. 5.

196. *Ibid.*

197. David Vienneau, "The Canadian Security Intelligence Service has been spying on the CBC," *Toronto Star*, August 19, 1994, p. A1.

198. *Ibid.*

199. Shawn McCarthy, "CSIS demands return of classified document," *Toronto Star*, August 23, 1994, p. A1.

200. "RCMP gives Star lawyer a warning," *Toronto Star*, August 24, 1994, p. A9.

201. *Ibid.*

202. D. Vienneau, R. Speirs, and S. McCarthy, "Ex-aide admits leaking spy note," *Toronto Star*, August 26, 1994, p. A1.

203. *Ibid.*

204. Kirk Makin, "Tory aide admits CSIS leak," *Globe and Mail*, August 26, 1994, A1.

205. Eoin Kenny, "Ex-Tory aide arrested for CSIS leak," *Ottawa Citizen*, August 26, 1994, A1.

206. *Ibid.*

207. "Mounties raid CTV news bureau," *Toronto Star*, September 3, 1994, p. A1.

208. David Harris, "Much to lose in CSIS probe," *Ottawa Citizen*, September 12, 1994, p. A9.

209. SIRC, *The Heritage Front Affair, op. cit.*, ch. XIII, p. 11.

210. "Un ex-fonctionnaire auteur d'une fuite ne sera pas poursuivi," *La Presse*, July 20, 1995, p. B1.

211. Allan Thompson, "Gray allowed to read report given to Lewis," *Toronto Star*, October 6, 1994, p. A10.

212. Ibid.

213. "Les actes du SCRS seront examinés à la loupe par un comité parlementaire," *Le Soleil*, September 13, 1994, p. C12.

214. Jeff Sallot, "Bristow inquiry missing Bristow," *Globe and Mail*, September 15, 1994, A.10.

215. "Deux nouvelles enquêtes sur le SCRS," *La Presse*, September 15, 1994, p. A9.

216. "Une enquête indépendante sur le SCRS est réclamée par des groupes," *Le Soleil*, September 10, 1994, p. A15.

217. "L'informateur Bristow: des allégations sont vraies," *La Presse*, November 30, 1994, p. A13.

218. SIRC, *The Heritage Front Affair, op. cit.*, ch. VI, p. 9.

219. *Ibid.*, ch. VI, pp. 2–4.

220. *Ibid.*, ch. VI, p. 12.

221. "[CSIS] used the investigative technique which offered the best value for money when it instructed the Source to report on the white supremacist targets." *Ibid.*, ch.. XIII, p. 1.

222. To wit: Steve Hammond (January 1991), Sean Maguire (September 1991), Tom Metzger (June 1992), John Metzger (June 1992), David Irving (November 1992), and Dennis Mahon (January 1993). *Ibid.*, ch. VI, p. 10.

223. Grant Bristow's contribution to the eighty threat assessments on white supremacist activities produced by CSIS since 1989 was qualified in a footnote to the SIRC report, which quotes CSIS: "While it is not possible to quickly attribute the contents of specific assessments to [the Source], the

intelligence from this individual is seen as a significant contributor." *Ibid.*, ch. VI, p. 11.

224. *Ibid.*, ch. XIII, p. 15.

225. *Ibid.*, ch. XIII, p. 12.

226. *Ibid.*, ch. XIII, p. 13.

227. *Ibid.*, ch. XIII, p. 14.

228. *Ibid.*, ch. XIII, p. 10.

229. Tu Thanh Ha, "CSIS probed Reform funding," *Globe and Mail*, December 16, 1994, A1.

230. David Pugliese, "CSIS spying on racists 'successful,'" *Ottawa Citizen*, December 16, 1994, p. A1.

231. Allan Thompson, "A peek under the cover," *Toronto Star*, December 17, 1994, p. B1.

232. Jean Dion, "La sainte colère de Preston Manning," *Le Devoir*, December 21, 1994, p. A1.

233. Clayton Ruby, "SIRC's intolerable 'limit of the tolerable,'" *Toronto Star*, December 21, 1994, Sec. B., p. A25. Barbara Jackman, a well-known Toronto immigration lawyer, also criticized the Review Committee for its lack of distance from the secret service it was supposed to be overseeing: "They have an ongoing relationship with CSIS that is part of their function and there may be a natural tendency for them to begin to accept the CSIS version of things." (Thompson, "A peek under the cover," *op. cit.*).

234. Ruby, "SIRC's intolerable 'limit of the tolerable,'" *op. cit.*

235. SIRC, *The Heritage Front Affair, op. cit.*, ch. V, p. 34.

236. *Ibid.*, ch. V, p. 35.

237. *Ibid.*, ch. XIII, p. 5.

238. David Vienneau, "Racist group had 'hit list' of Metro Jews," *Toronto Star*, December 16, 1994, p. A1.

239. Boei, "Blood on Jew's steps," *op. cit.*

240. Thompson, "A peek under the cover," *op. cit.*

241. *Canadian Security Intelligence Service Act*, Section 19(2)a).

242. Kirk Makin, "SIRC report triggers more questions," *Globe and Mail*, December 17, 1994, A6.

243. Derek Ferguson, "Report 'whitewash' of spy agency mole," *Toronto Star*, June 14, 1995, p. A3.

244. House of Commons—Subcommittee on National Security, "Evidence," *op. cit.*

245. "Spy watchdog blasted in report," *Edmonton Journal*, June 12, 1996, p. A12.

246. David Vienneau, "Liberals fault spy agency but urge no change," *Toronto Star*, June 20, 1996, p. A11.

247. Jim Bronskill, "Security service rejects call for tighter rules," *Ottawa Citizen*, June 20, 1996, p. E6.

248. "Spy watchdog concerned about safety of sources," *Ottawa Citizen*, July 22, 1995, p. A4.

249. Dale Brazao, "Star finds Grant Bristow," *Toronto Star*, April 20, 1995, p. A1.

250. "Affidavit of Tyrone Mason," *op. cit.*

251. "Ex-spy may face charges," *Edmonton Journal*, November 16, 1995, p. A8.

252. SIRC, *The Heritage Front Affair, op. cit.*, ch. IV, p. 10.

253. Mitrovica, *Covert Entry, op. cit.*, p. 115.

254. *Ibid.*, p. 172.

255. Brock Ketcham, "In Search Of Supremacists," *Calgary Herald*, February 9, 1997, p. A6.

256. Devin Clancy, "Running the Fascists Out of Town," *Briarpatch*, December 21, 2017.

257. Jack Lakey, "Hate crimes drop by 43% as leaders fade from view," *Toronto Star*, March 14, 1997, p. A7.

258. *Ibid.*

259. Mitrovica, "Front man," *op. cit.*

260. Colin Perkel, "Droege's death won't slow down extremists, ex-CSIS mole says," *Globe and Mail*, April 25, 2005, p. A9.

Chapter 9. Terror Threats, Courtesy of CSIS

1. Security Intelligence Review Committee, *Annual Report 1997–1998*, Ottawa, Public Services and Supply Canada, 1998, p. 37. Although the SIRC report does not identify the source by name, journalist André Cédilot of *La Presse* confirmed in an article published several years later that Breault was indeed the "controversial figure" in question (André Cédilot, "Il faut revoir la lutte contre le terrorisme," *La Presse*, December 15, 2001, p. A6).

2. André Noël, "Un drôle d'espion," *La Presse*, December 14, 2001, p. A7. I sent an access to information request to CSIS (#117-2016-197) to ascertain the exact date that Joseph Gilles Breault began acting as a "human source" for the intelligence agency, as well as the exact date that the agency ceased to use his services, and the total amount of money paid to him in this capacity, including reimbursement of expenses. CSIS would not "confirm or deny the existence of the records requested," citing sections 10(1)(b), 10(2), 15(1), 16(1)(a) and 16(1)(c) of the *Access to Information Act*.

3. *Ibid.*

4. National Assembly—Standing Committee on Public Finance, *Journal des débats*, 36th legislature 2nd session, Quebec City, National Assembly, October 31, 2001, www.assnat.qc.ca/fr/travaux-parlementaires/commissions/cfp-36-2/journal-debats/CFP-011031.html.

5. Richard Hétu, "L'avant-garde de l'islam," *La Presse*, February 1, 1992, p. A1.

6. *Ibid.*

7. "News film cast discredit on Muslims, groups say," *The Montreal Gazette*, March 30, 1988, p. A7.

8. Gazette officielle du Québec, October 17, 1990, 122nd year, no. 42, p. 3764; Jules Béliveau, "Un responsable des registres chez les Musulmans de Montréal," *La Presse*, December 2, 1990, p. A12.

9. Jules Béliveau, "Mouammar désavoué par des mosquées et des groupes musulmans," *La Presse*, April 9, 1989, p. B6.

10. Regarding the *Satanic Verses* affair, see the text I wrote on the subject (in French) in September 2007: http://archives-2001-2012.cmaq.net/es/node/28088.html.

11. Bruno Bisson, "Menace de mort contre Rushdie—Écrivains et artistes dénoncent le manque de fermeté du Canada," *La Presse*, March 10, 1989, p. A9.

12. Hétu, *op. cit.*

13. Andrew Duffy and Jennifer Gould, "Leader of revolt studied at Ryerson," *Toronto Star*, July 29, 1990, p. A1.

14. Andrew Duffy, "Trinidad assesses its tarnished image," *Toronto Star*, August 4, 1990.

15. On January 8, 1992, the government renewed the authorization it had given to Breault to maintain the civil status registries of the "Community of the Muslim Nation of Greater Montreal" (Gazette officielle du Québec, January 29, 1992, 124th year, no. 4, p. 706). Then, on April 24, 1993, the maintenance of the registries was entrusted to Said Youssef Fawaz … while Breault remained responsible for the conservation of said registries (*Gazette officielle du Québec*, July 28, 1993, 125th year, no. 31, pp. 5156–5157).

16. Irwin Block, "Anti-Semitic text removed from shelves after protests," *The Montreal Gazette*, November 27, 1990, p. A4. It should be noted that the CSIS informant was known as "Youssef Mouammar" in the media, although he used his birth name, Joseph Gilles Breault, when setting up commercial enterprises.

17. Raymond Gervais, "La crise politique algérienne divise les Algériens de Montréal," *La Presse*, January 13, 1992, p. A5.

18. Gervais, *op. cit.*

19. Amar Overdane, "Fanatisme débridé," *La Presse*, January 23, 1992, p. B2.

20. Noël, *op. cit.*

21. It should be noted that there were already doubts at the time about the true nature of the GIA. The French newspaper *Le Monde* did not hesitate to write that the GIA was "largely infiltrated, at least in its beginnings, by the Algerian security services" (Simon Catherine, "Le bras armé des islamistes," *Le Monde*, November 10, 1994, p. 14). In addition, two former members of the Algerian security services have documented the infiltration and manipulation of several Islamist guerrillas by the Algerian military-police apparatus. See Habib Souaïdia, *La Sale Guerre*, Paris, La Découverte, 2001, and Mohammed Samraoui, *Chronique des années de sang*, Paris, Éditions Denoel, 2003.

22. Éric Clément and Gilles Toupin, "Des appels au meurtre en Algérie proviennent bel et bien de Montréal," *La Presse*, December 14, 1994, p. A1.

23. *Ibid.*

24. *Ibid.*

25. Éric Clément, "La députée de La Pinière incite les médias à ne pas se laisser berner par les intégristes," *La Presse*, December 15, 1994, p. A10.

26. National Assembly, *Journal des débats*, 35th legislature, 1st session, Quebec City, December 14, 1994, p. 648.

27. Noël, *op. cit.*

28. Caroly Adolph, "Local group wrote hate letter: Jewish center," *The Montreal Gazette*, October 29, 1994, p. A3.

29. Éric Clément, "Personne ne s'accord sur le nombre d'intégristes musulmans à Montréal," *La Presse*, November 11, 1994, p. A5.

30. Adolph, *op. cit.*

31. *Ibid.*

32. Éric Clément, "La police de la CUM n'enquêtera pas sur les menaces que se lancent pro-Israéliens et pro-Palestiniens," *La Presse*, December 16, 1994, p. C13.

33. *Ibid.*

34. *Ibid.*

35. Éric Clément, "Menacée de mort pour avoir critiqué l'islam et le régime dictatorial du Soudan," *La Presse*, February 11, 1995, p. A9.

36. *Ibid.*

37. Noël, *op. cit.*

38. Normand Lester, *Point à la ligne*, Montreal, Les Intouchables, 2011, p. 175.

39. Noël, *op. cit.*

40. SIRC, *Annual Report, 1997–1998, op. cit.*, p. 36.

41. Lester, *Point à la ligne, op. cit.*, p. 176.

42. *Ibid.*

43. Paul Wells, "Public enemy or public servant?," *National Post*, December 15, 2001, p. B7.

44. Noël, *op. cit.*

45. Normand Lester, "Une enquête sur l'islamiste intégriste Youssef Mouammar," *Le Téléjournal*, Montreal, Radio-Canada, October 5, 2001.

46. Noël, *op. cit.*

47. *Ibid.*

48. *Ibid.*

49. Lester, *Point à la ligne, op. cit.*, p. 175.

50. Noël, *op. cit.*

51. Lester, *Point à la ligne, op. cit.*, pp. 175–176.

52. Noël, *op. cit.*

53. Christian Dore, "Sur la trace des rumeurs: Déstabilisant les entreprises, elles ont coûté 600 millions d'euros à Coca-Cola en 1999," *Le Figaro*, August 14, 2002, p. 2.

54. Michel Auger, *L'attentat*, Montreal, Trait d'union, 2001, p. 187.

55. *Ibid.*, p. 188.

56. Lester, *Point à la ligne, op. cit.*, p. 176.

57. Noël, *op. cit.*

58. "On each of the lines of the Montreal subway, there is a bomb," the communiqué warned. "If our texts are not made public on international radio and TV, the three bombs will be detonated simultaneously by three brother combatants at the time of our choosing (March 4 between 8 a.m. and 10 p.m.)" (Rima Elkouri, "Ben Laden dans le métro?," *La Presse*, October 3, 2001, p. E1)

59. "Real or not, threat tests hospitals," *The Montreal Gazette*, March 31, 1998, p. A3.

60. Éric Trottier and Yann Pineau, "Attaque appréhendée au gaz sarin: La Régie de la santé a-t-elle exagéré?," *La Presse*, March 30, 1998, p. A1.

61. George Kalogerakis, "Gas warning to hospitals 'a mistake,'" *The Montreal Gazette*, March 29, 1998, p. A1.

62. Trottier and Pineau, *op. cit.*

63. *The Montreal Gazette*, "Real or not, threat tests hospitals," *op. cit.*

64. Trottier and Pineau, *op. cit.*

65. *Ibid.*

66. Lynn Moore, "Letter castigates police—Accused by health official of misleading public on gas alert," *The Montreal Gazette*, April 3, 1998, p. A5.

67. CSIS, *Chemical, Biological, Radiological and Nuclear Terrorism* (Report No. 2000/02), Ottawa, CSIS, December 18, 1999, p. 7, http://infosect.freeshell.org/infocult/SCRS_2000_02.pdf.

68. André Duchesne, "Le Canada n'est pas à l'abri d'une attaque à l'arme biologique," *La Presse*, February 3, 2001, p. B5; Philippe Coste, "Charbon: un bacille facile à faire vivre, pour des utilisations artisanales," *AFP*, October 17, 2001. The Canadian Press story (by Jim Bronskill) on the CSIS document was itself picked up by three anglophone dailies: "Canada at risk of terror, CSIS warns," *National Post*, October 26 1999, p. A8; "Canada at risk for terrorism, report warns," *Edmonton Journal*, October 26, 1999, p. E14; "CSIS fears bioterrorism, nuclear attacks," *Ottawa Citizen*, October 26, 1999, p. A3.

69. Marie-Claude Girard, "Simulation d'attaque terroriste en juin à Montréal," *La Presse*, March 29, 2000, p. A8.

70. "Attaques biochimiques—Le Canada à l'exercice," *Le Soleil*, March 29, 2000, p. A11.

71. Helen Branswell, *The Canadian Press*, September 24, 2001.

72. Pascal Ceaux and Fabrice Lhomme, "Le procès de 24 islamistes soupçonnées d'appartenir au Takfir s'ouvre à Paris," *Le Monde*, September 29, 2001, p. 4.

73. "Un projet d'attentat à Montréal découvert en 1999," *Le Monde*, September 29, 2001, p. 4.

74. *Ibid.*

75. Bertrand Desjardins, "Le métro de Montréal, cible des terroristes islamiques," *Le Journal de Montréal*, October 1, 2001, p. 3.

76. Brian Myles, "Attentats dans le métro de Montréal: Un canular, assure la police," *Le Devoir*, October 2, 2001, p. A5.

77. Lynn Moore, "Terror trial cites metro bomb scare: Incident occurred in 1998: police," *The Montreal Gazette*, October 2, 2001, p. A3.

78. Brian Myles, *op. cit.*

79. Marie Tison, "Pour le SPCUM, le complot terroriste dans le métro de Montréal est un canular," La Presse Canadienne, October 1, 2001. On the French side, *Le Soleil* in Quebec City, *Le Droit* in Gatineau-Ottawa, *Le Nouvelliste* in Trois-Rivières, *La Tribune* in Sherbrooke, *La Voix de l'Est* in

Granby, *Le Quotidien* in Saguenay and *L'Acadie Nouvelle* in Caraquet, New Brunswick. At the same time, The Montreal *Gazette*, the Toronto *Globe and Mail*, the *Edmonton Journal* and the *Windsor Star* all published English versions of the story.

80. Éric Clément, "Ce n'était pas un canular: un groupe de ben Laden a bien menacé Montréal," *La Presse*, October 2, 2001, p. A1.

81. Jean-Robert Sansfaçon "Où étiez-vous le 4 mars 1999?," *Le Devoir*, October 2, 2001, p. A8.

82. Lester, "Une enquête sur l'islamiste," *op. cit.*

83. On December 14 and 15, 2001, however, the case was the subject of three articles in the print media, two in *La Presse* and one in the *National Post*. After these three articles, no newspaper ever mentioned the case again.

84. Noël, *op. cit.*

85. Lester, *Point à la ligne, op. cit.*, pp. 174–175.

86. Noël, *op. cit.*

87. The fire required the intervention of some 130 firefighters and the evacuation of 2,000 employees working in the building, which includes, in addition to the CSIS offices, those of the departments of Citizenship and Immigration, the Solicitor General, and Human Resources Development and Public Works. See: Raymond Gervais, "Les services secrets ont eu chaud," *La Presse*, December 22, 2001, p. F2; Sidhartha Banerjee, "2,000 forced out—Evacuees federal-building workers," *The Montreal Gazette*, December 22, 2001, p. A1; Jérôme Dussault, "Incendie chez les espions," *Le Journal de Montréal*, December 22.

88. Gervais, "Les services secrets ont eu chaud," *op. cit.*, The source of the fire was located in the crawlspace between the ceiling and the floor of the sixth floor, in the area occupied by CSIS. It should be noted that the firefighters were obstructed by CSIS security measures, which contributed to a delay of several hours in extinguishing the blaze, which was finally put out in the early evening. "Since the building is protected and not just anyone can enter, the firefighters had to bring all their equipment to the roof by ladders," wrote the *La Presse* journalist. *The Gazette* reported that this was "a major

problem for the firefighters." Coincidentally, a fire drill had been held in the same building two days earlier, which facilitated the evacuation. In addition, the fire started during the lunch hour, when many employees had left the building for their break (Banerjee, *op. cit.*).

89. One wonders to what extent CSIS allowed the Service de sécurité incendie de Montréal (SSIM) to investigate further. If CSIS did not allow firefighters to enter its premises to extinguish the fire, there is no reason to believe that it was more lax with the SIM investigators. As for the Montreal police arson squad, it is known that they were not called in to investigate the origin of the fire (Banerjee, *op. cit.*).

90. Andrew Mitrovica and Jeff Sallot, "CSIS agent destroyed Air-India evidence," *Globe and Mail*, January 26, 2000, p. A1.

Conclusion: State Secrets Suck!

1. J. Michael Cole, *Smokescreen: Canadian Security Intelligence after September 11, 2001*, Bloomington, iUniverse, Inc., 2008, pp. 73–75.

2. *Ibid.*

3. Security Intelligence Review Committee, *Broader horizons—Preparing the groundwork for change, Annual report 2014–2015*, Ottawa, Public Services and Procurement Canada, 2015, p. 18.

4. *Ibid.*

5. Emma Loop, "Canada's Domestic Spy Agency Doesn't Know For Sure Whether Its People Funded Terrorists," *BuzzFeed*, January 28, 2016.

6. Andrew McIntosh, "Présumé espion à la solde du Canada—De nouvelles révélations embarrassantes," *Canoë*, March 16, 2015.

7. This is what the author was told by the Bibliothèque et Archives Nationales du Québec in an email dated October 21, 2022.

8. Robert Fife, "CSIS violated its own rules in smuggling of British teens," *Globe and Mail*, October 11, 2022.

9. Robert Fife, "Ottawa won't say if CSIS operative who trafficked teens to Islamic State militants is now in Canada," *Globe and Mail*, September 15, 2022.

10. Adrian Humphreys, "Canada's spy agency accused of 'nabbing British children and trafficking them' to Islamic State," *National Post*, September 1, 2022, p. A1.

11. Colin Freeze, "PM backs CSIS amid claims of informant smuggling schoolgirls," *Globe and Mail*, September 1, 2022, p. A1.

12. Syrian-born Maher Arar is a Canadian engineer who, along with other Ottawa residents, was the target of a joint investigation by CSIS, the RCMP, and various Canadian police forces in the fall of 2001. During a stopover at a New York airport in September 2002, Arar was detained by US immigration police on the basis of information provided by the RCMP that was later found to be erroneous. He was then transferred by US authorities to Jordan and then to Syria, where he was detained and tortured for 374 days before being released due to lack of evidence. In January 2007, the Harper government agreed to pay Arar and his family $10.5 million in compensation for his ordeal.

13. Commission of Inquiry into the Actions of Canadian Officials in Relation to Maher Arar, *The Report of the Commission of Inquiry into the Actions of Canadian Officials in Relation to Maher Arar—Analysis and recommendations*, Ottawa, Public Services and Procurement Canada, p. 67.

14. Olivier Cassidy, "Couple could get max imprisonment," *The Province*, July 4, 2013, p. A4.

15. *R. v. Nuttall*, Supreme Court of British Columbia, 2016 BCSC 1404.

16. *Ibid*.

17. Keith Fraser, "Terrorism Charges—240 cops on bomb-plot case, jury hears," *The Province*, March 24, 2015, p. A14.

18. Geordon Omand, "Nuttall and Korody still a threat to the public, Crown lawyer says," *Globe and Mail*, September 8, 2016, p. S1; Ian Mulgrew, "Surrey couple freed as judge blasts 'farcical' RCMP sting," *The*

Vancouver Sun, July 30, 2016, p. A4; R. v. Nuttall, Court of Appeal for British Columbia, 2018 BCCA 479.

19. *R. v. Nuttall, op. cit.*

20. Mulgrew, *op. cit.*

21. Brian Hutchinson, "Alleged bomb plot foiled—B.C. suspects 'inspired by al-Qaeda,' police say," *National Post*, July 3, 2013, p. A1.

22. Ian Mulgrew, "Spy agency complicates terror trial," *The Vancouver Sun*, January 8, 2016, p. A4.

23. *R. v. Nuttall*, Supreme Court of British Columbia, 2015 BCSC 1125.

24. Keith Fraser, "Judge wants CSIS to obey her order," *The Province*, February 3, 2016, p. A9.

25. Keith Fraser, "Terror plot duo give up on CSIS records," *The Vancouver Sun*, April 15, 2016, p. A7.

26. R. v. N.Y., Ontario Court of Appeal, 2012 ONCA 745.

27. It should be noted, on the other hand, that Bill C-51 amended the CSIS Act to add a provision, paragraph 18.1(4)(b), giving the Federal Court the right of "disclosure of the identity of a human source or information from which the identity of a human source could be inferred," as long as such disclosure "is essential to establish the accused's innocence and that it may be disclosed in the proceeding."

28. The list of those "Permanently bound to Secrecy" also includes members and former members of the RCMP, SIRC, and some twenty other federal agencies, a complete list of which can be found in the schedule to the Security of Information Act. "Special Operational Information" includes: "the identity of a person, agency, group, body or entity that is or is intended to be, has been approached to be, or has offered or agreed to be, a confidential source of information, intelligence or assistance to the Government of Canada," as well as "the identity of any person who is, has been or is intended to be covertly engaged in an information- or intelligence-collection activity or program of the Government of Canada that is covert in nature." See Section 8 of the *Security of Information Act* for a complete list of "Special Operational Information."

29. Access to Information Request No. 117-2016-188.

30. CSIS based its decision on sections 15(1), 16(1)(b) or 16(1)(c) of the *Access to Information Act*. That said, some of the documents that were released do indicate that the Director of CSIS must seek "Ministerial approval for compensation offers that exceed the Minister's financial signing authority." Others reveal that CSIS senior officials must be informed of "any issue that could cause controversy or embarrassment to the Government of Canada."

31. McDonald Commission, *Second Report, op. cit.*, p. 539.

32. Cole, *op. cit.*, pp. 27–28.

33. *Ibid.*, p. 13.

34. *Ibid.*, p. 48.

35. *Ibid.*, p. 72.

36. Jeff Sallot, "Let police handle domestic security: group urges," *Globe and Mail*, April 6, 1984, p. 5; United States Secret Service, *Public Report of the White House Security Review*. Washington, DC, http://fas.org/irp/agency/ustreas/usss/t1pubrpt.html

37. *Review of the CSIS Act and the Security Offences Act*, Ottawa, House of Commons, March 26, 1990, p. 22:18.

38. Raj Persaud and David Canter, "Sleeping With the Enemy?," *Huffington Post*, March 4, 2013, http://www.huffingtonpost.co.uk/dr-raj-persaud/undercover-police-psychology_b_2806029.html

39. McQuaig, *op. cit.*, p. 11.

40. Fabrice de Pierrebourg, *Montréalistan—Enquête sur la mouvance islamiste*, Montreal, Stanké, 2007, p. 173.

41. Alain Bouchard, "Les tribulations d'un ex-agent double—De la griserie sur le terrain à… la prison," *Le Soleil*, November 18, 1996, p. A12.

42. *Ibid.*

43. "Re Unnamed person," 2020 FC 1190, canlii.ca/t/jht4n, para. 163–66.

44. De Vault and Johnson, *op. cit.*, pp. 246–247.

45. D. Brazao et al., "Portrait of the vanishing spy," *op. cit*, p. A1.

46. Bouchard, *op. cit.*

47. Gary T. Marx, "Thoughts on a Neglected Category of Social Movement Participant: The Agent Provocateur and The Informant," *American Journal of Sociology*, vol. 80 no. 2, 1974, pp. 423–424.

48. Keable Commission, *op. cit.*, p. 394.

49. Marx, *op. cit.*

50. Cole, *op. cit.*, p. 124.

51. *Ibid.*, p. 64.

52. Jeff Davis, "Oversight body for Canadian spies abolished," *Ottawa Citizen*, April 27, 2012, p. A6. The official name of C-38 is *An Act to implement certain provisions of the budget tabled in Parliament on March 29, 2012 and to implement other measures*.

53. François Lavigne, "We could use oversight," *Ottawa Citizen*, April 30, 2012, p. A10. Lavigne is one of the very few former CSIS agents—if not the only one—to have publicly denounced the anti-terrorist bill C-51, claiming that it granted too much power to the Canadian secret services and opened the door to abuse.

54. Bill C-38, part 4, s. 15.

55. An oncologist by profession, Dr. Porter was arrested in Panama on May 27, 2013, following an investigation by the Quebec government's Unité permanente anticorruption (UPAC). He was accused of accepting $22.5 million in bribes from the engineering firm SNC-Lavalin, related to the construction of the McGill University Health Centre (MUHC) in Montreal, where he served as president and CEO. He died of lung cancer on the night of June 30 to July 1, 2015, while still in custody in Panama. Arrested in 1989 in the United States after attempting to sell three military aircraft to Iran, Menashe was cleared the following year after indicating that he had acted at the request of the Israeli government. Relocating to Canada, he then did work for the Zimbabwe government, successfully framing

President Robert Mugabe's main opponent, Morgan Tsvangirai, whom he allegedly filmed plotting to assassinate the southern African state's leader. Douglas Quan, "Porter resigns as spy watchdog over business dealings," *Montreal Gazette*, November 11, 2011, p. A8; Brian Hutchinson, "Spy watchdog's 'peculiar deal,'" *National Post*, November 8, 2011, p. A1.

56. First elected as the Member of Parliament for Fraser Valley (British Columbia) in 1993, Strahl served as the head of various departments (Agriculture, Indian Affairs, Transportation) in the Harper government until 2011, when he left politics. Hélène Buzzetti, "Chuck Strahl quitte le comité de surveillance des espions canadiens," *Le Devoir*, January 25, 2014, p. A9.

57. Hugo De Grandpré, "L'ancien ministre Strahl dans l'embarras," *La Presse*, January 9, 2014, p. A8.

58. C-51, *op. cit.*, s. 50.

59. SIRC, *Annual Report 2015–2016*, op. cit., p. 18.

60. SIRC, *Annual Report 2016–2017*, op. cit., p. 25.

61. SIRC, *Annual Report 2017–2018*, op. cit., p. 23.

62. C-51, *op. cit.*, s. 51.

63. SIRC, *op. cit.*, p. 18.

64. SIRC, *op. cit.*, p. 12.

65. SIRC, 2015–2016, *op. cit.*, p. 18; SIRC, 2016–2017, *op. cit.*, p. 25; SIRC 2017–2018, *op. cit.*, p. 12.

66. SIRC, 2015–2016, *op. cit.*, p. 18.

67. SIRC, 2016–2017, *op. cit.*, p. 26.

68. CBC News, "Trudeau names parliamentary committee to oversee security, intelligence agencies", November 6, 2017.

69. McDonald Commission, *Second Report, op. cit.*, pp. 945–954.

70. "Deputy Prime Minister introduces bill to create committee of parliamentarians on national security," *Canada NewsWire*, November 24, 2005.

71. The name given to the alliance of the intelligence services of Canada, the United States, the United Kingdom, Australia, and New Zealand, established in 1946.

72. The official name of bill C-22 is *An Act to establish the National Security and Intelligence Committee of Parliamentarians and to make consequential amendments to certain Acts*. Note that the version of C-22 that was consulted is the one that was amended by the Parliamentary Standing Committee on Public Safety and National Security and presented to the House of Commons on December 9, 2016.

73. C-59, *op. cit.*, s. 4, 5, 7, 11, and 13.

74. *National Security and Intelligence Review Agency Act*, s. 8 para. 16(1), 17(1), and 18(3).

75. *Intelligence Commissioner Act*, s. 12–19.

76. *National Security and Intelligence Committee of Parliamentarians Act*, s. 8.

77. *Op. cit.*, s. 4(3).

78. *Op. cit.*, s. 4(7).

79. *Op. cit.*, s. 4(2).

80. *Op. cit.*, s. 32–33.

81. *Ibid.*, s. 29.

82. *Op. cit.*, para. 8(1)b).

83. *Op. cit.*, s. 27.1.

84. *Op. cit.*, s. 12–20.

85. *Ibid.*, s. 19.

86. Office of the Intelligence Commissioner, *Annual Report 2019*, p. 17.

87. *CSIS Act*, *op. cit.*, para. 20.1(17).

88. *Op. cit.*, s. 26.

89. *Op. cit.*, s. 12.

90. *Op. cit.*, para. 14a).

91. *Security of Information Act*, para. 8(1)a.1, a.2 and schedule.

92. *Op. cit.*, para. 22(1).

93. *Annual Report 2019, op. cit.*, p. 19.

94. Office of the Intelligence Commissioner, *Annual Report 2020*, p. 21, and *Annual Report 2021*, p. 31.

95. *Op. cit.*, s. 32(2).

96. NSIRA, *2021 Annual Report*, p. 18.

97. *Ibid.*, p. 17.

98. *Op. cit.*, para. 8(2).

99. NSIRA, *2020 Annual Report*, p. 19.

100. *Ibid.*, p. 61.

101. *Ibid.*, para. 6.

102. *Ibid.*, p. 19.

103. *Ibid.*, para. 18.

104. *Ibid.*, para. 16.

105. *Ibid.*, p. 61.

106. *Ibid.*, p. 19.

107. NSIRA, *2021 Annual Report, op. cit.*, p. 15.

108. NSIRA, *Review of CSIS Threat Reduction Activities* (NSIRA Review 2020-05), p. 20.

109. *Ibid.*, p. 21.

110. NSIRA, *2021 Annual Report, op. cit.*, p. 11.

111. NSIRA, *Review of CSIS Threat Reduction Activities—A Focus on Information Disclosure to External Parties* (NSIRA Review 2021-04), p. 6, footnote 15.

112. *Ibid.*, p. 11.

113. NSIRA, *2021 Annual Report, op. cit.*, p. 11.

114. *Ibid.*

115. *Ibid.*, p. 12, para. 72.

116. *Ibid.*

117. Jim Bronskill, "CSIS failed to fully consider human toll when disrupting threats, watchdog says," *Toronto Star*, February 18, 2023, https://www.thestar.com/politics/2023/02/18/csis-failed-to-fully-consider-human-toll-when-disrupting-threats-watchdog-says.html.

118. 2020 FC 1190, *op. cit.*, para. 4.

119. *Ibid.*, para. 154.

120. *Canadian Security Intelligence Service Act (CA) (Re)*, 2021 FCA 92, canlii.ca/t/jlbn8, para. 14–15.

121. 2020 FC 616, *op. cit.*, para. 260.

122. *Ibid.*, Annex C.

123. 2021 FCA 92, *op. cit.*, para. 22.

124. *Ibid.*, para. 24.

125. *Ibid.*, para. 26.

126. *Ibid.*, para. 34–35.

127. *Ibid.*, para. 43.

128. 2020 FC 616, *op. cit.*, para. 20.

129. 2021 FCA 92, *op. cit.*, para. 51–52.

130. *Ibid.*, para. 58–59.

131. *Ibid.*, para. 77.

132. 2020 FC 1190, *op. cit.*, para. 105.

133. *Ibid.*, para. 117 and 119.

134. *Ibid.*, para. 120–21.

135. *Ibid.*, para. 110.

136. *Ibid.*, para. 122.

137. *Ibid.*, para. 127–128.

138. *Ibid.*, para. 109.

139. *Ibid.*, para. 130.

140. *Ibid.*, para. 136.

141. *Ibid.*, para. 179.

142. *Ibid.*, para. 189–90.

143. *Ibid.*, para. 150.

144. *Ibid.*, para. 203.

145. *Ibid.*, para. 210.

146. *Ibid.*, para. 210 and 211.

147. *Ibid.*, para. 216.

148. *Canadian Security Intelligence Services Act (CA) (Re)*, 2021 FC 541 (CanLII), para. 70.

149. 2020 FC 616, *op. cit.*, para. 125.

150. *Ibid.*, para. 149.

151. *Ibid.*, para. 168.

152. *Ibid.*, para. 163.

153. *Ibid.*, para. 195.

154. 2020 FC 1190, *op. cit.*, para. 7.

155. *Ibid.*, para. 9.

156. *Ibid.*, para. 234.

157. *Ibid.*, para. 15.

158. 2021 FC 541, *op. cit.*, para. 84.

159. *Ibid.*, para. 95.

160. 2020 FC 616, *op. cit.*, para. 174. On May 12, 2021, three judges of the Federal Court of Appeal overturned Justice Gleeson's decision, but only on two grounds: 1) the file in which the breach to the duty of candour was found had not been properly identified; 2) the obligation of candour does not entail a waiver of the solicitor-client privilege (2021 CAF 92, op. cit.).

161. NSIRA also published a 120-page report on the same review: *Rebuilding Trust: Reforming the CSIS Warrant and Justice Legal Advisory Processes*, NSIRA Review arising from Federal Court's Judgment in 2020 FC 616.

162. *Annual Report 2021*, op. cit., p. 8.

163. *Ibid.*, p. 3.

164. *Ibid.*, p. 5.

165. *Ibid.*, p. 59.

166. *Ibid.*, p. 60.

167. *Ibid.*, p. 6.

168. *Ibid.*, p. 61.

169. *Ibid.*

170. *Ibid.*, p. 60.

171. *Ibid.*, p. 6.

172. *Ibid.*, p. 7.

173. In criminal law, where the police investigation leads to a charge, case law recognizes the right of the accused to receive any evidence relevant to the exercise of his or her constitutional right to make full answer and defence (*R. v. Stinchcombe*, Supreme Court of Canada, 1991, 3 S.C.R. 326).

174. Sections 196 and 196.1 of the *Criminal Code*.

175. "Mr. Big" operations are police investigations ultimately aimed at obtaining a confession from a person suspected of a serious crime, often murder, through manipulation and deception. The ploy usually consists of setting up a fictitious criminal organization, actually composed of undercover cops, with the goal of luring in the target, gradually building trust, until the day they are introduced to the apparent leader of the organization, nicknamed "Mr. Big," who will then try to draw them out by presenting them with an enticing future in a powerful and wealthy organization.

176. *R. v. Mentuck*, Supreme Court of Canada, 2001, 3 SCR 442, p. 471.

177. *Ontario (Public Safety and Security) v. Criminal Lawyers' Association*, Supreme Court of Canada, 2010, 1 SCR 815, p. 835.

Bibliography

Auger, Michel, *L'attentat*, Montreal: Trait d'union, 2001.

Austin, David, *Black Negroes, White Negroes. Race, Sex and Politics in 1960s Montreal*, trans. C. St-Hilaire & V. Dassas, Montreal: Lux éditeur, 2015.

Barreau du Québec, *Mémoire présenté par le Comité du Barreau du Québec sur le Bill C-157, Service canadien du renseignement de sécurité*, Québec: Service de recherche du Barreau du Québec, 1983.

Beal, Bob and Rod MacLeod, *Prairie Fire: The 1885 North-West Rebellion*, Toronto: McClelland & Stewart 1994.

Bell, Stewart, *Bayou of Pigs. Canada*. Mississauga: John Wiley and Sons, 2008.

Bernard, Dominique, *La Commission d'enquête sur des opérations policières en territoire québécois: portée réelle et limites du rapport Keable*, Master's thesis in political science, UQAM, 2008.

Boisvert, Anne-Marie, *La protection des collaborateurs de la justice: éléments de mise à jour de la politique québécoise—Rapport final présenté au ministre de la Sécurité publique*, Quebec: Ministère de la Sécurité publique, 2005.

Boyden, Joseph, *Louis Riel et Gabriel Dumont*, Montreal: Boréal, 2011.

Brodeur, Jean-Paul, «La Crise d'octobre et les commissions d'enquête», *Criminologie*, vol. 13, no. 2, 1980.

Brown, Lorne and Caroline Brown, *An Unauthorized History of the RCMP*, Toronto: James Lewis & Samuel 1973.

Bumsted, J. M., *Louis Riel v. Canada: The Rebel Years*, Winnipeg: Plains, 2005.

Butt, Michael, *Surveillance of Canadian communists: A case study of Toronto RCMP intelligence networks, 1920-1939*, PhD thesis in history, Memorial University of Newfoundland, 2003.

Canadian Security Intelligence Service, *Chemical, Biological, Radiological and Nuclear Terrorism* (Report No. 2000/02), Ottawa, CSIS, December 18, 1999.

Centre d'analyse et de documentation, *Front de libération du Québec 1963-1975*, Quebec City: Ministère du Conseil exécutif, September 15, 1975.

Churchill, Ward, *Agents of Repression: the FBI's Secret Wars Against the Black Panther Party and the American Indian Movement*, New York: South End Press, 2002.

Cléroux, Richard, *Pleins feux sur les... services secrets canadiens: révélations sur l'espionnage au pays*, Montreal: Éditions de l'Homme, 1993.

Cole, J. Michael, *Smokescreen: Canadian Security Intelligence after September 11, 2001*, Bloomington: iUniverse, Inc., 2008.

Commission of Inquiry into Certain Activities of the RCMP, Ottawa, Canadian Government Publishing Centre, 1981.

Commission of Inquiry into Police Operations on Quebec Territory, *Rapport de la commission d'enquête sur des opérations policières en territoire québécois*, Quebec: Direction générale des publications gouvernementales, 1981.

Conway, Marshall Eddie, *Marshall Law: The Life & Times of a Baltimore Black Panther*, Oakland: AK Press 2011.

Creighton, Donald, *John A. Macdonald: le 1er ministre du Canada*, trans. I. Steenhout, Montreal: Editions de l'Homme, 1981.

Cruise, David and Alison Griffiths, *Lords of The Line. The Men Who Built the CPR*. New York City: Viking, 1988.

Department of Justice, *Law Enforcement and Criminal Liability—White Paper 2000*, Ottawa: Justice Canada, 2000.

De Pierrebourg, Fabrice, *Montréalistan—Enquête sur la mouvance islamiste*, Montreal: Stanké, 2007.

De Vault, Carole and William Johnson, *The Informer: Confessions of an Ex-terrorist*, Toronto: Fleet Books, 1982.

Dion, Germain, *Une tornade de 60 jours*, Hull: Éditions Asticou, 1985.

Dion, Robert, *Les crimes de la police montée*, Montreal: Éditions coopératives Albert Saint-Martin, 1979.

Dobbin, Murray, "Thomas Flanagan's Riel: An Unfortunate Obsession—A Review," *Alberta History*, vol. 32, no 2, Spring 1984.

Dubro, James and Robin Rowland, *Undercover: Cases of the RCMP's Most Secret Operative*, London: Octopus Publishing, 1991.

Duchaîne, Jean-François, *Report on the Events of October 1970*, Quebec: Department of Justice, 1980.

Eaton, Scott C., *Capitalism on Trial: Section 98, the Communist Party of Canada, and the Battle for Legality in the Interwar Period*, Ph.D. thesis in history, Memorial University of Newfoundland, 2012.

Edwards, Peter, *Delusion: The True Story of Victorian Superspy Henri Le Caron*, Toronto: Key Porter Books, 2008.

Fidler, Richard, *RCMP: The Real Subversives*, New York: Vanguard Publications, 1978.

Forsythe, Dennis (ed.), *Let the Niggers Burn! The Sir George Williams University Affair and its Caribbean Aftermath* Montreal: Our Generation Press, 1971.

Fournier, Louis, *F.L.Q. Histoire d'un mouvement clandestin*, Montreal: Éditions Québec/Amérique, 1982.

Greer, Allan, "The Birth of the Police in Canada," in A. Greer & I. Radforth [eds], *Colonial Leviathan: State Formation in Mid-Nineteenth-Century Canada*, Toronto: University of Toronto Press, 1992.

Gwyn, Richard, *John A.: The Man Who Made Us. The Life and Times of John A. Macdonald*, Toronto: Random House Canada, 2009.

Hategan, Elisa, *Race Traitor: The True Story of Canadian Intelligence's Greatest Cover-up*, s.l., Incognito Press, 2014.

Hewitt, Steven R., *Old Myths Die Hard: The Transformation of the Mounted Police in Alberta and Saskatchewan 1914-1939*, Saskatoon: University of Saskatchewan, 1997.

Hewitt, Steve, *Spying 101: The RCMP's Secret Activities at Canadian Universities, 1917-1997*, Toronto: University of Toronto Press, 2002.

Howard, Joseph Kinsey, *Strange Empire: A Narrative of the Northwest*, St. Paul, MN: Minnesota Historical Society Press, 1994.

Jones, Charles Earl, *The Black Panther Party (reconsidered)*, Baltimore: Black Classic Press, 1998.

Kealey, Gregory S., "Presidential Address: The Empire Strikes Back: The Nineteenth-Century Origins of the Canadian Secret Service," *Journal of the Canadian Historical Association*, vol. 10, no .1, 1999.

Kinsman, Gary and Patrizia Gentile recount in *The Canadian Wars on Queers: National Security as Sexual Regulation*, Vancouver: UBC Press, 2010.

Le Caron, Henry, *Twenty-five years in the secret service: the recollections of a spy*, London: William Heinemann, 1892.

Leier, Mark, "Portrait of a Labour Spy: The Case of Robert Raglan Gosden, 1882-1961," *Labour/Le Travail*, vol. 42, Fall 1998.

Lester, Normand, *Enquêtes sur les services secrets*, Montreal: Éditions de l'Homme, 2002.

——————, *Point à la ligne*, Montreal: Les Intouchables, 2011.

Marx, Gary T., "Thoughts on a Neglected Category of Social Movement Participant: The Agent Provocateur and The Informant," *American Journal of Sociology*, vol. 80, no. 2, 1974.

McLean, Donald G., *1885 Métis Rebellion or Government Conspiracy?* Winnipeg: Pemmican Publications 1985.

Milot, David, "Histoire du mouvement marxiste-léniniste au Québec 1973-1983—Un premier bilan," *Bulletin d'histoire politique*, Montreal: AQHP/Lux Éditeur, vol. 13, no. 1, Fall 2004.

Mitrovica, Andrew, *Covert Entry: Spies, Lies and Crimes Inside Canada's Secret Service*, Toronto: Random House Canada, 2002.

Nicholson, G.W.L. and Mark O. Humphries, *Canadian Expeditionary Force, 1914-1919: Official History of the Canadian Army in the First World War*, Montreal: McGill-Queen's University Press, 2015.

Parnaby, Andrew and Gregory S. Kealey, "How the 'Reds' Got Their Man: The Communist Party Unmasks an RCMP Spy," *Journal of Labor Studies*, vol. 40, Fall 1997.

Pelletier, Gérard, *The October Crisis*, Montreal: Éditions du jour, 1971.

Penner, Norman, *Canadian Communism: The Stalin Years and Beyond*, London: Methuen Publications, 1988.

Philips, Alan, *The Living Legend—The Story of the Royal Canadian Mounted Police*, New York: Little, Brown and Company, 1957.

Report of the Royal Commission on Security, Ottawa: Privy Council Office June 1969.

Review Committee on the CSIS Act and the Security Offences Act, *Proceedings*, Ottawa: House of Commons, May 15, 1990.

Roberts, Barbara, *Whence They Came: Deportation from Canada, 1900-1935*, Ottawa: University of Ottawa Press, 1988.

Rodney, William, *Soldiers of the International: A History of the Communist Party of Canada, 1919-1929*, Toronto: University of Toronto Press, 1968.

Rutherford, Scott, *Canada's Other Red Scare: Rights, Decolonization, and Indigenous Political Protest in the Global Sixties*, Master's thesis in History, Queen's University, 2011.

Samraoui, Mohammed, *Chronique des années de sang*, Paris: Éditions Denoel, 2003.

Security Intelligence Review Committee, *Annual Report 1990-1991*, Ottawa: Public Services and Supply Canada, 1991.

——— , *Annual Report 1997-1998*, Ottawa: Public Services and Supply Canada, 1998.

―――――, *Broader horizons – Preparing the groundwork for change, Annual report 2014-2015*, Ottawa: Public Services and Procurement Canada, 2015.

―――――, *Section 54 Report to the Solicitor General of Canada on CSIS' use of its investigative powers with respect to the Labor Movement*, Ottawa: Public Services and Procurement Canada, 25 March 1988.

―――――, *The Heritage Front Affair: Report to the Solicitor General of Canada* (File No. 2800-54), Ottawa: Public Services and Supply Canada, December 9, 1994.

Souaïdia, Habib, *La Sale Guerre*, Paris: La Découverte, 2001.

Taché, Alexandre-Antonin, *Louis Riel et les troubles du Nord-Ouest: de la Rivière-Rouge à Batoche*, Montreal: Éditions du Méridien, 2000.

Waiser, Bill, *All Hell Can't Stop Us: The On-to-Ottawa Trek and Regina Riots*, Markham: Fifth House, 2003, p. 37.

Williams, David Ricardo, *Call in Pinkerton's: American Detectives at Work for Canada*, Mishawaka (IN): Dundurn Press, 1998.

Woodcock, George, *Gabriel Dumont: The Metis Chief and His Lost World*, Peterborough, ON: Broadview Press, 2003.

About the Author

Alexandre Popovic has been politically active in social struggles since the early 1990s. He has suffered police repression as a result of his participation in various protest movements; he subsequently began to represent himself in court. Intent on documenting the issue of police abuse, the author has sent more than six hundred Access to Information requests and has pleaded many times in front of the Access to Information Commission.

For over a decade, Popovic has been involved in supporting families who have lost a loved one at the hands of the police. In this capacity, he has participated in half a dozen coroners' public inquests as an interested party.

Basic Politics of Movement Security

J. SAKAI & MANDY HISCOCKS

978-1-894946-52-0 • 68 PAGES

$7.00

There are many books and articles reporting state repression, but not on that subject's more intimate relative, movement security. It is general practice to only pass along knowledge about movement security privately, in closed group lectures or by personal word-of-mouth. In fact, when new activists have questions about security problems, they quickly discover that there is no "Security for Dummies" to explore the basics. Adding to the confusion, the handful of available left security texts are usually about underground or illegal groups, not the far larger public movements that work on a more or less legal level.

During Montreal's 2013 Festival of Anarchy, J. Sakai gave a workshop about the politics of movement security, sharing the results of typical incidents of both the movement's successes and the movement's failures in combating the "political police" or state security agencies. He also discussed the nature of those state sub-cultures. This booklet contains a transcript of that talk, and of the subsequent lively question and answer period, along with several after-the-workshop observations by Sakai.

Mandy Hiscocks comes at the topic from her personal experiences organizing against the 2010 G20 Summit in Toronto. In this in-depth interview, reprinted from the radical Canadian political journal *Upping The Anti*, Hiscocks describes how her political scene and groups she worked with were infiltrated by undercover agents over a year before the summit even occurred. Hiscocks spent a year in prison as a result of these experiences, shortly after this interview was conducted.

ORDER FROM WWW.LEFTWINGBOOKS.NET

For the first time ever, a feature-length documentary is examining the issue of agent provocateurs and entrapment in Canada's national security apparatus. Inspired by Alexandre Popovic's *Manufacturing Threats: Case Studies of State Manipulation and Entrapment in Canada*.

MANUFACTURINGTHETHREAT.COM

KERSPLEBEDEB

Since 1998 Kersplebedeb has been an important source of radical literature and agit prop materials.

The project has a non-exclusive focus on anti-patriarchal and anti-imperialist politics, framed within an anticapitalist perspective. A special priority is given to writings regarding armed struggle in the metropole, the continuing struggles of political prisoners and prisoners of war, and the political economy of imperialism.

The Kersplebedeb website presents historical and contemporary writings by revolutionary thinkers from the anarchist and communist traditions.

Kersplebedeb can be contacted at:

>Kersplebedeb
>CP 63560
>CCCP Van Horne
>Montreal, Quebec
>Canada
>H3W 3H8
>
>email: info@kersplebedeb.com
>web: www.kersplebedeb.com
>   www.leftwingbooks.net

Kersplebedeb

www.ingramcontent.com/pod-product-compliance
Lightning Source LLC
Chambersburg PA
CBHW050548160426
43199CB00015B/2583